Rising In Consciousness

The San Francisco Lecture Series

Other Writings of Joel S. Goldsmith

RISING IN CONSCIOUSNESS

THE SAN FRANCISCO LECTURE SERIES

Joel S. Goldsmith

I-Level

Acropolis Books, Publisher

Lakewood, CO   Austell, GA

RISING IN CONSCIOUSNESS
THE SAN FRANCISCO LECTURE SERIES
FOREWORD AND INTRODUCTION
© 1997 Acropolis Books, Inc.

San Francisco Lecture Series
© 1954 Joel S. Goldsmith

Published by Acropolis Books, Publisher, under its *I*-Level Imprint.
All rights reserved.
Printed in the United States of America.

For information contact:
Acropolis Books, Inc.
Lakewood, Colorado

http://www.acropolisbooks.com

LIBRARY OF CONGRESS CATALOGING-IN-PUBLICATION DATA
RESERVED

Goldsmith, Joel S. , 1892–1964.
        Rising in consciousness: the San Francisco lecture series / Joel
S. Goldsmith.
            p.   cm.
        Includes bibliographical references.
        ISBN 1-889051-05-5 (hc : alk. paper)
            1. Spiritual life.   2. Mysticism.   I. Title.
BP610.G64   1997b
291.4'22 – – dc21   97–2586
                                                                         CIP

THIS BOOK IS PRINTED ON ACID FREE PAPER THAT MEETS
STANDARD Z 39.48 OF THE AMERICAN NATIONAL STANDARDS INSTITUTE

Except the Lord build the house,
they labour in vain that build it.
                                    —Psalm 127

"Illumination dissolves all material ties and binds
men together with the golden chains of spiritual
understanding; it acknowledges only the leader-
ship of the Christ; it has no ritual or rule but the
divine, impersonal universal Love; no other
worship than the inner Flame that is ever lit at the
shrine of Spirit. This union is the free state of
spiritual brotherhood. The only restraint is the
discipline of Soul; therefore, we know liberty
without license; we are a united universe without
physical limits, a divine service to God without
ceremony or creed. The illumined walk without
fear—by Grace."

                    —*The Infinite Way* by Joel S. Goldsmith

TABLE OF CONTENTS

TABLE OF CONTENTS

FOREWORD

Well remembered is the trauma that precipitated my determination to find and talk to God. I had always known that God existed. However, answers about life had to be found and they had to come directly from Him. Where would I find Him, and how?

Scriptures advise: "Seek Ye first the Kingdom of God" and "The Kingdom of God is within you." As the months passed and my search continued, a gentle sense of peace enveloped me. In my thirst to find answers, I was led to *The Art of Meditation* by Joel S. Goldsmith. In reading this book, a sense of recognition, agreement and joy overwhelmed me. I had found my way! The next year I found *Practicing The Presence,* and other books of Joel's soon followed. My consciousness was continuing to unfold and I longed to meet this man who was totally changing my life.

In 1960, a flyer announced that Joel Goldsmith would give a talk at the Wiltern Theater in Hollywood, California. Although only being able to find a seat in the back of a packed auditorium, I was there. After the talk, Joel adjourned to the lobby and was surrounded by people inquiring how to reach him and obtain further information. I carefully listened and noted his answers.

Forty years have passed since the incredible teaching and guidance of this man touched my life. The deep spiritual insights shared by Joel in his classes, tapes and writings have guided me through the variety of life's experiences. Joel's love for God is tangible, his explanations of spiritual principles straightforward, and his shared and spontaneous meditations penetrate the soul.

In reading this edition of *Rising in Consciousness: The San Francisco Lecture Series*, one can feel the power and flow of Joel's consciousness as when the message was originally given. If one has "ears to hear" and "eyes to see", the revelations so lovingly presented by this 20th century mystic can transform his or her life. In these times of external uncertainty, there is no greater gift of love and peace for humanity than the message found within these pages.

Lorraine Muns

INTRODUCTION

Rising in Consciousness: The San Francisco Lecture Series, by Joel Goldsmith, is a unique volume. Because it is the first in a trilogy of books, all presenting lecture series, it offers readers the opportunity to consider the work of one of the 20th century's great mystics from several points of view. First, the series of eighteen talks presented in San Francisco in 1948 is as dynamic a reading of Joel's message as any available. More interestingly, because of the context in time of these lectures, and because it is a part of a more expanded trilogy, readers are allowed an opening through which they can view the formative stages of a work we have come to know as the Infinite Way. *Rising in Consciousness* ("The San Francisco Lecture Series of 1948"), which is to be followed by *Consciousness in Transition* ("Metaphysical Notes," given within the same year), and *Consciousness Transformed* ("1963/64 Hawaii Hotel Talks") provides the reader with a kind of aerial map of an unfolding message. It also portrays a man, Joel Goldsmith, passionate about presenting Truth in as clear, practical and real a way as was possible. It is a close-up of a man and a message alive with the inner flame of Spirit.

It seems important here to place the lecture series that comprise *Rising in Consciousness* in an historical context. The year the lecture series began was 1948, a time when the figurative sounds of the hammers and saws of post-war rebuilding filled the air. Few in those days recognized the word, let alone the practice of meditation. Conscious-ness, or *higher* Consciousness, was a concept known only to the growing numbers of individuals who were studying Christian Science, any of the many metaphysical teach-ings, or Eastern based esoteric religions. These were a growing number to be sure, but their deepening realiza-tions were not generally broadcast and if they were, they elicited curiosity at best but more often, distrust.

To think that you could enter a lecture hall in those days and find a short, rather stocky man with greying hair and glasses, wearing a suit and what was to become a trademark string tie, holding the rapt attention of 75 to 100 individuals as he talked about creative meditation (the focus of the first San Francisco lecture) is notable and provides a clue to what was happening in the inner landscape of world awareness.

An acquaintance recently described her own experi-ence attending one of Goldsmith's lecture series in 1950 in Hawaii. "I was leaving church one day," she re-counted, "and a friend asked 'Are you going to the Goldsmith lecture?' 'Who is that?' I asked. As soon as she mentioned that name, something, I can't describe what, caught my attention. 'Well, he is a very spiritual man who talks about God in a new way . . .' Now she had my attention. 'That is what I have been looking for: yes of course I'll go!' " I asked this acquaintance what it was like to sit in a meeting room with Joel. Did everyone meditate? What was Joel like? "We were working hard to learn meditation in those days," she explained. "You see, we had not known about meditation before we started to work with Joel. So we did sit very still until Joel came in and went up to the dais and perched on a stool next to the podium. He looked around at us. And we were still for a bit and when he spoke I remember that everyone in the room was completely at attention. During the talk he would walk among us. It was like there was a current of electricity in the room." She continued, "We noticed in one of the later talks, that Joel stopped in the middle of a sentence and seemed to lift his head to one side. 'Oh,' he said. 'I am going to talk on another subject for someone here needs to hear this.' And Joel changed the talk right in the middle. God was certainly there that day."

This small reminiscence underlines the fact that each lecture and talk that Joel presented was aligned with the body of individuals who came to hear him. In reading the text of *Rising in Consciousness,* not only are readers aware that they are sitting in on what was an actual class experience, they soon come to know a student body, a living audience, that was present during that series. The motivation and yearnings of those seekers elicited the message that Joel was bringing through in each lesson. Because that relationship is so evident when reading the lecture series, readers can join in that relationship. It is as if the class that took place in a specific time and place is still a living, unfolding experience . . . and that is true. Those classes still unfold in ever widening circles of Consciousness.

Joel did not use notes when he spoke. Instead he spent hours of every day in meditation, in communion with "the Presence." This living connection was the source of his talks: not notes or rehearsals or planning. The individuals in the audience were not only hearing new material in each lecture, this *was* new material coming through Joel. It fit the composition and needs of the student body in attendance. It answered unspoken questions, healed troubled bodies and souls, and sustained each individual according to his or her capacity to receive.

As many know, Joel Goldsmith was born in 1892 in New York City. His family, who were of Jewish heritage, were more engaged by art, music and theater than religion. Joel left school after the 8th grade to travel the world working with his father. It was during this time that he gained an overview of a world in dis-ease. In his biography,[1] we read of him asking, "If there is a God, how could He allow his children to fall into such a state as this!" Like Buddha, who as Prince Siddhartha was stunned with amazement when he first saw suffering and death in the world, Joel's travels catalyzed a deep yearning to discover an underlying truth to all he saw.

Later, while still a young man, he experienced for the first time the mysterious nature of divine healing. Joel had gone to an acquaintance to explain why he would not be able to make an appointment: "I have to go abroad as my father is in London and he is dying." The acquaintance, who was in spiritual healing work, said, "Oh no, your father does not have to die." Joel, surprised, asked a question that was to change his life. "What do you mean he does not have to die?"

That question can apply to almost any human condition. We live in a world where death is inevitable in all its forms: the death of fortunes, of relationships; the death of our youth, our hopes; even our loves that grow lush blossoms in season, fade and are no more. Finally there is the ultimate and inevitable death of the body, a

---

[1] *The Spiritual Journey of Joel Goldsmith*, Harper and Row Publishers, 1973

death that is so overwhelming a prospect, few can talk about or even think of it.

Joel arrived in Europe expecting to bring back his father's body. In amazement, he found his father, vigorous and whole, standing on the dock to meet him. An incident like that for anyone—anyone, that is, who feels he or she is merely human—is not a miracle really, but a remembrance that there is more to life than what we see with our eyes. That kind of remembrance opens a kind of doorway that releases many questions: What *is* real? Who *am* I? That incident of healing marked the unfolding of an entirely new kind of life for Joel Goldsmith.

Joel had another experience a few years later: He arrived at the office of a Christian Science practitioner requesting help for a health problem; when he left the man's office a few hours later, he had experienced illumination. Joel would often recount, not without humor, that shortly after that experience, his customers (Joel followed his father's trade as a salesman) were coming to him not for merchandise, but for healing. "If you pray for me I'll be healed!" In those days the only prayer Joel knew was "Now I lay me down to sleep." It was that childlike prayer that launched a life of service in healing, teaching and revealing. Joel soon began his own healing ministry as a Christian Science practitioner.

In the mid 1940's, just a few years before the San Francisco series was presented, Joel came to a major turning point in his life. He had moved from the east coast to California. He was to say later, this move represented a transition in consciousness and that the physical move to California was merely a reflection of that. Soon after he arrived he was compelled to begin to write a small book titled *The Infinite Way*. Joel felt the publishing of *The Infinite Way* fulfilled what had been an active life of service as a healer and practitioner. By now, realizing that what he was hearing within and writing about could not be bound or encompassed by any organization, Joel had left the Christian Science Church. He was free: all was complete and, with this new message, his work was done. Now, on to a life of repose—meditating, carrying on a quiet healing practice, enjoying spiritual companionship. This was not to be.

Soon a family of three found their way to Joel and asked if he would give them a class. Though Joel protested that he was not a teacher, the family insisted that he had the message they needed to hear. After working with this family, several other couples began to arrive. Then that small group expanded into thirty, then fifty and more. Invitations to speak in other locations were extended and Joel's quiet semi-retirement ended. If it is possible to be reincarnated in the same lifetime, Joel Goldsmith was reincarnated with the publication of *The Infinite Way*. He was no longer, as his biography states, a man with a message but a message with a man.

The surge of activity that was beginning to overwhelm Joel's peaceful retirement saw the flooding into conscious awareness from hidden streams, a new way of life. That up welling of newness is the dynamic that is so evident in *Rising in Consciousness*. The book is more a lens magnifying a stage of evolution of a spiritual message than it is a book of eighteen lectures presented at a certain place and time. It is a way for readers to see how a revelator births a message; for that is exactly what was happening in those early lectures and class sessions.

During his classes, Joel reminded his audience that if they were coming to hear a great teacher, or to be uplifted, or to attain to a cloud nine or ten or eighteen, they were in the wrong place. He acknowledged that he was participating with this inner flow, this inner connection (the Source, the Christ, the Presence) and that was the resource for any talk or lecture. This was the message: how to attain that Presence. He spoke in simple, easy to understand language: no frills or preambles. "But," Joel would say, "don't look to me, the lecturer up on the platform. Use what I tell you, take a hold of these principles that are emerging in this very living lesson. Listen, hear me, absorb and practice these principles. *Then* you will discover that source . . . within you. Always within you."

This series of eighteen lectures, then, is more than another book on truth. It is a window into the formative years of a message that was to reach the far corners of the world. By the time readers experience the third volume of this series, *Consciousness Transformed,* (a compilation of Joel's 1963/64 Hawaii Hotel and among his last), they will understand that Joel was not presenting an absolute teaching but a way of life: "You cannot teach the absolute," Joel was to say. "You can only experience the absolute."

Joel's great unspoken gift to humankind is that he was not fixed to a particular method of presentation or even a particular message. He presented principles and always adhered to principles. That, in turn, allowed the filling out and fulfilling of a spiritual language that was always opening out the way to deeper realizations of Truth. What is God? What is man? How do we pray? What is the world? How do I heal? Joel always addressed these questions from the framework of principles he called *the Nature of God, the Nature of Prayer,* and *the Nature of Error.* "If you understand these principles," he maintained, "you have it all."

On this trinity, Joel unfolded, year by year, a message: a life's work of depth and purity, of richness and mystery. This is why his work has always been imminently accessible. Like great world Scriptures, this message changes with each reading; it yields to reflect the consciousness of the reader. How often do individuals reading a passage in one of Joel's many books remark in surprise, "I never read that before. How did I miss that? So that is what that means!"

That it was and is a living message, adds special interest to the concept of a trilogy of books each highlighting a particular phase of Joel's message. *Rising in Consciousness* along with *Consciousness in Transition* illuminate Joel's early class-work, the work that emanated immediately after *The Infinite Way* broke new ground in truth writings. *Consciousness Transformed* records the last years of his work. The world in 1964 was light years apart from the world of 1948 and by 1964 Joel was leading those "with eyes to see and ears to hear" into another realm–that of mysticism. To read and study the volumes of the trilogy as a whole is to gain an experience in dimension. It is much like the illustration plates in a human anatomy book: On one transparent page an illustration of the skeletal structure is drawn out in fine detail; the next transparent plate lays out the nervous system and the next plate the musculature, while still another depicts the organs. As the layers are placed one on another on another, a whole body emerges. A beginning biology student might well exclaim, "Yes, there is the skeleton but now look, see how the nervous system and the musculature and the organs all fit together. Now that I can see the whole thing I can begin to understand how this body works."

INTRODUCTION

Together the trilogy presents this same holistic overview of a living message. Since Joel's sole aim was to present an opening into Consciousness for all time, one that is never static, never fixed, never organized within or without, always yielding new mysteries, *Rising In Consciousness* sets a starting point for a more comprehensive understanding of a message that will always be unfolding.

The way presented by Joel Goldsmith—and remember that he said his was an old message, as old as time—is an infinite unfolding, not relying on a man, a message, or a name of a teaching; it is an unfolding that rests on an unchanging structure of principles. His life's work was to present these principles as simply as he could so that students could thoroughly embrace and absorb them. And the practice and dedication and commitment that had to follow, *that* would lead to the healing, regeneration and fulfillment; that would ensure that unfolding will always take place. This is what the eighteen San Francisco lectures teach.

In reading the opening of *Rising in Consciousness*, readers can envision sitting in that long ago classroom in 1948 in San Francisco, California. It feels appropriate to close this introduction with the opening passage of that first talk which so aptly mirrors the scope of the trilogy:

"Good evening. We are unfolding states of consciousness and our outer experience is never going to be any greater than our inner unfoldment. The only hope we have for greater health, greater success, greater harmony in our human relations is through the unfolding of our inner or real consciousness. So why not let us take today as merely the beginning of a week of unfoldment and see how much farther we will have progressed

in our understanding and in our outer experience by this time next week. . . ."

To read this volume *in relationship* with its companion volumes is to comprehend not only a week of unfoldment that is the San Francisco lectures, but a fifteen year unfoldment with *Consciousness Transformed*, that has become a fifty year unfolding; it is to know that *that* legacy of unfolding consciousness did not stop at fifteen years nor will it stop at three hundred years. How often did Joel quote the poet:

> *Truth is within ourselves.*
> *There is an inmost center in us all,*
> *Where the Truth abides in fulness; and to know*
> *Rather consists in opening out a way*
> *Whence the imprisoned splendour may escape*
> *Than in effecting entry for a light supposed to be without.*
> *— Robert Browning*

Joel taught his students to discover their own language of ineffable Spirit, their own "natural flow." The message contained in these eighteen talks is at the grass roots of this legacy of infinite unfolding.

Laurie Parker
Bellevue, Washington
May, 1997

~ 1 ~

CREATIVE MEDITATION

WE ARE UNFOLDING STATES OF CONSCIOUSNESS, and our outer experience is never going to be any greater than our inner unfoldment. If we have not developed spiritually to a greater extent by next week than we have at this point today, our demonstration of life and its harmonies will not be any greater or better next week than it is today. The only hope we have for greater health, greater success and greater harmony in our human relations is through the unfolding of our "inner" or "real" consciousness. So why not let us take today as merely the beginning of a week of unfoldment and see how much farther we will have progressed in our understanding and in our outer experience by this time next week.

Now, as to the meaning of the words "creative meditation." You and I have heard a lot about meditation and certainly we have read much about it, but this idea of creative meditation gives us something new to think about. Creative meditation goes a step further because in it, there must be an expectancy of a causative principle *and* a specific effect. Let us not forget that when we think of the idea, creative meditation, we are thinking of a creative principle at work; and we are thinking also of an effect that must take place—under, of course, one

1

condition: If the seed is planted in fertile soil; if our
consciousness is receptive and responsive to the truth,
and if our consciousness is not so cluttered up with the
idea of demonstration, with the idea of an effect of some
material good which we are expecting. If our consciousness is open to God and to the unfolding of divine
consciousness, that is the state of consciousness which is
receptive and responsive to the seed that will be planted
there during meditation.

That is the idea of creative meditation. You plant the
seed to allow the creative principle to act upon it and to
produce fruit after its own kind. In our creative meditation then let us above all be expectant of good;
expectant of an answer; expectant of a greater degree of
spiritual understanding and, therefore, of more harmony
in what we call our human experience. As you know, it
is not really a human, but a divine, spiritual experience.
The "world" has turned it into a material one and has
finitized that which is really the life of God made manifest
as you and as me. The object of meditation is to achieve
the spiritual life. Meditation of itself is but a means to an
end—and the end is the attainment of spiritual life.

Yesterday while I was in the chapel in Palo Alto I
took from the wall this statement: "The world is new to
every soul when Christ has entered into it."[1] That is the
purpose of meditation! As humans, we have become
separated from our source and this is what makes us
appear to the world as humans. Now we are opening
consciousness to where the Christ, the presence of God,
the spirit of God, can enter in and make us new. Listen to
Jesus when he says, "I can of mine own self do nothing[2]
. . . the father that dwelleth in me, he doeth the works."[3]
And Paul: "I live, yet not I, the Christ liveth in me."[4]

Just think, if I were sitting here as a human being and all there was to me was a mind and body, you would not benefit very much by that. There is only one thing that can bring some measure of unfolding spiritual consciousness to you, and that is the presence of God, the Christ that liveth in me, for which I am the presentation or vehicle. You, of course, are identically that same thing when you open your consciousness and let the Christ enter in, so that you also can say—and mean it—"I can of mine own self do nothing[5] . . . the Father that dwelleth in me, he doeth the works."[6] And, "I live, yet not I, the Christ liveth in me."[7]

Now the object of meditation is to still the human mind, to still the activity of the human senses to that degree which will permit us to become consciously aware of the presence of God, to become consciously aware of the divine activity operating in, through and as us—and, as a matter of fact, as our consciousness. It is to become consciously aware of the divine activity operating as our consciousness! God, the divine being individualized as the Christ, becomes our individual consciousness and that consciousness is the savior of the world—the savior of my world. Your consciousness is the savior of your world. Lift your world up from the material sense of existence into the spiritual reality! Your own consciousness does that when it is imbued with this Christ! Therefore, the purpose of this meditation is opening consciousness to that inflow so that it becomes spiritualized; so that it becomes the very Christ itself in individual expression.

On this thought of stilling the human senses or the human mind, do not believe for a moment that that means trying to stop your thinking process, because you will never succeed in that. No one ever has. But there does come a time to those who continue meditation, when the human mind of itself stops, when thoughts no longer intrude during meditation. But you cannot bring that about through trying to stop thinking. All you can do is to dam it up for a little while, and then it breaks out stronger than ever. What you *can* do during meditation is to learn to pay no attention to the thoughts that are going through your mind. These will neither harm you nor help you. And as a matter of fact, that is what we are learning in this work–that no amount of human good thinking will help, and no amount of human evil thinking will hurt. On this point, too, it is so natural for me to know and say this, that I often do not remember that there are apt to be those who have been brought up in metaphysical teach-ings that stress the sense of "right thinking," or "human thinking," or "learning to hold the right thoughts." What I say is in no sense in criticism or judgment or condemna-tion of that method or approach to living. Every path that we take leads up, up to the final one, which is God. I am not, therefore, speaking in contradiction or contradistinc-tion of any other approach. I am merely presenting what has been my individual unfoldment, which has been that the human mind is not a power. The human mind cannot create good and cannot create evil. It appears to, that is true. That is why we have the human world; that is why we have this metaphysical teaching–because there is this appearance of evil, and we think something is required to correct that view.

Two times two are four and no amount of human thinking will ever change that. Love is love, and nothing will change that. And so, while we are in meditation, if thoughts persist in coming to our mind, passing through our "upper story," let us not be concerned about it. Let these thoughts come and let them go. They may be personal and sensual too, but let us not pay attention to them. Let us remember to let them come and go of their own accord and pretty soon, for lack of feeding them, they will not come any more. We can starve them by learning to disregard them; and when we are disregarding them, we are keeping our real thought on the object of our work. The object of our work is a state of receptivity so that the Christ may flow in. That is the purpose for which we meditate. That is the object we hope to attain—the ability to have a conscious recognition of the presence of God.

Where the Christ becomes the reality of our being, we are then no longer in the human sense of existence but in the spiritual. And that is the first step, as I see it, on this spiritual path. Take your thought off of person, place and thing. Take your thought off of body, health, money or employment. Take your thought off of every human situation, right now, this minute, and send it to God! Center your thought, right now, on God! What is God? God is love; God is soul; God is life. You cannot define God. If you could, it would not be God. We are not going to define what God is. We are going to re-move thought from person, place and things, and say the word *God.* God—the divine consciousness of my being. God—the soul of my being. God—the law of my being. God—the substance of my being—the substance of all form. God—the creative principle of the universe; the law unto my being; God—the substance, the law of all form, of all formation; God—the substance, the law, the cause, and even the form of all effect; God—the sub-stance, the law, the life eternal of all form. You cannot separate God, life, from its form which you are!

God is the life of all form. God is the substance, the law, of all form. God is the spirit and soul of *our* form. God, appearing individually as you, constitutes all there is of you. God is the life of you, and that is why you are immortal—and now! Because God is the substance of your body, even your body is immortal! Your body is not flesh and blood as it appears to be. God is spirit and your body is spiritual. Your body is as immortal as your life, which is God! There is no reason for any body to ache and change, or decay and die. We permit that through the acceptance of the belief of a selfhood apart from God. We permit it through accepting God as the form of spiritual creation, but not the form and substance of all creation. God is the form, the substance, the law of all creation, including your body. Your body is not material. Neither is the food you eat material. It is spiritual. All that is material is our concept of creation. Creation itself is all God in the sense that God is the essence, substance, and form.

Now, in this meditation, we are not thinking of form or figure, of outline, color, grace, or body. We are thinking of God as the substance of all form, color, grace, outline, body. God is the substance of our being, the substance of the stone. God is the law of the stars and planets. The stars and planets are not a law unto themselves. God is the law unto them, as we are the law unto ourselves. And because we are infinite consciousness, the sun, moon, stars, and planets are embodied in us, and we are the law unto them. Yes, we are the law unto the stars, the moon and the planets!

This divine consciousness of ours, imbued with the Christ, is the law unto all creation. Nothing in this world acts upon us. We are the law unto all that appears in our universe. All of us are the activity of God; the universal I; the universal ego, individualized as you and as me. That is the law unto all creation. And so, in our creative meditation, we remember that our entire consciousness is filled with God. God as the law. God as the substance. God as the creative principle! And God appearing as effect. God appearing as form. God appearing to us as sun, moon, stars—as food, as pets, and as all other relationships on earth. So, while our consciousness, our main thought, is centered on that, these human thoughts that come and go are of no importance. Do not try to stop them or throw them out. Let them come and go, and they will fade out. I promise you, they will fade out. It is only a matter of practice.

Now as to our class beginning next week—and that is just an opportunity to continue this idea of meditation. For many years I practiced and taught metaphysical healing, not as a class teacher but merely as an individual, a practitioner, who taught those who came for help and for healing; I taught only those who wanted the teaching in addition to the healing. The day finally came when I made the decision never to teach again, and when I made that decision I heard a laugh inside of me. It really was a laugh, and I heard it right out loud. And this voice said: "Oh, yes you will! You will teach, but you will teach those I send to you, and you will teach them what I give you to teach." I did not question that, but neither did I understand or know how it would come about. Then, one day, a lady who had been coming to my office for help asked me if I would talk to a small group on the subject of the Bible. I said no, that I was not teaching. But the calls kept coming for several weeks, and finally I thought I would make an exception and for four nights would talk on the Bible. And those four nights have stretched out to this present time without the interruption of even a single night.

And so I have found it to come literally true. I have not sought students, and those who came have come of their own accord, either through reading my writings or through recommendations. So I feel impelled to say regarding these classes, that those who come to them must not come expecting them to be lectures, or expecting a good time. If the object is to be achieved which we have set out to achieve, it is really going to be work for two solid weeks—good, strenuous work! Why? Because here again, unless consciousness is enriched; unless it is changed or unfolded in a spiritual way, the outer experience will be no different. Unless one is prepared to really put in conscientious work, so that at the end of the class they can say, "I am farther along in spiritual development," it will be of no use to come to the class—not unless one is thinking beyond the immediate day or the immediate problem, beyond the meditation to realization. Let us then accept that the object of meditation, the object of my being in the spiritual realm is that I may become consciously aware of the presence of Christ, and become that which I am—the light of the world. Let us dedicate ourselves to that now.

In my own work when this began, I went through three months of inner initiation. It took place every morning from five to seven. It was a magnificent experience and one that can never be shared with anyone. It was in that period that it was shown to me that the only purpose of our existence on earth is to be the light of the world; to be a path or a way, to show these others who are what I was before the ordainment—a seeker—so that they may rise above the human sense of existence.

Now remember that everyone in the human world is faced with the belief of a physical body. They are faced with the belief of physical supply. And right now, they are being faced with the belief of atomic bombs and rumors of wars. In the human picture there is no way of avoiding those experiences or of rising above them. The only way is the spiritual way, and the spiritual way is that way where the Christ becomes the reality of our being! And when we begin to look out from the standpoint of God, the sum total of all creation, then we are fulfilling the greatest law ever revealed by Jesus Christ—the law of forgiveness. There is no greater law than that of forgiveness. Remember, love God with all thy might and love your neighbor as yourself. That neighbor is every human being on earth, every animal, every plant! And there is no way you can love them while holding them in condemnation.

In this meditation, then, see and understand that God is the life, soul, mind, not only of friends, but of all so-called enemies. And, in that way, you will eliminate all enemies. Jesus said to Pilate, "Thou canst have no power over me, unless it came from the Father in heaven."[8] That is our answer to enemies or enmity of every form whether appearing as man, sin, disease, or lack. Some of you who heard me in January will remember how many times I stressed this fact: that this law of forgiving, this law of forgiveness, is the real law of demonstration. This ability to see God as the mind, the life and soul of enemies as well as of friends. Why? Because not only in the Old Testament, but all the way through the teachings of Jesus, we have this reminder—the first commandment is the secret of life. Only one God, only one life; the life of every one of us; the life of

our so-called enemies. God is the only mind, and therefore God must be the mind of what we call enemies!
Only one God, and only one creation—and all spiritual!

In that meditation, can you not see that as long as your
consciousness is filled with this oneness—one God, one
creation, all oneness, you are opening your consciousness
for the inflow of the Christ? There is no other way. Love
is the way and love is truth, and truth is the ability to
become aware of God as the form and formation, the
cause and effect of all that appears as our world! Thus our
objective is embodied in these meditations: "The world is
new to every soul when Christ has entered into it"[9] . . . "I
can of mine own self do nothing",[10] "The Father within,
he doeth the works"[11] . . . "I live, yet not I, the Christ
liveth in me."[12]

Let us now sit in silence and take any or all of these
three thoughts as the central theme in our consciousness.
Paying no attention to the human thoughts, we center
our thought on these and when we have finished, we can
feel that we have become connected to the divine source
of our being.

As a help, may I offer you this: You are familiar with
the illustration I have used on the subject of supply and
will know immediately what I mean. I said that the
oranges growing on the orange tree are not our supply,
they are not even the supply of oranges. They are the
effect, the result, the fruitage of supply. Supply is the law
that operates *in* and *as* the tree. You can take away all
the oranges and as long as that law is in operation, you
will have more oranges. Now to think of the oranges as
supply and try to hold on to them or even give them
away and think you are giving something is foolish. You
are not giving a thing away because they are multiplying

rapidly all the time. And so, with that as an illustration, you will remember that everything you see is only the result of the law of God! You will remember that behind the visible is the law of God producing and reproducing. That which is visible to you, whether money or whatever, is but an effect of supply—it is not supply. It is only an effect of supply! Supply is the consciousness of good within, and as long as we have that, we have what we call dollars.

Now, in the same way, when we look at people do not look at them and think of them as good or bad or sick or well. Look through the individual and see that every individual is just the product, the result, the presentation, the vehicle through which or as which God is appearing. Remember not to put value on oranges, or dollars, or people! And even the good that appears to come through them, while being grateful for it, look behind to see the actual source through which it comes. No one is good of himself. Every bit of good you have ever done has not been a result of your own nature at all. We are neither good nor bad in life—it is God shining through. We of ourselves have never been charitable or kind; that is a quality of God shining through. And although we have those qualities, it does not mean we have them of ourselves. *It is God.*

Evil is not a quality of itself, either. There is no such thing as a concrete evil. Evil is just God shining through. It is our misinterpretation of it that causes it to appear to us as evil. There cannot be the first commandment, "Thou shalt have no other gods—powers—besides me,"[13] and evil. There cannot be infinite good and evil. So the evil we behold is only a negative appearance, concept, false idea of that which is real and which is God, good.

Jesus said: "Thou couldest have no power over me unless it be given to thee of the Father."[14] And so now, as we look at the individual, let us look through him, and see that only God is appearing through him or as him, and there is no evil. God is the only power to whatever is given effect. The same with oranges and dollars. Do not let us see those as supply, but as the effect of the law of God, which *I am* . . . the effect of the law of God–which I am!

~2~

Unfolding Consciousness

This is a continuation of our class yesterday, a continuity of unfolding consciousness. We are taking up where we left off, and, as a matter of fact, carrying right on as we will for the rest of the week.

When John was in prison he sent word to Jesus: "Art thou he that should come?[1] Is this the promised Messiah?" And Jesus did not tell him that he had been authorized or ordained, or had received a license to be a rabbi. He said, "Go and show John the things you have seen, that the sick are healed."[2] Our only authority for the work we are doing is its result, and that result must be healing, the healing of the problems of human existence! The work of healing through the spirit is never the healing of a body; never the healing of a physical condition. That is the result, but it is not the work. The work is the spiritualizing of consciousness. The work is spiritualizing consciousness, spiritualizing thought, opening consciousness to the receptivity of God. That is the work in healing.

In the presence of God there are no problems, and so when you are standing, actually standing, in the conscious awareness of the presence of God, you have no sins or diseases to overcome. Of all of Jesus' statements, the greatest is, "Seek ye first the kingdom of God . . . and all these other things shall be added unto you."[3] Now the kingdom of God, the realm of God, is consciousness. The spiritual atmosphere of God is the kingdom and when you are in the spiritual atmosphere of God, all the harmonies of this world, of heaven and of earth, are added unto you.

The subject of healing work is a very interesting one and there are many approaches to this practice, but I can only speak of that which has revealed itself to me. Healing work is accomplished entirely through silence! The treatments, so called, of oral explanation or the written word, are merely little ladders which we use to climb up to the point of silence. Sometimes they are necessary, most often they are not. After one has been in this work for awhile, in this study and practice, it is almost unnecessary to use the mental argument for healing. It is possible to just close the eyes and quickly get into an atmosphere of silence and watch the healing work taking place. Then later on, it is possible to maintain that silence consciously even while doing the ordinary things of life: driving a car, writing, reading, housekeeping, or gardening.

It is possible, then, to maintain that spiritual atmosphere regardless of what is seemingly being done with our body or our mind; the healing work takes place whether or not we are actually engaged in the work of bringing it out. Think of the atmosphere of Jesus' thought when the woman pushed through the throng. He did not know she was there seeking a healing. He turned around and she had been healed. It was her coming into the atmosphere of that consciousness and doing so in faith, that healed her—which brings up a very important thought here. What is the patient's duty and part in a healing?

In my writing, I have made it very clear that ninety-nine percent of the responsibility for healing is on the shoulder of the practitioner, and I really believe that it is. The practitioner should assume the responsibility for the healing work—not that any practitioner can guarantee one hundred percent healings; but the real responsibility for the healing work rests with the practitioner. The reason is this: healing is accomplished through a spiritual state of consciousness! And the practitioners who live, work, and have their being in that spiritual atmosphere will do beautiful healing work and they will do it in proportion to the degree in which they live in this spiritual atmosphere. True, you can do healing work even while being part of the human sense of life, but to do really great works it becomes necessary to come out and be separate. It becomes necessary to come out and live on the higher plane.

Again, you can enjoy a movie, good music, family life, and home, but it does mean that in that spiritual existence the things of the human realm have little or no place. There are wonderfully sweet things in this human life: family, music, art, literature. One can find opportunity for enjoying these without coming down to the level of much of the world's pleasures and pains.

And so, the practitioner who lives in the highest degree of spiritual consciousness will give out the highest sense of spiritual atmosphere and do the best healing work. And this atmosphere has no relationship at all to sanctimoniousness. It does not mean that at all. As a matter of fact, often when that kind of attitude is present, we may question how much spirituality is there, because true spirituality is humble. True spirituality makes you realize that we are all one under the skin, whether a master of two thousand years ago, an ancient rabbi, or a priest of today. All one under the skin! Also, spirituality has nothing to do with a lot of religious learning. True spirituality has to do primarily with the degree in which an individual has realized the nothingness of evil and the presence of the Christ.

We have taken as our theme Paul's statement: "I live, yet not I, the Christ liveth in me."[4] And Jesus' statement: "I can of mine own self do nothing, the Father within, he doeth the works."[5] So, in that atmosphere, in that realization of this inner presence, this inner power, is the beginning of spirituality. And when that comes, it brings with it the other end of the same stick—the realization that what appears as sin or disease is not power. It is really just the universal belief of a selfhood apart from God. It is really only the accumulated human beliefs of the *materia medica* and theological world. All these, banded together, form a mental influence so strong as to become almost mesmeric—and then we see the streetcar tracks coming together in the distance and believe it is so. We see the sky touching the mountain and believe it is so. We see a snake where a rope really is, and we wonder what kind of a miracle-performing treatment will change the snake into a rope. None of our treatments will ever change the streetcar tracks, the sky sitting on the mountain, or the rope that looks like a snake. Our treatment is only the realization that the tracks are already normal and harmonious; that the sky has never sat upon the mountain; that the rope has never been anything other than a rope. So that realization of the nothingness of error is the second part of the revelation that comprises spiritual consciousness. When we no longer hate or fear error in any form, when we no longer love it—then we will find we have attained at least a great enough measure of spiritual consciousness to begin doing healing work.

Now back to the patient's part in this work: First of all, patients make it very difficult when they persist in remaining in the same frame of mind they would hold when going to a doctor, where they acknowledge a physical disease to be their claim and expect some piece of matter to cure or remove it. In approaching a practitioner for healing, that should not be. The attitude that is most helpful is that of, "Show me how to find the Christ. I know that whatever of sin, discord or disease may be present in my thought or in or on my body, represents only that degree of the absence of the conscious awareness of God." And so the attitude of the patient should not be to describe all the symptoms, but rather to open consciousness to the receptivity of truth—the presence of God. "I live, yet not I, the Christ liveth in me."[6] Their real attitude of mind should be, "Open this truth to me. Show me the presence of God. Reveal the omnipresent Christ that already is my own consciousness, but of which I am not yet aware!"

That is the help which should, first of all, come from the patient approaching a practitioner for healing. Then, of course, comes a willingness to try, so far as possible, to keep thought away from the problem and on the spiritual things of life. "Thou wilt keep him in perfect peace, whose mind is stayed on thee."[7] That is not merely a Bible quotation. That is the actual truth! God does keep us in physical, mental, moral, and financial peace in the degree that our thought is off the problems of life and on the spiritual realities. How, we ask, can we do that? That comes through hearing a teacher or

practitioner with some measure of spiritual consciousness to whom we can turn to be lifted up. "I, if I be lifted
up, will draw all men nigh unto me."[8] And there again
is the practitioners' need to stay on that high level day
and night, so that everyone who turns to them may be
lifted up immediately into that consciousness wherein
they are able to discern spiritual harmony manifested as
health, harmony and supply.

Then too, there is the study and reading of inspirational literature. There now is metaphysical literature to
meet every taste and every consciousness and everyone
must find that which meets his or her own state of
thought. There are those who require only the highest
spiritual and inspirational literature. Only that which
keeps their consciousness high in God meets their need.
There are others who are just as earnest, just as desirous
of finding God, but cannot respond to that type of
literature and require more of the mental type, which
makes them think and reason. Again, there are those
who require that which will center their thought on
prayer and devotion. It does not follow that that which
was recommended to you will meet your need. There
are types of literature that we might read which are not
meant for our own particular state of consciousness, so
it would be just as well to leave them alone. Each one
must find that which meets his need. It does not follow
that that which was recommended to you will meet your
need. Each must and will find his own literature.

As you know, in my own case, I have written that
which represents my state of consciousness as it applies to
the spiritual life—and I must tell you that I cannot read that
all the time either. No. I feel that I like to delve around and
find something in the thought and consciousness of others

who have come along this way; some beyond. Further, as part of this work, let me mention in passing–not that I have any interest other than to show you my own trend of thought–that I find a great deal of good in Marchette Chute's books, *The Search for God* and *The End of the Search.* They seem to answer something in me along the lines of scripture. In the same way, for years and years I have enjoyed Allen Boone's *Letters to Strongheart* and *You Are the Adventure.* They are inspirational in nature and help to keep thought on a higher level.

So, another point for those seeking truth and healing is, as much as possible, to keep their thoughts away from the ordinary radio programs, ordinary types of reading, and ordinary types of movies, to keep more on the spiritual, the mental plane–and that will keep consciousness open and receptive for the inflow of God.

A third point is to associate, as far as possible, with those on the same path. There is nothing more helpful to our mutual progress than a meeting like this–*nothing.* "Where two or more are gathered together in my name, there am I among them."[9] When people come here seeking nothing from each other, with no thought in their minds but receptivity to the Christ, you may well know that the Christ is here to fill that need. No one in this room has come here to get a thing. Each one knows there is nothing to be gotten of a material nature, only an atmosphere of the Christ for all to share. And when we come together in that mental attitude of expectancy, that mental attitude of consciousness open for truth, God, love, what can result but good? And so every meeting we can have together on this level of spiritual thinking is advancing our own progress. But that must also be tempered with judgment, as it would do me no

good and you no good, to go around from practitioner
to practitioner or teacher to teacher just because they are
presenting a mental or spiritual message. Jesus gave us
the recipe for that years ago: "My sheep hear my
voice."[10] You, in your prayers, will be led to those
practitioners or those teachers who can meet you on
your level of consciousness, just as in my prayers I
attract to me all those who are able to receive this
particular message. Not because it is the best message or
the highest, but because it is *my* message, the only
message I know. And only those who can receive this
message should be drawn to me. And you should allow
yourselves to be drawn only to those who can meet your
spiritual need—who have the particular bread for you.

I said to begin with, that the subject of healing work
is interesting because it has nothing to do with a "process." It has to do with silence. Healing work has to do
with *silence!* You know, and I know that sin, disease and
lack are unrealities! They have not, and never have had,
a real causative principle, no more than the mirage on
the desert could show forth real water or a real city. Sin
and disease have no causative principle! The reason for
that is that God is the only cause. God or mind or soul
is the only creative principle. Therefore, all that can ever
have real being is the effect of God, the effect of Spirit,
the effect of Soul. So, all that exists in the realm of sin or
disease must necessarily exist as an illusion or false sense
which we have, for the time being, accepted. Knowing
this, we know that when we turn to the Christ for healing,
we are not really turning there with a prayer that God
"take away" this disease or this sin. We are not going to
God for anything of a physical nature. We are going to
God, the eternal Spirit, so that its divine, omnipresent

wisdom may dissolve for us the illusion of sense–the illusory picture which at the moment is appearing as sin or as disease.

The things of God are foolishness with men, just as the things of men are "foolishness with God."[11] We do not go to God to tell him what claim or what disease is to be removed, or what sin or what limitation or lack, nor do we go to God to explain our need for money or employment. We go to God for one purpose–to hear the still, small voice. If we have any other purpose in going to God, let's drop it right here and now! If you had a sin or a disease that God could remove, then God would not be God, but a brute. He should have removed it long before you ever prayed for help! The fact, then, that you still have a problem is proof that you have no problem that God could have done something about or can do something about. Remember this.

The only thing you are entertaining is a false sense of God and God's creation and the only place you go to have that corrected is to God, but not to tell God that your need is physical, or mental, or moral, or financial. It is not necessary in any way to try to enlighten God as to the nature of your problem, or to tell the practitioner what the pain is. In this approach to spiritual healing, a diagnosis plays no part. It is never necessary for anyone to tell me where the pain is or what organ is affected, or even the name of the person requiring help. I too, "can of mine own self do nothing."[12]

Now, ask yourself: "If I, of my own self, had the power to heal anyone, wouldn't I be doing it this very minute instead of spending my time talking about it? There is nothing I can do of my own self and so I am in the same position that Jesus was in when he said this."

But, the Father within, this spiritual consciousness, this divine Spirit can and does dissolve all error—all appearances of error. Every form and phase of discord is overcome, destroyed, eliminated by the conscious realization of the presence of God! And so, both by practitioner and by patient, let it be remembered that the work is done through the silence—not necessarily though, through sitting with eyes closed and waiting for God to do something; that is not always silence, although it is sometimes a good preparation.

Silence is a state of our own receptivity, our conscious awareness of our own being, whether with eyes closed or whether driving a car. Silence is that state when the consciousness is alert and the ears are open and receptive for that still, small voice. And we prepare for that state of receptivity, for that state of consciousness, by going into meditation or the silence, when we awaken in the morning. Meditation is but one facet of this beautiful gem called Christ healing—just one facet of it.

We must learn when we awaken in the morning, sometimes even before we are out of bed, to turn within, become silent, remembering just some passage as: "I live, yet not I, the Christ liveth in me."[13] Thus we make room right there and then for the entrance of the Christ to be the guiding stream; the guiding point of consciousness; the healing influence in consciousness throughout the day. Make room for this healing influence on awakening in the morning! Let the first thought be that of opening consciousness to the inflow of the Christ, the Father within. These "statements" will not do anything for you. Too many people are walking up and down this earth, making affirmations and repeating quotations like that, and nothing happens. All of these statements are of very little help, take my word for it: It is the conscious realization of the presence of God that does the work! It is the actual feel of the presence of God. It is coming to that place where you can feel God within you, can feel that Christ within, can almost understand Paul when he said, "I live, yet not I, the Christ liveth in me."[14] When you feel that, you have achieved the consciousness of the presence of God!

And then you have the divine healing influence, that which goes before you to make the crooked places straight, that which walks beside you and behind you as God, as your guide and your protection. Thus, you carry with you your own healing influence so that all who meet you during the day feel the Christliness of your thought. It has nothing to do with you as a person; it has nothing to do with the fact that you are a good human. It has to do with the fact that Christ sits on the throne!

Your consciousness is open to the Christ, and the divine presence is there and is felt, when you have attained the conscious awareness of the presence of God. Throughout the day we should take as many periods as our time or our work will permit. Take five minutes out to go to the washroom for a few minutes, and be patient and let that silent influence come upon you again. Because it is that silent influence, that healing influence, which does the work for you and for all who contact you in your day's work. And remember: It does go out before you to make the crooked places straight. Now then, that silence which you have through these short periods of meditation–that silence becomes the healing Christ in your thought, and that does the healing work.

Now, for a few moments we will go into an actual silence, an actual period in which we will realize that we

are all in one place, are all one mind. And we will take
for our thought: "I live, yet not I, the Christ liveth in
me." Gently and peacefully, we will let that thought
circulate and percolate through our consciousness
awhile. Remember, you have dedicated this week to the
achievement of the presence and power of God. We are
not ending this meeting at two o'clock. We are continuing this meeting right through tomorrow and the next
day and the next. And so, we are carrying out of this
room with us until tomorrow, this continuing unfolding
consciousness of the presence of the Christ. The realization will be that of harmony, of peace. Outwardly, it will
appear to our neighbor as if we have had a healing of
some physical or mental or moral or financial discord,
but we know that that did not happen. All that happened
is that the Christ flooded our consciousness and showed
us that there is no sin, disease, lack, or limitation. Do not
permit yourself to think of your problem between now
and tomorrow. If it comes into your thought, insist that
it get behind you and stay behind you.

We are going to have no time in this twenty-four
hours to think of problems. Your mind is going to be
stayed on God: "Thou wilt keep him in perfect peace,
whose mind is stayed on thee."[15]

So, the manner of thinking of God can be something
like this:

God, the divine intelligence of this universe, is the intelligence of all mankind, whether appearing as man, woman,
child, animal, or plant, visible as life–the fruit of life. God, the
divine soul of this universe, is the soul of all mankind. God,
the Spirit, is the substance of all form. There are no material
forms or formation. Everything that has form has a spiritual
form and God is the substance of that form. Any appearance

contrary to that spiritual form is illusion! God is the mind of every individual. Anyone appearing to have a mind apart from God, anyone even claiming to have a mind of his own, is nothing more nor less than a temptation to accept a mind apart from God.

Do not be tempted. Do not fall into temptation! Whenever you see any sign of insanity or mental sickness, realize immediately that the temptation is coming to you to believe that man has a mind apart from God: God is the mind of this universe and of all men; God is the soul of every individual; God is the eternal life of every man, woman, child–in heaven and on earth. God is the life of every individual who has ever lived on earth now, or ever will live on earth. God is the universal life of all being, therefore there is no diseased life and no dead life. All life is eternal, immortal and omnipresent to those of spiritual vision, and those of spiritual vision are those who have come into this agreement that God is Spirit, the substance of all forms. God is the substance of all formation and the law of all formation.

Let that be with you until tomorrow.

~ 3 ~

PRACTICING THE PRESENCE

THERE COULD NOT BE THE PRESENCE OF GOD and the absence of any quality of God. And that brings me right up to a couple of notes I made for today: To begin with, how many are familiar with the term "mortal mind"? Wouldn't this be a wonderful day to begin to give up the use of that term, to drop that term from your vocabulary? It has served its purpose and has had its day. Actually, there is no such thing as mortal mind since there is only one mind and that mind is God. At best, then, this thing that has been called mortal mind is not an opposite of divine mind, because divine mind, being infinite, could not have an opposite, and so this so-called mortal mind could be only suppositional.

I have said to you that when you are in meditation try to give your words a specific meaning of your own. There is nothing more harmful than the use of quotations as such, because they become hypnotic in their action and will result in no benefit to you at all. Take, "I live, yet not I, the Christ liveth in me."[1] Now to begin with, this sounds beautiful; but actually, if you have not come to some conclusion as to what the Christ is, how do you know what it is that is living in you? Especially if you have not come to some understanding of that word, "Christ"? Christ does not mean what the orthodox

27

church means: a man who lived two thousand years ago. Christ means the spirit of God that is in man; the spirit that animated Christ Jesus; the spirit that animates you. The word Christ may not mean a thing in your life, and may even set you back to some theological belief. And so it would not be wise for you to even use the word Christ unless you, yourself, had arrived at some meaning of it that made it a living presence to you!

It so happens that the term "the Christ" registered very deeply with me right away. Something struck deep within me–I do not know why–and from that day to this it has been the guiding force in my life. Why? Because I do not associate it with a man named Jesus but with something to do with God itself, the universal mind or soul, an individual presence, an individual feeling of within-ness, and so the Christ to me can become very real. Then, when I go into the silence and realize, "I live, yet not I, the Christ liveth in me,"[2] I know what I am repeating. I am being what Jesus meant when he said, "I can of mine own self do nothing,[3] the Father within me doeth the works."[4] I know that I am that living Christ presence.

To repeat what Jesus said, "I can of mine own self do nothing, the Father within, he doeth the works," to repeat this is meaningless to me. I only know what he means from the fact that I know what the Christ is; and I know that he means this divine presence and that he is not thinking of some great being. I know that he is thinking of the same essence, or being, or spirit within that he meant when he said, "I live, yet not I, the Christ liveth in me." If, then, you take a quotation into your meditation or into your daily life, be sure that you do not use it as a quotation. Try to get some original meaning for yourself so that it lives for you.

Mortal mind, if you use the term as such, will present to you some evil mind or some mind other than God, or some presence or power other than God—and mortal mind is not that at all. At best it means the sum total of human beliefs. There are two words that we can use as substitutes for mortal mind which will mean something so beautiful to you that it will help you in your healing work every time you are presented with a need for healing for either yourself or others. The words are these: "appearance" and "suggestion." Let us say that we are out walking on the street and we see some evidence of error—drunkenness, immorality, accident, sin or disease. Now, let us translate that, immediately, into the word "suggestion" or the word "appearance"! Why? Because if you do, you will have caught it right then and there. The error does not exist as an actual condition; it does not exist as a man; it does not exist as something or some person, but only as a false appearance. And when you recognize it as that, it disappears. You have seen through it and destroyed it because its only reality was in you believing it to be something or someone.

Whenever, then, error presents itself to you as somebody or something, if you are quick and alert and say, "That is neither something nor somebody. It is nothing but a suggestion of a selfhood apart from God, an illusory picture,"—that quickly you will have met it! The sick person will jump to his feet; the drunken person will become sober. I can tell you this only because years and years of evidence have proven that it is true.

So, when a call comes, just to recognize, "This is neither a person, a thing or a condition, but a suggestion only, and I am not going to accept it,"—that ends it! That is where your instantaneous healings come from. An

instantaneous healing will not take place if the practitioner first sees it as a person, thing, or condition, as a
disease, or as mortal mind. The only way you can dispel
the illusion of sense is to recognize, instantly, that you
are dealing with appearance or suggestion.

Remember the illustration in my writings of the
streetcar tracks coming together in the distance? That is
not a condition. Nobody has to sit down and give a
prayer or treatment to adjust the streetcar tracks. What
we are called upon for is the recognition that it is only an
appearance and we can stay right on the streetcar. The
same with the sky "sitting on" the mountain. That exists
not as an actual condition to be met, but only as a
suggestion coming to the one who is seeing it. The same
with the mirage. There has never been a mirage to wet
the sands of the desert. No mirage city has ever grown
or been torn down. That exists only as appearance, an
illusory sense, a suggestion of a condition apart from
what is familiar to the normal senses.

Now, all these things are really what is meant by the
term "mortal mind." The only trouble is that instead of
it indicating the nothingness of what we seem to see all
around us, it frightens us into believing we have something to get rid of. It would be wise for those who can do
it, to remove that term from their thinking and substitute
for it this thought: error in every form is only appearance or suggestion. Then you know you do not have to
reach out to do something to it. And that leads me up to
the most important part of the whole work: Healing
work has nothing to do with healing you of disease, sin,
fear, lack or limitation; it has to do with my not accepting a false appearance as reality. If I accept that appearance or suggestion of error, then I am in the same boat

as those who are believing that it does exist, and we cannot help each other, for it will be the blind leading the blind.

The only difference between a patient and a practitioner is that the patient momentarily believes that some suggestion or appearance exists as an actual condition, whereas the practitioner has come to see that what is appearing as sin, disease, or lack is nothing more than illusion, appearance, suggestion. He treats it that way and quickly drops it.

Out here is the presence of God. The presence of God is therefore present as each individual. The fullness of God is here as each individual. It does not take the whole world of people to come together to form God. Each individual is the absolute allness of God individualized here, just as every number one is the allness of one, every number two, the allness of number two. Appearances testify otherwise as we say, "Here is a male and here is a female, here is a person of years, here is a person of immaturity, and here is a child." Again appearance! It is not true. Every individual is the fullness and the allness that is God. "Son, all that I have is thine."[5] That makes it very clear and true. All that I, God, have is thine. And, "Lo, I am with you always."[6] The fullness of the I is with you, any premise to the contrary being only an appearance–illusion–false sense. It is not true. One with God is a majority. So then, every time you come face to face with an individual who will not accept any limiting appearance about you, you must have some measure of healing. It must be so.

Every time there is a lecture, from two to twenty or more are healed and that is a matter of receptivity. It is a question of the realization that you yourself are the fullness. The realization of that on the part of you and on the part of the teacher is the oneness with God that produces the healing. Now behind this is the truth that God is all and the truth that God, the infinite one, appears as me. It appears as you and as me, as the dog, the cat, the bird. But it is still the one! You are that one. I am that one. You are the fulfillment of that one. I am the fulfillment of that one. You may say that this is a treatment I am giving. Any statement of truth is a treatment to the false appearance. I am not making these statements in the sense of giving a treatment, but in the sense of presenting the truth of being. I have no intention of healing anyone or anything; no idea that God, whether appearing as one or as another, has need of healing. And you are that God appearing. You are the life eternal, I am the life eternal. And that is true of everyone!

Where we come into trouble is this: we have been educated into the belief that we are finite—human beings. And so we come seeking some good. One person seeks health, one companionship, one supply, and one a home and therein lies the error. And incidentally, that is the reason for delayed healings, for slow healings, and for failures in the healing work.

If everyone, even those who today call themselves patients, will acknowledge that they are not coming for healing but for the revelation of their own fullness, their own completeness, they will hasten the day of their healing. When you come into a library or to any metaphysical center or lecture, you are not really coming to be filled because that would be an acknowledgment on your part of a vacuum within your own being: "I am empty, or half empty. Fill me!" That is not true. You are already the fullness of being, and the reason you are here is a part of my demonstration. You are here to bless me. I myself would not be very happy here with an empty room, and so it is a part of my demonstration. We are really blessing each other. "Where two or three are gathered in my name, there am I among them."[7]

Can you see that it would not be possible to have a whole room full of empty people wanting to be filled by one person, or that I, as one person, could fill them? No, we come here in a sort of exchange courtesy. You are part of my demonstration and I am part of your demonstration. We are part of the fulfillment of God. We are really God fulfilling itself and this is our meeting place. It is only by the courtesy of time and effort that I am the one sitting up here on this platform. Next year it may be you, and whether or not it is, is a matter of your own choice. Anybody can sit up on this platform who chooses to, who wants to dedicate their life.

Never believe for a moment that this great spiritual truth of the ages has been given to us for my benefit or yours. That is really the most selfish part of this whole scheme, the belief that in some way God is going to bless you or me for our sake and then let us go about our business a little healthier or a little happier. That cannot be true.

"I am the light of the world,"[8] and you see, I am the light of the world for the benefit of all who at this moment may seem to be enjoying some phase of darkness. And when they are no longer enjoying it, they will come out from under. In the same way, you are the light of the world, regardless of appearance. The allness of God permeates you, but not for your own sake—only that you may be the light of the world *to* the world. We all have friends, families, neighbors and many of those have not come into the light of this truth, and it is for that purpose we are here. To be a light so that they may see by our example the fruitage of spiritual living, not that you or I may benefit.

In the scheme of God, I am sure it is unimportant whether I individually ride the wave of prosperity or not. The only possible reason that God could have in prospering me is that you might see the benefits of the spiritual path and reach out for it. Likewise, there is only one reason that you should show forth health and wealth, and it is not so you can have a more peaceful mind or a less painful body. It is only that, *as* the light of the world, others will see that that is the fruit of the spirit and thus you will lead them in that way. It would be a very simple thing for all of us to be healthier and wealthier than we are if we could agree from here on, to stop trying to demonstrate these for ourselves. If we could give up the attempt to be healed or enriched today, we would come naturally into the grace of God. Our very efforts to heal and be healed are the stumbling blocks in our path. The harder a practitioner works on a case, the less chance there is of bringing out a healing. Healing is not a thing of labor, but of love, of grace. Health, wealth and harmony are the grace of God! No one has to work for it, pray for it, or be deserving of it. No one need learn to be a better man or a better woman. All of this comes as the grace of God, and grace is made manifest in proportion as we stop thinking of ourselves and our problems and start thinking of God, start thinking out to the world.

Here is one good way to make a beginning. If this presents anything of a new nature to you because of other reading that you have been doing, don't throw it back at me untried. Try it! Give it a chance to work in your consciousness, and then see whether or not it bears spiritual fruit. People coming for help are thinking of themselves as human and even if they are thinking of themselves in a spiritual sense, they are thinking of themselves as something less than God itself, thinking of themselves as effect. The hint I want to give you now is: reverse that and think of yourself as cause, and see how much help you need after that! Think of yourself as the causative principle of life. Think of yourself as the *is* unto your own being, the law unto your own body, the law unto your own business. What is my authority for that? I come well authorized! It is the whole of the teachings of Jesus Christ comprising the Gospel according to John: "I am the way, the truth, and the life"[9] . . . "I am the resurrection"[10] . . . "I am the water and the wine" . . . "Hast thou been with me so long, Philip, and hast not known?"[11] . . . "Thou seest me, thou seest the Father that sent me"[12] . . . "I and the Father are one."[13] Try that and see if it does not work! See if it does not free you from fear.

You cannot be healed of fear while you believe there is a law outside of you. Even if you think it is a law of God, you cannot be healed of fear. Who knows if you are going to connect up? Maybe it will miss you. If, however, you are the law of God, how can you escape from yourself? "If I make my bed in hell, thou art there."[14] Yes, if I am in hell then God is too, because I and God are one. Try that, and see if you can ever fear after you have decreed yourself to be the law; to be the life, the mind, the soul of God—all in one.

When you come into this library, when you go out to a movie, when you go into a restaurant or a cocktail bar, never believe that there is a good or bad atmosphere depending on where you are. There is no atmosphere even in this library of benefit to you, no atmosphere in the cocktail bar that is bad for you. You carry your own atmosphere! You are the law of God. When you come into this place you are the law of God, the presence of God. You carry the atmosphere of health and of wealth, and everyone in this place will see it and benefit by it. The same in the cocktail bar, hotel, prison, asylum. You carry the atmosphere of health and wealth because God is your life, your soul! I carry the atmosphere of my being with me, and it blesses not only me, but all who come within the range of my body, the range of my thought. They must be blessed even if they touch my coat, because I am permeated with the atmosphere of God. God is the mind, the soul, the substance of my body, the law of my body. There is nothing to me but God, and if you are seeing me as less, you are seeing what your own vision has created. There is only God here and that is all I can see out there!

The longer we see male and female, health and sickness, wealth and lack, the longer we postpone the day when we realize that we ourselves are the law unto ourselves. Words are sometimes very powerful and often we come across statements that bring out intense and great truths, even when of themselves they may not seem to have been written or spoken for that purpose. I am thinking of three such statements with which I am familiar in the writings of Mrs. Eddy: "Christian Scientists, be a law unto yourselves, that mental malpractice cannot harm you." There is a direct indication that you can be, and as a matter of fact *are*, a law unto yourself. You are the law, and the only malpractice is the so-called thinking we speak of as beliefs. No one can malpractice. There are only these universal beliefs which you will accept unless you yourself realize that *you* are the law.

"Take possession of your body, and govern its feelings and actions." Not a word about turning it over to God. She tells you to take possession of it and govern its feelings and actions. "Only the mind of the individual can produce a result upon the body."

I have never lost those statements and the essence of them because it carries us back to the original treatment, the original statements of Jesus: "I am the resurrection[15] . . . I am the truth . . . I am life eternal." He made himself the law unto his own being. When Pilate said: "Knowest thou not that I have power to crucify thee?"[16] Jesus answered: "Thou couldest have no power over me unless it be given to thee of the Father."[17] Why? Because Pilate himself was the law of God, and Jesus knew it—and his knowing that Pilate was the law of God proved it impossible to kill him. To crucify him, yes—and then only because he gave his consent to it. Remember, Jesus gave his consent to that crucifixion. He probably wanted to show forth that you can destroy even the human sense of life but you can do nothing to what is real; and this he proved.

Likewise with you. This human world can do to you anything that you will permit it to. It can crucify you and can set you free. But it must have your consent. No one can die without giving their consent to it. Whether you know it or not, believe me; I have seen that nobody dies until they give their consent. They may not say openly, "I am ready to die," but they do say, "Oh, what's the use?" or "I'm giving up." That is really the consent. In the same way, no one can be a failure until they consent.

There are certain conditions in the world that may knock a man down, but until he gives his consent to the failure, he will rise above all obstacles and be stronger than ever before.

It is a matter of your own consent. And the reason? You yourself are the embodiment of all the God power there is! There is no law of God that can act upon you. You are the law of God that acts upon your business, your body, your family relations and as a matter of fact, on the atomic bomb. There is no atomic bomb that can wipe you out except with your own consent! If you are now agreeing or fearing what will happen under atomic warfare, you are really now digging your grave.

If you are accepting this teaching of Jesus Christ (which was not original with him), remember that he was only one of our great teachers. This teaching has been on earth in many forms before, even in print. There is nothing new about it. We, in this age, have been given this truth not only in a form we can accept, but with signs following that prove it is a healing work. We can prove that a person like yourself can just by a little study and acceptance of a few old truths, be a healer, a practitioner, a reformer, if you will, anything you want.

I have seen almost every type of disease healed, almost every form of insanity met. I have seen wonderful things in this world, enough to be able to testify that this is a miraculous work. A person with no other background than your own can go out and do it. We have, in this generation, the signs following that we are the Christ as well as Jesus, Buddha, Shankara. You are the Christ. As much as Jesus, if you will only acknowledge it and claim it! You, within a day, a week, a month,

or a year can be doing the same healing work that is
being done by the finest practitioners in the metaphysical world. It is a very simple thing. It comes as a result
of knowing two things. The first, that I am the very
presence of God! I need no other law to act on me for
good. I am the embodiment of all the law of good that
God ever gave to individual being. And second, all there
is in the way of evil, so-called, is not a reality. It is an
appearance or suggestion, and all I have to do is recognize it as an appearance and let it go! That is the second
part that is necessary to know and understand in order
to be a practitioner—hypnotism! It is enough just to know
that you are *not* called upon to heal cancers or tumors or
blindness or lack or limitation. You, as the practitioner,
must be the unhypnotized person who knows there is no
such thing as an externalized cancer or tumor, blindness
or lack or limitation. How could there be, if God is the
cause or principle of the universe, and all that God made
is good?

That which constitutes a practitioner, therefore, is one
who knows these two things: All that God is I am; "Son,
all that I have, is thine."[18] Anything else is an appearance, a suggestion of a selfhood apart from God. And
the person who sits back quietly and realizes, "Thank
you Father! I don't have to sit here and remove disease
or heal it. I only have to be unhypnotized enough to
know that God is the life, God is the mind of this
individual." I am the law of God in action. Every
individual is the law of God in action. And so, if you will
(and remember we have now been three days on this
path bringing to light our true identity in which is
neither sin nor disease), begin by reversing your own
beliefs about yourself! That you exist as an effect of

something, that you exist as an image, reflection, or idea. You do not at all! You exist as the very presence of God, the very allness of God—individually manifest here for the glory of God. No, not for your benefit or mine, but to show forth the glory that is God.

Begin now! Instead of wanting some law that is going to miraculously make you healthy, wealthy and wise, be that law! Forget about mortal mind and see that everything that comes within range of your vision is appearance. Right where that false appearance is—right there—is reality, the universe of God, perfect, entire, complete and only awaiting your recognition! "I live, yet not I, the Christ liveth in me."[19] All that is real of me is the Christ. Anything else, that which is visible to senses, is but our limited view of the Christ which I am.

~ 4 ~

REALIZATION

As WE FINISH THE FIRST HALF OF OUR FIRST WEEK, we lead up to that place where we recognize that we exist as mind, or consciousness, or life eternal. Nothing is more important in the working out of our problems of health and other problems of human existence, than the knowledge of who and what we are. As long as we believe we are some finite person and that there is a law of good that can operate for us, we are apt to believe that we in some way have become separated from it, or might be separate and apart from it, or may not find it or connect with it. Or for the same reason, we may believe there is a law of evil that can act on, or through, or in us. The truth is, there is no law of good that can act upon us that we can use and contact, either through study or prayer.

We are our own law—that is what we must realize. We ourselves are constituted of the law of God. We are the law, the mind, the intelligence of our universe, the intelligence of our body; the intelligence of our business, of our entire universe. If there is any discord or inharmony it is because we have recognized some power apart from God. We have acknowledged ourselves to be other than that God being. This probably is the most important part of all metaphysical revelation—the nature of our true being. Unless we can see that we exist as mind

41

or consciousness, we will always be asking something or someone or some law to act upon us or through us.

I am life eternal. "I am the way, the truth, the life."[1] Now this, of course, does not refer to what ordinarily appears to us as humanhood. No human being is God or even the Christ. But God is the intelligence and the law that constitutes you. What we behold out here as humans is but our mistaken or false concept of the real you, the real me. It would certainly be sacrilegious to think of some person who is stupid, dishonest, deformed, and say, "You are God." God is the sum total of you, and all that appears contrary to that is the illusion or false sense or suggestion we talked about yesterday. Let us not forget that when we are working in the realm of spiritual unfoldment, we are not starting from you and going up to God. We are starting with God and coming forward to that which is the individualization of God, that which is never visible to the human eyes. We cannot see, hear, taste, touch, or smell "you." You are consciousness and all that is apparent to me, to my physical sense of you, represents my distorted view of you. Therefore the only way I can ever touch you really, is in spiritual consciousness.

I wonder if any of you felt that last night? Somehow in working here, you have been really beautiful and sweet in this work and I feel a great sense of love for you. Last night, before retiring after meditation, really and truly, as a group, everyone was with me and I could feel that great sense of love coming in and going back and forth, and I can truly say I lost all sense of humanhood, and could feel and touch the divine in you. I wonder if someone was having a healing, because it was so easy to reach you.

That is not possible with the human senses, but with the spiritual sense I can reach and touch and commune with the spiritual sense of you. That is the real sense of communion and that is where healing work takes place; not in calling you a human being, a divine idea, but in reaching through the appearance to the reality. That is when healing takes place. When through that spiritual sense I have contacted the reality of you, it is not so much that you are mind or God, as that God is all the reality or mind there is of you. That God, the universal good, is the individual life, mind, soul of you and of me.

So starting with God, we come down to its individualization and find it to be you. Therein comes this great law of forgiveness. It is so easy, when we look at people as humans, to find something in them that needs changing or altering or improving or condoning. Sometimes we feel so self-righteous when we find someone doing something we think is wrong and we say, "I can forgive them." This is all part of the human picture and will heal nothing. True forgiveness is not sitting in judgment on a person, first finding them to be wrong and then deciding to forgive them for being wrong. True forgiveness is in closing our eyes and getting within, in the spiritual sense of things, and there getting in touch with the reality of that individual and finding that all reality is God and there never has been a sin or a mistake or anything to overcome. Even if you did correct the sins and faults of your friends or loved ones, you still would not have accomplished much in a spiritual way. When you blot out the picture of all humanhood, the good as well as the bad, and get close to the center of being, close to God, you will find that sooner or later, when you open your eyes, those friends or relatives will no longer be the erring individuals they now appear to be. And we will go into the manner of accomplishing that.

For the balance of this week, those who are working with some problem of health or anything else, please drop it and don't do any more mental work on whatever your immediate problem is for the balance of this week. Follow out the schedule I am going to speak of in a moment, and let us see what happens to that problem by dropping it. Do no mental work, do not take it into your thought, but as often as it presents itself to you, turn from it and say, "No work will be done on that. 'Get thee behind me, Satan,' "[2] and persist in that attitude for the balance of this week and possibly into next week. Absolutely refuse to do anything about it. If it has the power to destroy you, let us find out about that now. You will find that the problem has no power to crucify you or set you free—no power and no existence. So for the next few days, or as long as we are working here together, let us not take up your problem, whatever its name or nature, but carry out what now follows:

In healing work, we have what appears to be a patient, a practitioner, and a God. And whether or not you consciously think of it in this way, there is this picture retained in thought that the patient sits here coming to the practitioner over there, and probably the practitioner is going to God and God is going to come down to the patient, and will complete the circle and now we will have a healing. There is no such relationship, no such thing as patient, practitioner, and God, nor is there such a thing as patient and practitioner. So there is no patient coming over here to a practitioner and no practitioner reaching over to the patient—no such relationship as that.

I am going to explain now what this relationship is so that we can do our work. If there is anyone you know who asks you for help, or anyone you need to forgive, or if you need to unsee the error handling them, this is the way you will work—and watch the results!

In the earlier days, when a ship wanted to reach shore, it radioed its message to the main station near Washington, D.C. and that station relayed messages back to the ship. They found in certain storms, however, and especially if the wind was in the wrong direction, that this big, powerful station of the government in Washington could not reach the ship that wanted to receive the message. It would not carry through. They could not send it in a strong enough manner to reach that ship. Just about this time, there was a little amateur ham radio operator a few miles along the coast and it turned out he could reach any of the ships regardless of storms. A little, weak ham station, and he could reach any of the ships. So it got to be a habit when the big station could not reach the ships, to tune into this little ham radio operator and let him send the message out to the ship and for awhile these men never stopped wondering why their big, powerful station did not reach through and this little station could. One day it dawned on them that this was a mystery, so they went to him to find out. He said, "It is very simple! You see, you are sending your message from your station through the air, through the storm to the ship, and if the wind is against you, you have great resistance. I send my message straight up into the air and let it fall down to the ship."

Now in a good deal of mental practice, strangely enough, there are still attempts made by practitioners to reach out from their thought to your thought. Of course, in the early days of metaphysical practice, that was the only known method. It was the earliest discovery in mental practice; it was really a matter not so much of mind over matter as mind over mind. You can still find literature telling you that the practitioner must work until he overcomes the belief in the patient's mind and then, when the patient's mind is healed, that is the healing. That is suggestion, hypnotism, one mind controlling another. Most practitioners have long since outgrown that method because not only is it not a very good one, but it often does not work. It is difficult to send a message straight through from one person to another. The best way is to reach God and let the message drop down from God to the individual needing it.

The example in this case is not quite the same as the example of the wireless. We do not send any thought up to God because really, here in this chair sits all there is of both God and man. "I and my Father are one,"[3] so if I want to reach God, all I have to reach for is the spiritual center of my own being. When I reach the spiritual center of my own being, strangely enough, the patient gets the benefit of the healing. The patient has done that first by placing himself, through his request for help, into oneness with my consciousness—into this oneness.

You must remember that none of this is entirely explainable in a human way. To illustrate: I have seen healings of cats, dogs, and birds, and I know they are much easier to heal than human beings as it is not possible for them to ask for help or for them to even desire help of a metaphysical nature. How, then, does that healing take place when they have not asked for it and are not even spiritually minded? The whole point is this: Everything that comes within range of my consciousness is part of my universe and therefore takes on the atmosphere of my consciousness. Therefore, if I take into my consciousness that which appears to the world as a cat, dog, bird, flower, or crop, it automatically takes on the complexion of my consciousness.

It is the same way with what we call problems. I have never been guilty, and never will be, of sending a thought out to any individual, nor will I ever hold a thought for anyone or about anyone. Then, when I am thinking of you or if you ask for help, or by virtue of your being where there is something in the nature of truth or God which you are seeking, you become one with infinite spiritual consciousness and its healing activity.

As I am not interested in making you a better or healthier human, but in bringing you into the divine reality of you which is God, I pay no attention to you as a human being. In this sacred and secret part of me, in communion with God, all who are part of my consciousness with any degree of receptivity, come into that outflow of God. Sometimes the patient says, "I got your thought." They did not. What they received was an impartation from God itself in the center of their being. Why? The God at the center of their being is the God at the center of your being, and so I do not have to reach out to you or find you out in space. Whether you are in the room with me or six thousand miles away from me, the spirituality of you is right in here—right within my own soul consciousness. That is also true the other way. Right in the center of your being I am. No one can deny that this "I am" is God. Right in the center of your being God is, and as God is all there is to me, that is where I am and that is where you are.

My oneness with God constitutes my oneness with every spiritual idea of God. That is why I am never

separate or apart from my spiritual good, whether
health, wealth, successful activity, co-operation, students,
dollars, a house to live in, or transportation. Regardless
in what form these spiritual ideas appear humanly, I am
one with them. Not because I am one with a lot of
people or things but because I am one with God, which
is the embodiment of all–spiritually. Always remember
this: that your oneness with God constitutes your
oneness with every spiritual idea.

You can never be without companionship, without
friends, without a home, without a relative, without
transportation, or a room in a hotel. You can never be
incomplete in any way once you have realized that your
oneness with God constitutes your oneness with every
spiritual idea. "I and the Father are one,"[4] and "Son, all
that I have is thine."[5] Just remember this promise. "All
that I have is thine!" Why? My oneness with the Father
makes all that the Father has, mine.

Now you may ask the question, "Why am I not
demonstrating it, since it has been proven true?" The
answer is this: Realization. The statement is not enough;
the quotation is not enough. There are loads of people
making these statements, and I read yesterday that in the
last twelve months nineteen million Bibles have been
printed. If these quotations or these statements of
themselves were enough, think how many copies of the
Bible there are in the world! The statement, "Son, I am
with you, and all that I have is thine," is not demonstra-
ble until you yourself have realized it. That is your work
as a metaphysical student and it makes no difference
what branch of metaphysics you are following, or what
teacher or teaching. The last analysis is that you must
come to the realization of truth itself.

The truth is true, but its only benefit to you is in proportion to your realization. Therefore, we have these periods of meditation, of silence, of sitting by ourselves and pondering these Bible truths and metaphysical truths until we arrive at the moment of realization. But the correct letter must precede the realization and above all, realize that there is nothing for you to demonstrate or get.

You are yourself the fulfillment of all that God is. "All that God has is thine!" But until you make this contact with the infinite invisible within you, until you come to realize that you have nothing to get or to acquire or to achieve—not even more understanding of truth—there are no more truths for you to learn. You will only hear the same ones over and over again, and always it will be the same truth. There is nothing of a deep nature for you to learn. There is only the realization to be attained, and the first realization is, "the kingdom of God is within me,"[6] and I must learn to contact it or to find it there.

When I want to help you, I don't want to think of you as a human being or as a patient, or as a student, or as a man or woman. I want to close my eyes and reach God within me. When I have reached God within me, I have reached the spiritual center of your being and it will awaken and quicken you to the reality of your being. That is what happens in spiritual treatment. It is getting within to God, to the center of my being and of your being.

When it is said that the kingdom of God is within, it does not mean that God is within your body, although it is within and without. It cannot be localized. I can go within and realize that what appears to be within is my consciousness; that center of being which is God from which all good finds outlet. I can really touch here, within my own being, that God-center within my own consciousness and, having done that, I have touched the spiritual reality about you. That is where we get all of our healings of sin and sex desires, the unnatural phases of human existence. We cannot overcome those humanly. Much as we would like to be rid of them, we cannot humanly, and through willpower they would only return in stronger form.

When we touch the spiritual reality of being, it releases all of the soul force, the soul power of you, and that is a beautiful process where all false desires that are present are melted away and dissolved. It is not that we say, "I am going to heal you of smoking or drinking." Personally, I do not care what you do. I don't do it because once this refining comes, it takes all of the other away. As I find the spiritual center of your being, you will find that you are not smoking or drinking and you will find many of your tastes being refined. You won't even like the same books or movies because this beautiful soul-sense has released and come out into active being.

It is all there in the center of your being now. There are no persons so depraved, so sinful, that they have not the whole of the Christ at the center of their being. If there is the least desire in them to be free, they can be freed. Whether or not they ask for it, they are always sending out an invisible call. Once your spiritualized senses are aroused, you can feel these calls, can sense the people who are calling for help when they don't know it themselves. They are reaching out for God, for spiritual awakening. By not trying to be a do-gooder to reach out and heal them, but by reaching in to your own being and touching the God of you, you have touched the God of them and have set them free.

No demand that is ever made on you is made on your human understanding. You can meet any demand made on you by realizing that it is not made on your human ability to meet it. If you were asked for ten thousand dollars this minute do not feel, "I wish I could." Feel that the request is not made on you as a human. It is made as it was on Jesus when he was asked to feed five thousand. He could not have fed the five thousand out of his human possessions. He could not have healed the multitudes out of his human wisdom or knowledge. Only the Christ of the individual, this infinite invisible which is the center of our being, can meet every demand whether physical, mental, moral, or financial.

Never permit yourself to say, "I wish I had enough understanding to help." You will never get that much understanding. The Christ, the reality of you, can meet it here and now. Take those individuals into the center of your being by turning, not to them, but to the God within you and realizing, "All of this God energy, all of this Christhood, *I am*." And you find that you have freed them. For every financial problem, turn to the Christ within you, and it will meet the need. How, heaven only knows, but heaven does know. All of this is a part of impersonalizing good. All is a part of making ourselves infinite. How? By realizing that infinity is the reality of us. Infinity is the reality of us, and infinity, which is the center of our being, can meet every demand that can ever be made upon it.

Because realization is necessary, there must be some way that we, as humans who have not been trained to find that center of our being, can attain it. There is a way. That is the development of the listening ear; the development of that state of receptivity. Remember always, to keep this ear stretched out a little bit, as if you were always waiting for something that is just beyond earshot. Keep that open all the time, whether doing housework or at business or at church or driving a car. There is always a way to reserve one little place in your consciousness to keep a listening attitude. As you develop that, you will find yourself receiving not only messages by the power of the Christ, but guidance, leading, direction. You will never make a false step after you have developed this listening ear or state of receptivity. It is, however, a matter of practice. We get so busy in our human things that our whole thought is centered on the outer world, and that is the smallest part of our world after we have touched the Christ. However important you think life is, you will find it is not significant.

Every one of us is a part of God's plan and very few of us are fulfilling even one tiny bit of it. Raising a family or building a house is not part of God's plan, but we have not found God's plan and so we are busy at these other things. Even teaching metaphysics is not a part of God's activity. God's activity is imparting directly from itself to you and to me all this metaphysical knowledge that we need. We have been side-tracked and believe we can help each other out this way, but develop the listening ear, and you will find yourself a spiritual job to do in this work. You will find yourself receiving spiritual guidance, a spiritual direction; first in the path you are now on, you will become a better business person, a better housekeeper if you are receiving divine guidance. But from there on, you will be going up the spiritual scale into those things which are really a part of the activity of God.

For the balance of the time we are working together you are not going to work on your problem. But if the opportunity presents itself, work on the problems of as many others as present themselves. Be willing to give help for those who ask and have no hesitancy in giving it regardless of the degree because you, as a human, cannot give it. It is only in the degree that you touch the divine of you that your help is effective.

In your meditation, your periods of quiet, keep your thought centered on the idea that the Father is the causative principle. The Christ of God is your own consciousness. When you touch that, you touch the Christ of every individual in the world; and more particularly, you touch the Christ of everyone within range of your human experience. Then, remember that your oneness with God constitutes your oneness with every spiritual idea. Whatever name or nature, if in your experience at this moment you need some divine idea, contact with some person or book or teacher or teaching, be assured, your realization that your oneness with God constitutes your oneness with every spiritual idea will bring it forth to you even from across the sea, if that is what is necessary.

~5~

CARRIERS OF THE DIVINE MESSAGE

EVERY SINGLE WORD THAT IS SPOKEN and every moment of silence is the same thread of continuity, of spiritual consciousness expressing itself. And it expresses itself in words, in thoughts and of course, its most powerful mode of expression is silence. Truth, when expressed as silence, is the most potent. Our thoughts and words are very weak substitutes for the real teaching, the real receptivity which comes through the silent and still activity of our soul. The activity and spontaneity of Soul is best apprehended in silence.

Now this truth of course, is nothing new. It is as ancient as the ancient of days. I would like to begin this morning, and I hope to end this morning, with a brief reading from some of my own more recent works. It sets the idea that we will carry through the day:

"They stalk through our minds, these people of the past, leaving in our
thoughts the impression of their thoughts and acts; of their desires and aims;
of their hopes and of their faith—and ofttimes of their accomplishments and
failures."

"For us, they relive the history of the ages, telling and retelling the struggles
of mankind; of its comedies and of its drama."

55

"The philosophy and the religion of all eras pass by as in review and we watch
them pass from the freedom of inspired thought to their imprisonment in
church and interpretation."

"We follow the flight of the universal Light as it inspires the meditations and
prayers of Buddha, Jesus, Shankara, John and Paul; we see its illumination
touch the consciousness of inspired souls—and again we witness the sad
spectacle of this Light being chained by men in personalities. What is this
Light men seek to personify? Why does not man push aside the veil covering
his eyes that he may behold the impersonal savior and physician?"

"Purifier of the individual soul and healer of the personal body—glorious
Light of all ages - nameless, formless, universal, impersonal - oh man!
Enlarge your vision and behold it here and now. It walks beside you by
day and sits by your side at night; on your journey it travels as guide and
protector; in your work it serves to inspire and direct. Open your
consciousness, now, and let the Presence in!

This light, this power, is the impersonal Christ. This Christ has been made manifest all through the ages in various forms and has appeared in what appears to us to be many people. We have had, in ancient days, very wonderful teachings presented to the world—spiritual teachings by Buddha; the great light of Shankara in

India who gave to the world the great absolute truth. There is today none in the world as absolute.

It is the realization, it is the teaching of the I, not only as God, but as the individual you and me. It is given forth in such terms as "I am" or "I am that." At any rate, the main message is I Am. That same I is God. That same I is individual you and individual me. That which appears to our senses as human beings, as the baby that is born or the old man or woman that dies, that is not the I. As a matter of fact, that is not you or me; that is our false sense of both God and man. That is the limited and finite view–the false view. Something that has crept into belief and we have identified ourselves with it, until now we begin to say, "I am sick, I am well, I am poor, I am old." And all this time I am is God.

It is a matter of identification, and Shankara realized it through identification; he knew "I" to be the infinite, individuality of all men. That teaching was given again, and for the first time in what we know as the Western world (although actually speaking, the holy lands are not directly in or of the Western world) as the teaching of the Master Christ Jesus. And here you have that teaching in all of its purity. You have that teaching, not only as absolute teaching, but you have it completely identified with our individual existence and with our daily affairs. Those who even glimpsed this teaching earlier than Jesus gave it out more as teaching, more as an unfoldment or revelation, rather than as a practical, useful thing for our everyday living. But Jesus brought it right down to earth; made it produce food for the multitudes; made it produce tax money; made it bring sick bodies back to health and dead ones back to life.

Jesus really made this teaching practical. He gave it to us in a form that, if we will be willing to reach, willing to

dig a little, will make it clear to us and also practical to
us. Now take the Gospel according to John. You will
find it there that, "I am the way, the truth, and the life"[1]
... "I am the bread, the wine and the water ... I am the
resurrection ... I am life eternal."[2] Just a little later, you
will find him saying to Philip, "Hast thou been with me
so long, Philip, and has not known me? Thou seest me,
thou seest the Father that sent me.[3]" "I and the Father
are one."[4] Now had that teaching referred only to Jesus,
it would have set up again someone to worship; someone separate and apart from our own being. But Jesus
never implied or taught that he was separate and apart
from the great truth of being, which was universal. As a
matter of fact, he fulfilled Bronson Alcott's definition of
the true teacher—"the true teacher is one who turns his
followers away from himself and makes them lose faith
in him that they might find the truth in their own being."
Jesus fulfilled that description of the real teacher. "My
doctrine is not mine but his that sent me"[5] ... "If I speak
of myself, I speak a lie[6]".... "I of mine own self can do
nothing."[7]

Now Jesus, when he spoke in that manner, was
speaking of what appeared to this world as his humanhood, just in the same way that any teacher of this day
would have to say the same thing to you: "Do not build
me up as a personal savior, but look to this Christ of your
own being." Any true metaphysical teacher today must
turn all attention from himself or herself as a person, to
the universal Christ which is the divine idea of son of
God, which is your own consciousness.

You remember what we said yesterday about this
healing work: There is no healing that goes forth from a
practitioner to a patient. The consciousness of the practitioner and the consciousness of the patient is one and

the same consciousness, and that consciousness is God. Not like one of my friends who used to say: "Joel, there is only one mind and that mind is yours." That is true in a sense. There is only one mind and that mind is my mind—but then I am big enough to take you in too. That mind is your mind. It is the infinite called God, and it is infinite in its individual expression to you.

Just as number twelve carries the same fullness of the number twelve whether appearing as twelve dollars or twelve apples or twelve acres, the fullness of the twelve is included in every manifestation of twelve. And so the sum total of God is manifested in what we see as the individual you and me, or else the Bible is wrong. It says: "All that the Father hath is thine . . . *all* that I have is thine."[8] That must be seen as a literal truth. All that is included in the Godhead; all that is included in that which we call infinite consciousness, or God; all that is included in what we call individual you and me!

There are people on earth today who are artists, writers, sculptors, painters and architects. We can do as little or as much as we wish to. We are the outlet. We are that place in consciousness as which the allness of God may appear if we will only let it, because actually we are the sum total of all the qualities and activities of God. God is the life, the eternal life of our being. That is the teaching of Jesus Christ. "I and my Father are one";[9] "I am in the Father and the Father is in me." That is the teaching that ultimately we are going to manifest here.

John, the beloved disciple, got this vision: In the beginning of the book of Revelation, he tells us the message was dictated to him by Jesus. We understand metaphysically that it was an impartation to him of the Christ, the Christ which he at the moment was translating as the human Jesus. When people are under illumination, under divine guidance, very often it will appear to them in the form of someone they can identify such as the man Jesus. Why? Because we have seen photographs or paintings or pictures of someone known as Jesus, and the moment the Christ appears to us, we set it down in that form. Actually, nobody in modern days has ever seen the form or figure of the man Jesus because they would have no way of identifying him. The man Jesus was not a white man. He was very brown or almost black, the same color as the Arabs of today or the ancient Hebrews of his own day; very few people in their spiritual illumination have seen such a form. Mostly we see it as some modern Nordic or American form. When a Hindu is illumined and feels the divine presence of the Christ with him, it is more apt to be Buddha, or Krishna, or Mother Kali. However, whether it appears to us as a dark skinned Jesus or a light skinned Jesus or a Buddha or a Shankara, actually it is the Christ which our finite sense presents to us as some form tangible to us at the moment. It may not even have to appear as a religious personage. Here is an illustration of a true story:

On Friday nights, the vice-president of a bank in Long Island usually carried all the payroll to be distributed Saturday morning to the factory. It was always his custom to take a shortcut through a vacant lot on his way home. This particular night as he cut into the vacant lot, it came to him that he had forgotten something. He turned around and went back but he could not find anything he had forgotten, he could not remember a thing. He said to himself, "Must have been a mistake," and started out again. This time, he went through the vacant lot and had no feelings in any way. The next day, the paper reported that a man had been held up and killed on that lot about that time. Some time later, they caught the man who was responsible and this banker, remembering the incident, thought: "I wonder if he was not waiting for me?" He received permission to go down to speak to the prisoner who said: "I know you . . . where you work. You were the fellow we were after but when you came back the second time with those two other fellows accompanying you, we knew we were licked." He had had no one with him. He had a divine sense of protection, the omnipresence of the Christ, and that appeared at the moment in just the form he needed. He did not need the form of Jesus but two sturdy guards in the way of guides. Now where was the Christ? It was in the banker's consciousness all the time! It was always within. Let us remember that as we come a little farther along. John who beheld the city not made with hands, and Jesus who beheld the kingdom of God on earth—both saw the real vision of the Christ.

This is just a personal opinion and no one need accept it or believe it. It happens to be my belief that John was the only one of the disciples, probably the only person of that period aside from the Master himself, who caught the full and complete vision of spiritual life, of heaven on earth. One particular point in his revelation that makes it clear to us is his understanding and realization that heaven and earth were here, and that there was no real power of evil and that heaven and earth are one, not two.

That is brought out clearly (and I hope every one of you will have the opportunity of reading that wonderful revelation) in Marchette Chute's book, *The End of the Search*. I do not know of any translation or explanation of Revelation equal to hers. It is so clear, so concise, so absolutely real that you can almost feel the earth disappear under your fingers as she is describing all of these errors, or what the world calls error, disappear and melt into the oneness of the Christ.

You will remember that Jesus made it clear that this unfoldment of spiritual truth is not truth over error, not good over evil, not God over devil. That was the great mistake of the Hebrew scriptures: this great belief that there is great power that overcomes all other powers, a great power, a great wisdom, or a great intelligence that does away with sin or disease or opposing armies. That is the whole history of the Judaic people of the early days, this belief in a great, great power which has power to destroy all evil powers. Jesus never gave us that teaching—Jesus went much higher. He went into the realization that as God is spirit and spirit is all, there are no lesser powers. No reality to evil.

You have that clearly given in the wonderful lesson before Pilate, when Pilate said: "Knowest thou not that I have power to crucify thee or to set thee free?"[10] And Jesus answered: "Thou couldst have no power over me unless it be given thee of the Father."[11] And, of course, that other great example where Peter cuts off the ear of the servant because they were going to take the Master to prison, and Jesus tells him: "Put up thy sword. Those that live by the sword will die by the sword."[12] If you are going to use material power to help you to live, you are going to die by that same material power. If you think for a moment that you are going to live by some form of human power or human good, whether in the form of money in the bank or an army at the front, or medicine or surgery, you will find that ultimately you will also die by that.

Unless you find your safety and security in spirit, in God, you will always be battling error in some form and you will be using one form of error to overcome or destroy another form. The Hebrews, when they were using what they thought was the Lord Jehovah to overcome the armies of the aliens, were living by the sword–by human power–and ultimately that same power was going to destroy them. There is an example of that in our own modern history: Those familiar with world events will remember how England and France built up Hitler so he would be able to rise up and destroy the Russians and thereby save England and France. When they got him built up just enough, he turned on them. That is the history of the world. If you live by the sword, you will die by the sword. Never think that you will benefit at someone's loss.

All mortal, material power fades out ultimately but when you come to the Christ, to God or truth, you don't come to a power that will overcome your errors. You come to the only power there is, in which there is no error. That is the real secret of the Christ message: "Thou couldst have no power unless it comes from the Father."

Put up your sword. If you are going to live by the sword you will die by the sword! Paul carried this teaching of Jesus out into a greater part of the world. Up to the time of Paul it was believed that this message was really only for the Hebrews, that they were the only people ready and there was no use giving it to anyone else. But Paul had a broader vision. He saw that you could carry it out to the world and give it to all who had a ready consciousness. That readiness of consciousness had to do only with your individual unfoldment.

This metaphysical message is not reserved for any particular people. The Jew is as able to receive it as the Gentile; the Muslim and the Hindu as the Christian. But

only those of all faiths can receive it who have a prepared consciousness. You could be a Christian and, if
your consciousness were not ready for this truth, you
could not fully appreciate it. It is not a matter of race or
religion but of individual salvation, individual readiness.
It is a matter of consciousness.

Paul carried the message out and what was the
message he carried? "I live, yet not I, the Christ liveth in
me."[13] And remember Jesus? "I can of mine own self do
nothing."[14] In other words, Jesus saw this great power in
a personal sense as the Father while Paul caught it as the
spirit of God—he caught the Christ in him. Again, the
name means nothing. What counts is whether you can
catch the sense or feeling of an inner presence, an inner
power, a something higher than your humanhood. The
Chinese, Lao Tzu, caught the vision and called it the
Tao; Abraham called it Friend; Jesus called it the Father;
Ramakrishna called it Mother Kali; Paul called it the
Christ within. The term you use is of no importance.
What is important is, do you catch an inner feeling, an
awareness, a light or a glow within? If you do, it makes
no difference what name you call it or whether you see
it as personal or impersonal. It is *It.*

All through the ages, you find that men have appeared and re-appeared with some measure of this
Christ. All have not seen it in its fullness, but nearly all
of these people have seen some degree of it. It is abroad
in the world again today, and again it is abroad only in
the measure of the understanding of the individual who
is presenting it. There is probably no such thing yet, as
a full and complete revelation or unfoldment of it but
you will find this mystical trend, this mystical message of
oneness, the one power, running through many of the

modern teachings. You will find another sense of it running through Allen Boone in his *Letters to Strongheart* which brings a great sense of the inner relationships that touch us in our animal kingdom; you will also find that mystical light from the ancient ages up to the present, and finding such a welcome that such books as *Perennial Philosophy* by Aldous Huxley and *Men Who Have Walked With God* by Cheney, have become best sellers.

This teaching, therefore, is abroad in the land, and now we come to probably the greatest piece of good fortune that we can know, which is that we have been born into this age where the mystical teachings are reaching the highest level ever before known, except probably in the experience of the Master and John (and then only in their individual experience). In this age it will be possible for you and for me to attain heights of understanding and demonstration never before known, except for one or two individuals. The reason for it is this: It is in this age, for the very first time, that the nature of error is being made known to the world at large. You will all agree with me that if it were not for some form or phase of error, none of us would be here. Some form or phase of error has driven us into meta-physical teachings, and error will continue until its true nature is known. Why? Because if error as sin or disease existed as reality, we would be in the same position as the Judaic teaching of looking for a God to overcome sin and disease. We would be looking for a great power of good to help us overcome some power of evil; for the truth with which to fight error; for a God to do battle with the devil. And, in the degree that we do that, we are back in the Judaic age.

So, in this era, we are learning that the nature of error is not something of a real nature to be overcome or destroyed but is purely illusion, a belief, a supposition that has been built up in human consciousness. And we are not now on the path of destroying error but merely on the path of knowing that it does not exist as a reality. The mirage of the desert, the skies sitting on the mountain, the tracks coming together in the distance, the snake instead of a rope, all of these are to show, not that there is a God, a power to correct or destroy these, but that these have no real existence.

We are living in the age when we are no longer going to look for a cause for disease because we know that disease has no existence, no reality. Have you ever stopped to think how many practitioners there are in the world who, contrary to medical beliefs, fail to come down with the infection and contagion coming to the practice in which they are engaged? How wonderfully they go through their practice without catching these diseases! This would not be if these diseases were realities. Now the work that we are engaged in is only partly the realization of the oneness of God and man because, at least intellectually, we all know that and accept it. And so we have just one step further to go and that is to realize it.

The main work we have to do is to come into the awareness, the actual consciousness of the nothingness of what appears as sin and disease so that we no longer criticize, judge or condemn those who at this moment seem to be indulging it; rather, we stand back and smile, knowing the unreality of it and also the ultimate freedom of those who even at this moment, appear to be ensnared with it.

Now in our old theological form of living we may have turned to the man Jesus and looked to him for our help, or if we were of other faiths, we may have looked to the God up in the sky. But, from this moment of our entering the world of spirit, we will look to no person. We will look to this impersonal Christ, the Father within; the Christ that liveth in me. Even though we turn to someone for temporary help–to a practitioner or a teacher for help or teaching–we are not going to believe that the mind or consciousness through which they are speaking is other than our own. We are not accepting the belief that the power that brings our healing is coming from any truth other than our own consciousness. If you see the consciousness of your practitioner or teacher as other than your own, you are cheating yourself of entrance into heaven. Heaven, or harmony, is divine, but it is your own consciousness, and it is within your own consciousness that all of this begins.

Here we have the Master: "If I go not away the Comforter will not come to you."[15] You know that even the disciples, after being with him for three years, brought their hard cases to him. You would think that after three years with him, they would have known enough to meet them themselves. They had to run to Jesus. Jesus knew and saw that and so he told them: "If I go not away the Comforter will not come to you." Now in the same way, sooner or later, some practitioner or teacher is going to say those very words to you. "If I don't get out of your life, you will look to me forever and you had better find this thing in your own consciousness!"

And so those practitioners and those teachers who, today, are turning you more and more and more to the consciousness of your own being, to the divine emanation of your own being, to the absolute and utter reliance on the Christ of your own being, they are truly showing you the way to heaven. The way to heaven is the way to your own consciousness. Let us not forget that. Never transfer power to your practitioner or teacher, even when you appeal to them. Even if the practitioner or teacher calls it forth, know that the help, ultimately, is coming from within your own consciousness.

THE NIGHTINGALE OF THE EAST

Amidst the flowering lands of a garden in Egypt, sat a nightingale
 of great beauty. Its soaring song filled the oasis with lilting
 melody. Its song was a carol of love; a message of peace from out
 the heart of the infinite, stilling the waves of the world of sense.

Knowest thou, O bard, of the peace that fares forth with thy song?
Knowest thou the strife that is stilled by the melody from thy throat?

The nightingale knows not of the power of its song, and less of the
 unrest that is quieted by its sound.

So should ye be as the song of God pours from you—the willing
 carriers of the divine message, yet unaware of the power of your
 being, and still less aware of the troubled hearts you quiet with
 the melody of love.

Joel Goldsmith

~6~

BE A BEHOLDER

BE A BEHOLDER! BE A WITNESS! Whenever I meet Allen Boone for luncheon and ask him how he is, he tells me, "I am alive, and that counts ninety-nine percent." And I can see that everyone here is alive and, after a whole week of this, I think that is ninety-nine percent! The other one percent you will get resting over the week-end.

It must be clear to you, after all of this week's work, that the principal point of what I talk and write about is that what appears to us as error in any form is really not error at all; that there is neither a sin nor a disease that has to be overcome; it exists only as an illusory experience, a mental belief. If we were dealing with disease as a reality, as something which is cause and has an effect, we would have to know a lot more than we do about the body and the things that cause bodily ills; but because we do not handle our healing work from that standpoint, it must be clear that if we are having any results at all, it must be because sin, disease or error do not exist as a reality that must have something done to it.

The more clearly you can perceive the unreal nature of any form of error, the closer you will come to being free of it soon and to attaining a spiritual consciousness which is the most important point of all. This healing work which we are doing in this age and at this period of our unfoldment is not really the most important reason we have come to earth. We have not been born into this world just to do healing work, any more than Jesus came to earth to cure people's ills or raise them from the dead. The chances are that Lazarus, even though raised from the dead, passed on sometime later and only a change in the date on the tombstone was involved. And you, too, will find that so far as the actual healing was concerned, all that happened was a change of date on your own tombstone.

It was in 1928 that I lost all desire for the things of the earth in the sense of their having or making any demands upon me. I still enjoy good music, good friends, good books and good food, but they are no longer a necessary part of my experience. I am in the world but not of it. I enjoy them all but do not miss them when they are not in my experience, when they are separate and apart from me. I have become aware of something in you that I can commune and tabernacle with, and it makes no difference what your degree of education, what your financial and your social background is. I have touched a place in your consciousness where we can be wonderful friends together. I know you more or less as you really are. I can love everyone on this earth–I had a very hard time hating even Mr. Hitler! It was not easy for me to hold harsh feelings toward him. I have seen something in men and women that is beautiful, even when outwardly they may not be manifesting it at the time. The chances are that some of those individuals who are not manifesting it today, will sooner or later be showing forth that it was there all the time–that which this spiritual transition has enabled me to see now.

Why is it necessary that we come to that place? It lies in this: You have nothing that I desire or envy you for or would go out of my way to get. I can enjoy mental, spiritual companionship with you but there is nothing of any nature you have that I can desire or want. I cannot hate you or be too sorry when you are away from me. We are just good friends at all times. Now, imagine a world of such relationships! That is the only way we can end wars. Don't ever think for a minute that any of these treaties are going to end wars; that ending armament is going to end war. When war came in 1939, Britain was unprepared. That did not prevent war. None of the human things will prevent war, because regardless of how wonderful a human you may be, or how wonderful those humans who function as the heads of our government may be, tomorrow we may have villains there and they can overthrow in one generation all the good that has been built up over a dozen years. Now since that is true, the answer is that either there will have to be world peace, individually and collectively, or there will be wars. And if peace, it will have to come when each individual realizes his oneness with God, and realizes that all the good he is to receive must come from God, and not from another individual.

This spiritual unfoldment does not make crackpots of us. We do not arrive at the point where we say, "Our good does not come to us through each other." It does. I may sit here today talking—someone else tomorrow—and you may receive good through them that you are not receiving from me or any other teacher or speaker who comes here. Whatever good you receive will come from God! You are always attracting your own good, and that good comes from your own consciousness! But until you can receive it directly, you will have to receive it through a practitioner, a teacher, or a book.

My supply comes to me directly from my own consciousness. No one is responsible for my supply. I receive it directly through my own consciousness. However, today, you may be the avenue through which it comes to me. You may be that point of consciousness receiving good through me, and thereby I receive my good through you—but not *from* you. I am independent of you, and if you contributed nothing it would take nothing from my supply, and if you did contribute today and then never showed up again, it would make no difference to me. The infinite consciousness which I am will provide my supply for me, and as long as it is necessary to have an avenue or channel, that avenue or channel will be supplied. The same with you. As long as you have need of a book, a teacher, a practitioner or a teaching, that need will be supplied to you. It will always appear as man, woman or book but remember, it is coming to you because your own consciousness is attracting it to you and for you.

Now, when you realize that all of your good flows from your own consciousness, you can no longer be envious or jealous of another's possessions, or have a desire for them, or even a mild wish for them. Why? Because you can have all you want by opening your own consciousness and letting it flow in! When you and I, as individuals, come to the place where I have nothing that you desire and you have nothing that I desire, where we feel that the infinity of good is flowing from our own individual consciousness—that consciousness which we call God—then we can see how little strife there will be. There is no other way! Only through an illumined spiritual consciousness, one which knows that the place "whereon I stand is holy ground,"[1] can we bring this about. Why is it true that the place whereon I stand is holy ground? Because I and the Father are one, and wherever I am, God is. We are not two. We cannot get separated from each other.

The place whereon I stand is holy ground! If I make my bed in hell, "thou" art there, in the sickroom, the prison, the asylum, or the poorhouse. If only you can realize God as your own individual being! You will very quickly find a change of consciousness that will attract to you all of the good, not only necessary for your development, but an abundance of it. I am not come merely to supply your needs but that you might have life, and life more abundantly—health and wealth without measure! There is no limit to the amount of health and wealth we are permitted to have under spiritual law, but there really must be that spiritual illumination. So remember that in this healing activity, our work is not to make you a healthy or wealthy human, but to bring spiritual illumination to you and then these other things will be added unto you. That is the messianic promise. "Seek ye first the kingdom of God and his rightness, and all these other things will be added to you."[2]

In this message, as I interpret it, we have two important quotations from the Bible. (And here I remind you again: Don't think that by memorizing and reciting them, they will do anything for you. They will not, and if they do, it will be too bad for you for it will not be permanent.) When the essence or substance of these quotations becomes part of your own consciousness, when you really understand them, they will begin to live for you and function for you eternally.

First: "Take no thought for your life." You may refer
to that entire passage in Luke 12:22–32. Throughout all
of my writings I stress as the vital part of your
unfoldment: "Take no thought!" That does not mean to
become mentally lazy or to sit back and wait for some
mysterious God to come and work for you. The "take no
thought" attitude is not one of mental indolence nor one
of blind faith. The "take no thought" attitude is the very
contrary; it is one of mental alertness and spiritual
expectancy. Jesus winds up that passage with the statement that, "your heavenly Father knoweth what things
you have need of"[3]. . . "and it is his good pleasure to
give you the kingdom."[4]

Now, when you are living in the constant realization
that God is your very own consciousness, God is the
mind of you, and that this mind or consciousness of
yours knows your need and is forever fulfilling it, you
cannot become lazy, sit back and call for an unknown
God to do something for you. Neither can you just go
about your human business and expect that all good will
flow in. It is only as you live in a state of spiritual
expectancy, spiritual alertness, having a spiritually open
ear as if just beyond earshot was that divine message
waiting to come in, and you are always at the standpoint
of waiting to hear it! And you develop that state.

The second quotation is: "Not by might, nor by
power, but by my spirit."[5] No opportunity there for
being mentally lazy or sitting around waiting for good to
happen to you. "Not by might!" It is not the physical or
mental effort that you make, it is the spiritual awareness!
It is the realization of spiritual power functioning in you
and through you and as you that does the work. Making
this transition from the human method of living and of

supplying oneself with health and wealth, to the spiritual–the re-birth–requires that God, at all times, be the central theme in your consciousness.

"Take no thought for your life, what ye shall eat, what ye shall drink, or wherewithal ye shall be clothed."[6] However, "Thou wilt keep him in perfect peace, whose mind is stayed on thee!"[7] You have got to think, but don't think about things you need. Think about God. The more you realize God as the mind and soul and spirit of your being, the more you realize God as the soul of you, the more you are really thinking correctly about God, and keeping your mind stayed on him.

God is not a God afar off. He is nearer than hands and feet, closer than breathing: "I and the Father are one."[8] Right where I am sitting, or standing, or walking or talking, there God is unfolding and expressing itself as me, and I am dwelling in thought on God when I am realizing that truth.

"Seek ye first the kingdom of God and his rightness, and all these other things will be added unto you."[9] Seek the consciousness of the presence of God and all things will be added unto you! This is being a beholder. And we go about it something like this: Probably heretofore, we were good, hard, physical workers, depending on our good, hard physical work to do things for us. Maybe we prided ourselves on being a faithful worker, a conscientious worker in the human way. Perhaps as we came into metaphysics, we became faithful mental workers and gave ourselves, our families, our friends, good mental treatments. All of that was a stepping stone up to this. Now we are not going to use our physical or mental work as the springboard for our good. We will use our spiritual unfoldment, our spiritual consciousness, and we

will do it in this way—and watch this closely over this
weekend.

Be a beholder! Watch, as if you were looking over
your own shoulder as to what God was going to bring to
pass in your experience; the God that is right where you
are. Watch everything that you do, everything that you
hear, everything that you are thinking. The God that sits
at the center of your consciousness knows all that is
going on, and we are sort of watching over this shoulder
to watch God appear in form and unfold as our experience. To illustrate: God is not something separate from
the form in which God appears; God is the substance
and essence of that form! How is that?

God has brought this group together? That, in my
language, would be separation and duality. It would not
be correct. God has not brought this group together.
God has appeared here *as* this group. God has unfolded
itself to me *as* this class! There is not God and this class.
There is God appearing as this class! Likewise, God has
not sent to you a practitioner or a teacher; God is now
appearing to you as a practitioner and a teacher. There
is no separation between God and me. God has not
"sent" me. God appears as me. God has not sent you to
me. God has appeared before me as you. And that is
oneness, not duality.

Now, in the same way, God does not send me my
supply. God appears to me as my supply. God is not
only my supplier, God *is* my supply! If, at this moment
I see God as food on the table, that is merely my interpretation of God appearing. Let us call that the added
things. Actually, God is unfolding *as* my supply. Do you
follow that?

There is no separation, no division between God and
my good! God did not send a contact to me like Miss

Buck and the Andersons.[10] God has appeared to me as
Miss Buck and the Andersons. I cannot separate God
from Miss Buck and the Andersons. God appears as
these to my individual consciousness.

This is very important because now, as you watch
your life unfolding, you are not going to see a group of
human people coming into your experience, or a lot of
dollars. You are going to see God coming in infinite
form and variety. No matter what form it appears in–it
might be a vacation trip, a new teaching, or it might be
an unfoldment within your own consciousness, it might
be spiritual illumination–it will be God appearing to you
directly. You may see it in the form of Jesus Christ; or
your mother; or your father. It will be God appearing to
you in a form that you can understand. Never separate
God from any of the forms in which God appears. God,
being infinite, appears in infinite forms and variety. God
did not always appear in the same form to you and may,
because of the infinity of God, never appear twice the
same. That will never end. Life cannot end at a hundred
years, for life, being infinite, must appear in infinite form
and variety.

This will also help you in your healing work: There
is no such thing as God and your body. Your body is
another one of the infinite forms in which God, the
divine substance and essence of the universe, is appearing. Your body cannot decay or decompose unless you
accept the universal belief that you have a material body
which functions in time or space. God is the essence and
substance of you as flesh and blood and bone! They are
only our translation or interpretation of the divine Spirit
appearing in all its forms. They are God appearing as
body. It is the same spirit and substance that your mind,

your consciousness is made of, only in one of its infinite forms and varieties.

For instance, beauty can appear as a daisy or as a rose. It must appear in its infinite forms and varieties. One is not more beautiful than another. The sense of beauty may be better in one than in another. We do not all appreciate the same form of beauty. We do not really connect up spiritual experience with the human forms in the sense of trying to demonstrate a place to live or trying to demonstrate an automobile. That would be taking thought for "things." Yet, there is a connection. As you become conscious of God appearing to you in infinite forms and varieties, it will always appear in the form necessary to your understanding at that particular moment. And if your need is what we call a house in which to live, an automobile, or a seat on a railroad train, it will appear to you in that form. It will be God appearing, but you will translate it into that form at the moment. Never must we, in this work, do mental work for any "thing." Never must we dishonor God by turning to God for improvement, employment or home. We do turn to God for the consciousness of the presence of God in any and every form, and if it happens to be a needle and thread, if that is what our need is at the moment, God must appear in that form. But let us demonstrate it in the conscious awareness of the presence of God in every form, in its infinite form and variety.

"Seek ye first the kingdom of God and his rightness, and all these other things shall be added to you"[11] . . . "Take no thought for your life, what ye shall eat, what ye shall drink and wherewithal ye shall be clothed"[12] . . . "Your heavenly Father knoweth what things ye have need of and it is his good pleasure to give you the kingdom!"[13]

He has not appeared before this because you have been violating this messianic teaching. You have been trying to get things and persons and places. And while violating the messianic teaching, how can you come into the promises? This is a principle! This is a law! You either fulfill the law or you do not demonstrate. The law is that you must not be trying to demonstrate person, place, or thing but grace.

"Seek ye first the kingdom of God." Take no thought for these other things. Why? Your heavenly Father, your divine consciousness, never farther away than your own breathing, is knowing your needs and supplies them. How? By might? By struggle? No! By my spirit!—by the natural flow! And here let no one misunderstand me and go out of here and say that I said you do not have to do anything. I am a hard worker; I work twenty-one hours a day, day and night, but I am not working for anything. I am doing the work that is given me to do this minute. I cannot be lazy under this messianic promise. I don't believe Jesus was lazy. The spirit forces you and does not leave you alone to become lazy. It may give you rest, but never can you be lazy.

When we say, "Not by might, nor by power but by my spirit. . . . Take no thought for your life, what ye shall eat and what ye shall drink," we do not mean, "Move out to the country and let God do it!" We mean this: "Instead of being concerned for the things of the world, be concerned with God, and do what is given you to do and do it the best you know how!" So even though we have said take no thought, when a call comes for you to do something, be alert and do it! Not because you are

responsible for the result, not because your human
activity is of itself important, but because your human
activity is merely your carrying out, on your level of
consciousness, the divine command!

If you are not living up to your own highest sense of
right, fulfilling every obligation to meet your highest
sense of right, then, somewhere, you are falling down in
your spiritual understanding. When Jesus said, "Who is
my mother, my father, and who are my brethren?"[14] it
was not that he was a negligent son or brother. He was
bringing out the great truth that his greatest responsibility was to those who were seeking the spiritual path of
God, and nothing must interfere with that. That done, he
could go back and be any kind of a son—and he would
want to be a good one. We must never allow our human
obligations or family to interfere with our spiritual
unfoldment; that would be dangerous to our own
growth. It means that we will have to place our family in
some spot where they can be taken care of yet not be
permitted to interfere with our own development or
growth. That would be the end of our own spiritual
development. Nothing must interfere with that.

We are told about the man who went out to find "the
pearl of great price,"[15] and then sold everything he had
in order to get that pearl. If it is spiritual development
that is pounding away at your consciousness, and it is,
that is why you are here, because something of a spiritual nature is trying to break through and will not let you
rest until you have arrived at that point. If, then, you
have to sacrifice at this moment some material good in
order to achieve that spiritual unfoldment, be prepared
for it! You may have to sacrifice much to attain this
spiritual development, but when you have achieved a

measure of it, you will find you have everything else you need in the world.

So, no sacrifice of material comfort or welfare is too much to pay for the pearl of great price and I know there are too many people who really believe they should be able to keep all of the material comforts and attain their spirituality as well. It will not work! It will not work. Look at the lives of Paul, Jesus, John, or of anyone who ever attained spirituality and see how little they gave to material living. But, this will not take you away from normal living. It may interfere with the normal routine for awhile, and it is worthwhile! It is a new kingdom! It does take you away from people. It is that you no longer care what their background is, you learn to find the spiritual point in everyone—and then you have something in common with all.

To the commandments, Jesus could only add, "Love thy neighbor as thyself."[16] How? We could not, if that love had anything to do with physicality, educational, social or financial background. It is only as we meet all on a spiritual level that we can love them, and I mean love! It is only as we can look through physicality, look through Dunn and Bradstreet, because those are the barriers that separate us from each other.

Now again: Be a beholder! Our attitude is always that of being at a place, as in a movie, and watching the picture unfold. You know that the entire movie is really complete on the roll of film. You watch it unfold and, in the back of your mind, you know there is a happy ending already prepared. You are going through all the headaches, heartaches and grief only to end up with a smile when the lights come on. We, as a beholder, are in much that same position because it is God unfolding as my existence. I know that there is a happy ending in sight, even if I have to go through a world war or two—even if I have to go down to death's door or come to a place where, for a few days, I haven't enough money to pay for food. None of that is important because I know that God is unfolding this story of my life and, therefore, it is going to be a happy ending. I am not concerned with what part of the picture I come in on but only with the happy ending.

I can only live one minute at a time, and my mind is not on it. I would wonder how, when, and through whom. You might listen to a thousand teachers, and nine out of ten would have nothing for you. There is only one, here and there, that is meant for you. It is not that they are not good, those others; but for you there will be only one or two along life's pathway that will meet your particular state of consciousness. You will get a grain from each one, but as to your real teacher or teaching, there is only one of those.

In my whole life, there is only one state of thought that has registered with me. Occasionally there have been others, but always: "I and the Father are one." Anything along that line will find in me a wonderful state of receptivity. My only teacher is the state of consciousness that is repeating to me, "I and the Father are one"[17] . . . "Son, all that I have is thine"[18] . . . "The place whereon I stand is holy ground"[19] . . . "take no thought for your life, what ye shall eat or what ye shall drink[20] . . . not by might, not by power, but by my spirit."[21] All those things meet a response in my consciousness, and a dozen people have written along that line. That is my teacher, not a man, woman or book. My teacher is my own state of consciousness, of oneness.

I say to my classes in Hollywood, "Please don't bill yourselves as my students, or me as your teacher. Try to remember that your teacher is your state of consciousness expressing itself in infinite ways of spiritual impartation." That is your teacher. Whether you find it in these books or someone else's, makes no difference. Stick with it! Don't mix up a lot of different things. You can read a lot of different books, but stick to that particular teaching which brings out a response.

The term is used in the Bible, "Ye are God's witnesses."[22] Be a witness! "Be a beholder!"[23]—a beholder of God's unfoldment as your experience! And, as you behold, you will find that you truly have to take no thought. As a matter of fact, there is no way you can take thought. Every minute you will be given something to think about. The right way to do this? Learn to be a beholder, as if you were looking over your shoulder. Myself, I have a sort of feeling in my office in the morning: "I wonder what the Father is going to put on my desk today? Whatever it is, it is going to be God appearing, and I am going to take care of it!" I have built up this consciousness of always knowing that God is unfolding, appearing to me in some form. You can do the same thing. You can build yourself up as a beholder, so that every day when you awaken, you say, "This is God's day. I wonder what pictures he is presenting to me today?" When you begin to see that it is God presenting the pictures, you are coming to the first commandment, "Thou shalt have no other gods before me."[24]

In the world of religion, there is a God and a devil. No church in the world has not got a God and a devil. In the world of philosophy it is good and evil. Here is where we separate from every religion and every philosophy. We take the First Commandment literally—only one power! One cannot turn around now and say, "I wonder what evil influences are acting in my experience, what evil powers?" That must be ironed out here and now. You might, instead, awaken in the morning with the idea, "I am going to watch what God unfolds to me." In everything that unfolds, realize it is God doing it, so if you do not feel well—there is no mortal mind! You can say, "I wonder what lesson God wants me to get out of this? In what way have I missed the direction and God is pulling me back?" Again, no presence and power apart from God.

Awaken in the morning knowing that God is appearing *as*, is unfolding your experience—and never deviate. And if you have bad news or an accident, don't be tempted, don't be double minded and say "this is error." Nothing but God is appearing, and if it takes a pain to make me re-interpret it, it will have to be that way. We are standing on the First Commandment, as those who are in the class will learn next week.

We are not going to admit that the movement of the stars and planets can do anything to us. We are going to acknowledge God, the mind of our own being, as the governing principle, governing the movement of the stars and the planets. We will acknowledge no lesser power acting upon God's own power. In the same way, we will not acknowledge that error can do this to me, or ask why error is doing this to me today. There is no error except such as you accept into your own experience. God is the only presence and the only power and everything that is happening to you today, this minute, is happening as the result of God operating in, for, and through you *if* you will acknowledge him in all ways—and it did not say in all "thy good ways." Acknowledge him in all thy ways. Acknowledge God as the only actor in your experience, as the only presence, the only power, the only law, the only substance, the only cause, the only effect. God, God!

The divine infinite consciousness which is your consciousness, is the infinite, eternal life which is your life! Acknowledge no life apart from your God life and you will never have the experience of dying. It will never happen to you if you stick with your First Commandment. God alone is universal life, God is the reality of my being! Don't separate God from its forms. God is not sending something to you. God is appearing to you in infinite form, in infinite variety, and in infinite experience. God is appearing to you *as!*

There is not desk and wood here. You cannot separate wood from desk. The wood is appearing as the desk. There is no such thing as Joel Goldsmith and his body. I and my Father are one. I and my body are one. I am the consciousness which appears as this body! I and my body are one. My body will never die. It never will age and decompose. I know that my state of consciousness is always held to God; always held to the spirit of truth, and is forming me every single day. And because there is no time, it will go on doing that forever.

You see, nothing is appearing to you except God in infinite form and variety. Therefore, God is appearing to you–as body! You may, at this moment, be entertaining a material concept of your body, and you must change that. Your body is spiritual. It was formed of the substance of God, or consciousness, and if you want to change your body, change your concept of your body and then your body will respond. Why? Because your body is just a product of your mind.

~ 7 ~

Conscious Oneness

I have said: "If there is no change in our consciousness during the week, there will be no change in our outer experience the following week." Now, in proportion as some change toward truth takes place in your consciousness, in that proportion there is some improvement in your outer affairs—either in your health, your family relations, or in your supply. It would be as impossible for you to be in the same place today that you were a week ago as it is to toss raisins into your bread dough and not have raisin bread. That which goes into consciousness must come forth as manifestation. That which becomes a part of consciousness as truth must appear as manifestation. There is no such thing as truth and manifestation. Truth itself appears as manifestation.

Spirit is not something separate and apart from the forms it assumes. Spirit is the substance and the "form" is its manifestation. Therefore, if truth appears in or as our consciousness, if truth appears in or as the spirit of our being, it must also appear as manifested form. Therefore please remember this as the foundation, the real point, of recent talks: that all improved states of consciousness *must* appear as improved demonstrations or experiences. And today we come one step further. Unless we consciously make the decision to act or live in some higher way, on a higher level, we are not going to live or act or have manifestation on a higher level. We cannot sit back passively and say (or believe), "There is a God or law that is going to do something in me, through me, for me or to me," just as we have learned not to believe that there is an evil law or an evil power. There is no such thing as a law that acts upon us except that to which we give power to through our belief.

You can accept any belief and make it a law unto yourself. There is no power in the stars or in the stars' acting upon us, but you can make a god of anything you wish. You can pick up a piece of metal, or a penny, and call it a good-luck charm and make it so. You can go to Canada, Salvador, places in the United States, and make a god out of some piece of metal or bone, and in the measure of your faith derive some benefit from it. Always you are a law unto your own being, and there-fore, you can make a god out of anything and, tempo-rarily at least, benefit by it. But that is not the law of God and it is not permanent. There is really no law, no law of evil or of good, that acts upon you.

Why? You are yourself the embodiment of all law! All that God is, *I am.* Is that one of my pet teachings or beliefs? No. The Bible itself tells us: "All that I have is thine[1] . . . The place whereon I standest is holy ground[2] . . . I and my Father are one[3] . . . I am with you always."[4] Therefore, all that God is, I am. God is the law and the substance of the universe, therefore my oneness with God makes me a law unto my universe—my world.

God, the indivisible God, becomes the individual law unto your own being through your own state of con-sciousness. God becomes the law unto my being through my state of consciousness. Sometimes we watch friends or family making terrible mistakes, at least to our sense, and we would love to reach out and prevent them from doing so. There is no greater error that we could be guilty of, because we would be interfering with another's individual demonstration of his own being. Each of us, ultimately, will come into heaven, into the kingdom of God, but we are going up by different routes. There are some people so constructed that they can make this a gradual and beautiful ascent into heaven without discords to "push" them. There are others so constructed that unless they get into a lot to trouble, they will not find themselves coming into heaven. Their troubles drive them on. Unless some of us get to the place where the doctor says, "You are finished," we will not give up our outer pursuits and find our way to God. So, serious diseases have often been the way, the cause, of driving us to God. With others it is poverty. Whatever it is, the ultimate result will be to bring us into heaven. And so, if you could interfere with the demonstration of an individual at a given moment and make him take a better path, you may not, in the end, be doing him a good service. You might settle him temporarily in a better human sense, but then comes that fear again.

I sense there are so many people here who have never found God; so many are really content with the human sense of good they are experiencing—good health, good supply, a happy time going to church. There they are, on that level. They know there is a God intellectually. But, when you have found God, all of these phases of human or mortal conditions drop away. We no longer have to be told to be better humans. Our part now is to realize that God is the law unto our being and for that reason we ourselves must make the decision in what way we

will go. If you have made the decision to take the
spiritual path, then you will find many temptations to
lead you away from it and you will have to be very firm
in your determination to let nothing interfere with your
progress spiritually.

There are many demands on you when you take that
path. There may be a teacher seven hundred or seven
thousand miles from here whom you just have to reach,
whom you have to find at this point of demonstration.
That calls for time and for money and it is up to you to
make the decision whether you are going to sacrifice
some material form of good in order to follow your
spiritual leadings. Again, it may have to do with family
cares or family matters. Something, in some way, will
always intrude itself to interfere with your progress–if
you will let it.

In the Bible we have wonderful unfoldments given to
us as to the value of spiritual teaching. We have heard it
called "the pearl of great price."[5] When you find the
pearl of great price, the particular teaching that says to
you, "This is it, this is the way," then stand by it and
make your demonstration of finding it, of achieving it,
until the unfoldment or revelation of God has come to
your consciousness. When you have touched even the
hem of the robe of God, you will no longer need books
or teachers. We will, however, still keep reading and
going to church now and then, not because of spiritual
enlightenment and not because we need them. Rather,
because of the joy we experience through the exchange
of spiritual views. It is for that reason we read such
books, associate in class with people on the same path,
and associate ourselves with teachers of this path. Not
because we need them, but because there is never a time

when we are not benefiting from the exchange of ideas. The real purpose of our new realm is to come into the conscious awareness of the presence of God; that must be made our point of decision–then it must be carried out.

We will always be in this world even though we will not always be of the world. This work is not meant to take anybody out of the world or to make of anybody an ascetic or a hermit. On the contrary, it is meant to make us the "light" of the world and that light has no right–ever–to be hidden. Therefore we will always be in the world, but not of the world.

TITHING

How can we demonstrate being in the world and not of it? To teach you just one phase of it today I am going to take up the subject under the title of "tithing" or "giving." Sooner or later we all are going to learn the value of gratitude, but that is only one little facet in the vast subject of love. Tithing is something that carries us to our highest sense of gratitude.

Ordinarily, tithing is taken to mean that if we give ten percent or so of our income to some charitable or spiritual purpose, we will in some mysterious way have pleased God and so will be rewarded. I think, personally, that this is one of the most dangerous teachings that can be given out, for the simple reason that there is no word of truth in it and ultimately it will find us without a prop. There is no virtue in giving when there is any sense of a future tense connected with it. If our giving, whether in contribution to a charity, a church, or a teacher, carries with it any sense or thought that we will receive some benefit from it, it is best not to give. No.

Giving should always be from the standpoint of gratitude for that which already is, for that which already has
been established from the beginning. For instance: We
cannot get health and we cannot get wealth; we cannot
get happiness or peace. Those things were established
from the beginning! They were part of your consciousness and they will unfold in proportion to your turning
within for that unfoldment, and in proportion to your
devotion to the spiritual sense of life.

Now, if you can feel a sense of gratitude for that
message, for the avenue through which that message is
brought to you, and if, out of the fullness of your heart,
you feel that sense of gratitude that impels you to give
your "mite" or your last penny, then you will find that
tithing is one of the greatest blessings ever given to
human consciousness. There is no greater blessing than
tithing when it is the outpouring of a sincere sense of
gratitude for the revelation of God as your individual
experience. Certainly tithing in that sense is gratitude,
and gratitude is one of the facets of love.

But there is an even stronger law than that which goes
with tithing. Humanly you believe that your present
income is the limit of your income, and humanly you do
not know how to increase it. If you did, you would be
doing so. Now, when we begin tithing, we certainly
declare that this tithing is not coming from "our" income;
therefore it has to come from God. It is not from "me," it
is from God. It is God's support of the activity of truth in
human affairs or in human ways. Let us assume for the
moment that God, imparting truth to human consciousness, compels us to interpret that impartation as a book or
church or teacher. (You must understand here that God
"needs" none of these avenues: God needs no mediator.)

God and you being one, all of this could be taking place in your consciousness without any "person" talking to you, without any person writing a book. Therefore, the fact that we are here, that these avenues are here, is our authority at this moment to interpret it as God's imparting of his word in this manner, through these channels. Why? Only that you require these channels for the word of God to reach you until the time comes when your oneness with God—your conscious oneness with God—enables you to accept the message without all of this. Therefore, since that is true, there must be these means provided in the meantime. And when we say that "God provides them" that is not really true. God knows nothing about human teachers or teachings, human places or human worships. For if God had made our churches, none would ever have been bombed or burned. These we create through our necessity for them.

We are not yet at that point of consciousness where we sufficiently realize our oneness with God so as to receive these messages without meditation, therefore we need these places and teachers and books. However, inasmuch as there is nothing personal about it, let us call that the activity of mind or God, and let us see that the activity or mind or God interprets itself to us as teachers, churches and books. Then let us see that the activity of God, acting through or as us, must support that enterprise.

Let us agree, then, to call it a transfer agent for good, and say, "I will contribute this particular sum every day or every week to this spiritual purpose, not out of 'my' income or the kindness of my heart, but merely as a transfer agent for good, 'God', maintaining its own infinite activity." Soon you will find that not one penny of that tithing will be coming from your pocket and you will

find, further, that your income will ultimately increase–
not merely to make up that amount, but to go much
further than that. We are saying this only to point out to
you what actually does happen, for you are eventually
going to carry this much further. You will ultimately
declare that every family obligation you have–or any
other obligation–is not your personal responsibility but
that of the Christ, and is, therefore, not to be met out of
your personal income.

Thus you will become the transfer agent for supporting your family or friends or relatives abroad, and so on.
You will find none of it will come from your principal if
you catch the central point: that no personal demand is
ever made of you, but on the Christ. Not that the Christ
supports the activity of this life, this job, this teacher or
this book. No, no! You, yourself, through your consciousness of this activity of God–good–have brought to
you those who, to your sense, are avenues or channels
of support! You must make a conscious decision that
you will be the transfer agent. As soon as you are
presented with a need or the call, you will accept that
the Christ has made a demand on the Christ of you and
that you can fulfill it, not out of your personal income,
but out of that which the Christ gives you.

We read in the Bible that the widow had only a
morsel, yet she fed the prophet. Had the supply come
from the little she had, it would never have sufficed. But
the demand was not made on her personal supply. The
demand was made on the Christ! Again, four or five
thousand people sat around waiting to be fed by Jesus
with a few loaves and fishes. Jesus was never in a
position to feed so many people from his personal store
of supply–never! Unless Jesus had been able to see that

the demand on him was a demand on the Christ itself, that it was the Christ making the demand on the Christ, it could not have been done.

And again, he healed the multitudes. If any individual ever gets the idea that he has enough human understanding to heal a disease, heaven help the patient! No. Every call for healing is a call on the Christ, and all a practitioner can ever do is be an avenue through which, or as which, the Christ is acting to dispel the illusion of sense. It makes no difference if multitudes reach out for that, even if multitudes right here reach out for healing. It would not be a personal or human man that would respond. But the Christ, acting or appearing as me, could just as well meet the demands for a thousand as for one. The Christ is unlimited.

Never believe that any "human" being has any quality of his own that will produce a healing—or that any of you have enough money to support churches or practitioners or teachers. As the Christ, any one of you could support churches or practitioners or teachers; but as the Christ, any one of you could support all of this activity. You have only to consciously accept the responsibility. You have only to say, "Father, I accept the responsibility to meet my generous share of the activity of the Christ movement here through me." But that does not mean you have the personal responsibility of supporting them. No. All the responsibility you have is to make the conscious decision that you are part of this work and that just as the Christ is operating through the lecturer or teacher, so the Christ is operating through you, for the benefit of this whole Christ activity.

Let us remember this subject: Tithing. It makes no difference whether you make the decision to give ten, five or one percent, or twenty percent of your income. The point is, you must consciously make the decision to be a part of the spiritual activity of the world and to fulfill your part in it! If you are called on for a healing—yes, if you should be called to come right up here on this platform this morning and finish the talk—be ready! If that call is made on you, it is only the Christ making a demand on the Christ, and any of you could fulfill it by consciously making your decision to be a part of the Christ life. There is a reason why all of this is important and it is not that of becoming healthier or richer humans. No, it is that you come into the realization of your Christ destiny and stop being even good humans.

We read in the Bible: "The earth is the Lord's and the fullness thereof."[6] How much of that is yours? All of it! All of it. Do you see what I am trying to get at? Not to make you a richer human, but to make you aware of the fact that the entire kingdom of God is yours! "*The earth is the Lord's and the fullness thereof.*" All that belongs to the Father belongs to you! You will never know that while you are counting it in dollar bills. You will know it only when you completely release yourself from the belief that you "have" so much and "have not" so much. When you begin to make the acknowledgment that all the earth belongs to the Father; but all that the Father hath belongs to you—"Son, *all* that I have is thine!"[7]

What is the most essential point in becoming aware of God? And that really is the most important question that can ever be asked. What is the most necessary step for us to take in becoming aware of God? Well, the most important step for us to take is this: To acknowledge God to be all there is to us. When we acknowledge God to be our mind; when we acknowledge God to be the life of us, the soul, the spirit of us; when we make the acknowledgment that God is the only element and only activity and the only law of our being, then we have taken the most essential step in becoming aware of God.

There is no selfhood apart from God. God is one, infinite, indivisible, appearing as each individual. The all-ness of God appears individually as "you." You are not a part of God. You are not a particle of God. It is not like the "drop with the ocean." There is not that relationship at all. You are the all-ness of God! *You* are the all-ness of God! The all-ness of God appears individually as you. It is like the all-ness of the number twelve appearing in every number twelve, whether as pies or grains of sand. Always the entire number contains the total value of twelve. Just so, the totality of God appears as individual you. You are all the mind, all the life, all the intelligence. You could not be "more" life, more immortality. You are immortality. You always have existed and always will exist and you cannot be more immortal than immortality, cannot be more truthful than being truth. No, either you are all of truth or you are not truth. Can a person be ninety-nine percent mortal? No, either you are mortal or you are not mortal. There are human degrees of being mortal, but that is not immortality. The same is true of every facet of God. You cannot be partly intelligent and yet be of God. You are the sum total of intelligence. Therefore, God's infinite intelligence is your individual intelligence. And so, the most essential step is "I, of mine own self, am nothing. God is the all-ness of me, the mind, the life, the soul, of me." Then let that come through your so-called human consciousness to make itself known as awareness.

It is for this purpose we have meditation, reading, lectures, class teaching. All of these are avenues or means through which you become aware of your oneness with God, become aware of God appearing as the sum total of you. The purpose of class teaching, lectures, reading and metaphysical literature, is only to bring you to the awareness that you are now what you always have been–the fulfillment of God! To repeat, the most essential point in becoming aware of God is making the acknowledgment that God is the sum total of me; God is the substance of my body, the actual substance of my body. Otherwise we would have God, infinite all, and a human body.

Now to come to a second point in becoming aware of God, and this deals with the subject of sleep and how to arrive at the condition of requiring less of it. That, of course, cannot be made a matter of human will (for we would wreck our human sense of health that way), but must be a matter of spiritual demonstration. However, this state can be achieved by practice. In my case the practice was this: For more than twelve years I have never had more than three to three and half hours of sleep at night and sometimes much less. Yet I have had no sense of needing sleep or of being tired and here is the reason: The temptation comes at bed-time to jump into bed in a hurry and get some sleep and this is the first temptation that must be overcome. Sit down for at least three to five minutes before getting into bed and just open your consciousness to God in the sense of, "I and the Father are one, and where I am is the conscious awareness of that." Open consciousness to God! It may be for only three minutes, but don't go to bed without doing this. Now, instead of lying in bed and thinking about the problems of the day or of what must be done tomorrow, lie there in the thought of conscious oneness with God, and, with this thought, fall asleep.

You will eventually find that instead of sleeping the whole night through, you will wake up in the middle of the night. And there is the time when the first really difficult steps begin. When this happens, get up out of bed whether it is hot or cold, have something warm to drink if you like, but get up! And for three or five minutes feel that conscious oneness with God. Then, if you feel like going back to bed, go ahead. In this way you are gradually filling yourself with the presence of God, and by degrees you will overcome the necessity for that state of *un*-consciousness we call "sleep."

The night before last I had not the faintest idea what would present itself to me Sunday morning. I awakened out of sleep with this statement: "Seek ye first the kingdom of God,"[8] and then, in big letters, "*and his rightness.*" For the first time in my life I understood those words. We all know what human life is: a little extra income, a little extra wisdom, a little extra health. But what is "his rightness"? What is the spiritual sense of health, the spiritual sense of supply, the spiritual sense of good? And there we have the whole secret. My lesson for the following day unfolded from there on. Imagine waking up out of a deep sleep and having the whole thing appear! The appearance of sleep was not unconsciousness but a rest for the body. And, in sleep, the inner mind was functioning. That is the place to which we ultimately come and not merely to a point of staying awake, more or less, for the greater part of the day. The place we come to is that of conscious intelligence, whether awake or asleep, and when that comes to you, it does not make any difference whether you stay in bed eight or ten hours out of the twenty-four. It does not really matter as long as you are *consciously* functioning; as long as rest is merely a resting of the body. The operation of God can go on while the eyes are closed and you are seemingly asleep, but not if you go to sleep *un-*conscious.

When I retire at night, I make the decision that everyone who reaches out to me for help must touch the Christ of his being and get Its help. It is not my human knowledge, but the divine consciousness of me with its Christ which helps. And this divine consciousness never sleeps. When I make the decision not to turn off my contact with those who are looking to me as a practitioner; when I consciously realize that everyone who reaches out to me during the night is reaching out, not to Joel Goldsmith, but to the Christ of me, and that Christ is awake and healing *now*, he gets his help. That help comes because of the fact that even in my sleep, I, the reality of me, am not asleep. My body is at rest, my human thinking is at rest, but the consciousness of me which is God, the Christ of me which is the form of God, is ever awake and ever healing. So don't look at our work as an attempt to sleep less hours or to be in bed a shorter time. The point is to come to the conscious awareness of the Christ. And I have given you the way to do it.

To sum it up: First, before retiring, have two or three minutes meditation to establish your oneness. Then when you get into bed, do not allow yourself to think about today's or yesterday's problems. Spend that minute before you fall asleep maintaining your conscious oneness with God. If you wake up in the middle of the night, don't try to get back to sleep, but jump out of bed for a few minutes and sit in meditation. Then, if you feel like it, go back to bed. Or if you feel like writing or like cooking, do that. This should become a matter of habit. Our life is again an adventure! It must no longer be lived according to the old standards. Life is an adventure if there is something worth looking forward to rather than just falling into the habit of living twenty-four hours a day in some routine manner. What to do about sleep? Don't be concerned if you feel more comfortable when you are in bed eight hours out of the twenty-four. But don't let it become an unconscious sleep. Make your rest a conscious oneness with God so that it becomes merely a rest, and your healing and creative work goes on.

~8~

HARMONY THROUGH ONENESS WITH GOD

THIS SUBJECT IS JUST THE SAME SUBJECT that we have been listening to for several thousand years—that of spiritual living, of our spiritual relationship with God, of bringing God into our individual experience. The subject is old, the presentation is always new; it is always appearing in new forms. Truth is a state of consciousness. Really, it is a state of infinite consciousness. God is truth. God is infinite. Consciousness is infinite. But because of that very infinity, it has infinite ways of presenting itself to us.

Back in the days of Krishna, probably the earliest known recorded history of truth, the presentation came in the form of the word "I." Always it was I speaking out through some individual—so much so, that often people deified the man, the individual who was presenting truth (God) only because of the use of the word I. That same thing happened later when Shankara, somewhere around 200 B.C., culled out from the Oriental scriptures the great secret and again presented it with the word "I." Only this time he went a little further and said, "I am that . . . *I am that.*" Here again, people also thought that a man was calling himself God. He wasn't. It was God announcing itself to individual consciousness. Then came the days of the one that we recognize as the

Master, Jesus of Nazareth. He presented the same story:
"I am the light of the world!"[1] And with that, people said
he made himself equal with God and that he thought it
not unseemly to do the works of God. "Let's crucify
him!"[2] they cried, yet all he was saying was that I–the
infinite law of being, the infinite creative principle of the
universe–I am your very own consciousness. I am the
very life of you! I am the very mind of you!

He wasn't calling a human being that. He was very
careful to say, "I can of my own self do nothing.[3] My
doctrine is not mine, but his that sent me."[4] He made a
great distinction between the man who was appearing as
the messenger, and the I that was presenting itself as the
message. But the human mind at that time couldn't
accept it any more than it had accepted it in its previous
appearances on earth.

Now, the revelation that the I is God, that God is the
soul of the individual, appears many, many times in the
history of the world. Each time it ends with misunder-
standing and sometimes with crucifixion; but because it
is the truth, it is going to present itself over and over and
over again until we individually accept it and do not
glorify the human self-hood, or think that it of itself is
something great. Rather, it will present itself in the same
message but in different ways, until we so readily
recognize it that we permit that little I, or ego, to be
crucified; "to die daily"[5] as Paul has told us, until it is out
of the way.

So, this "I that I am," Jesus also termed "the Father
within." And when we wish to contact that, when we
wish to become one with it, when we wish to bring it
forth into our individual experience, we know now–or
we should know–where to go. We do not have to

worship in such and such a holy mountain, nor yet in that holy temple out there in Jerusalem. We are taught that that kingdom is within our own being. Now we look at a musician and if we look with our eyes we believe that he draws music out of the instrument. But if we look at him with our understanding, we know that the music is drawn from the musical consciousness that is within his own being. The instrument is but an instrument, but the source of the inspiration, the source of the gift that is within the soul of the individual, that is God. One brings it forth as music, another as architecture, another as painting. Where is that gift all the time? It isn't outside in any mysterious God. It is always within the depths of our own being and it is brought forth when we are finished with the world. We find that when our hands are no longer needed for the care of little children and a household or a business, then we are able to go within and bring forth our gifts of art or healing.

Within each one of us there is a gift. As Paul tells us there is only one spirit that animates us all, but that spirit brings itself forth in different ways. One of us is given the gift of healing, another that of the law, another that of preaching. Each one, if he searches deeply enough within his own consciousness, will find some mode or method of expression uniquely his own. We may go outside to teachers for guidance, but we can't go outside to teachers for inspiration.

That same law holds true in this great work which we call spiritual living. You may go to a teacher, you may go to a book, for guidance and help along the way. But you can't go to a teacher or to a book for God. You have to go to your own soul, to the innermost depths of your own being. Never believe for a moment that any man or any woman or any book can reveal God to you. All these can do is show you the path along which you may travel until you get back into the kingdom of your own being, into the kingdom of your own soul, and there find God.

Perhaps you know the story that is told in two different ways. One is an ancient Hebrew teaching and the other an ancient Hindu teaching, but the story is the same in both cases: There was a disciple who went to his master and asked, "Please Master, show me God. Let me know God, let me be in God's presence." Over and over he appealed to his master but the wise master did nothing about it except smile and say, "Yes, in time. In time." Then one day, the master felt that the time had come. So he said to his disciple, "I am going to take you to our secret and sacred temple. There are three rooms in this temple but I can only take you into the first. After that, you are on your own. If you find the way, you will ultimately find God. If not, it will have to be another time." The disciple found himself alone in a room that was empty except for a golden statue of Jehovah God. And after the disciple got accustomed to the idea of this room, the feel of it, he felt something wrong. He said, "No, this isn't it. The atmosphere is too heavy here. I will have to go further." So he found his way into the next room. After entering the second room, he commenced to breathe more freely. As he got accustomed to the surroundings, he saw that again he was in an empty room except for a statue of Jehovah God made of crystal. He felt the lightness of that crystal, he felt the lightness of the atmosphere of the room and he said, "This is more like it!" But after awhile, he realized that even though this was more like it, it wasn't it. So began the search for the entrance to the third room. You know he found it and you also know what he found. He found himself in an empty room—completely empty. There was nobody there but He!

That's the story of the search for God. Eventually, we become one with God when we come into the realization that "I and the Father are one!"[6] We have to turn within our own being to find it. Where will you find happiness or peace, or contentment or security, if you do not find it within your own being? Certainly not in wealth. There have been untold numbers of people of wealth who have not found happiness. In fact, no one of wealth has ever claimed that the wealth itself brought happiness. If there weren't other conditions present, the wealth in itself was nothing. Happiness has to be found within.

There have been people who have found a degree of happiness in marriage. But it was only a degree. There came the same thing, ultimately; that realization of incompleteness—until someone finds within himself this great quality of oneness, this great quality of at-one-ment, this sense of completeness because of the divine being, the Father within. Now, Paul termed this "the Christ." He said, "I live, yet not I, Christ liveth in me."[7] And, because he could tabernacle with that Christ, because he could commune with it, because he could live with it, he had the secret of life.

John, of course, tells us of "the temple not made with hands."[8] John tells us of the invisible universe. Where is that invisible universe? Where, except within our own being? And is it really invisible? No, it isn't. It's really visible, really tangible. But only to spiritual sense! The eyes can't see it, that's true. The ears can't hear it. It is invisible only to material sense, but very visible, very real and very tangible to the inner senses. The value of this is great. The value of this is that it is the secret of life. With it, with the attainment of the realization and understanding of it, we come into every scriptural promise and its fulfillment: "Lo, I am with you unto the end of the world."[9] That's that invisible I, that invisible Presence, not present in the golden statue nor in the crystal statue—only visible as emptiness to the outer senses but completely satisfying and filling within. "I am come that ye might be filled."[10] Filled; filled full—fulfilled! That you may have the "real thing!"

But that I is God, that I is the Christ, the son of God. And your awareness, your conscious awareness of that truth, is your communion between that which is your outer self and that which is your inner spiritual self. Someday this outer self will disappear and all that is left then is the inner reality and in that moment you hear Jesus say, "And hast thou not known that when thou seest me, thou seest the Father that sent me,[11] for I and the Father are one?"[12] By that time he had overcome the world. By that time he had overcome his dependence on the things and thoughts of the outer world. By that time he had attained complete communion with this great inner being.

Spiritual living itself is the life lived by grace, not by might, nor by power. It isn't life that we experience with trials and tribulations and hard labor; on the contrary, it is a life in which we find all things appearing to us in the order that we need them, sometimes before we ourselves are aware of the need. That is living by grace. And that living by grace is attained only when things and thoughts have been overcome. We have not overcome the world while we are trying to improve or increase the material sense of our world. Just having more money or a heart or liver that functions as we think it ought to, that is not the attainment of spiritual life or immortality. True, it is obtaining a better human experience, but at best it is a temporary one. The attainment of spiritual life is that state of being in which we live by grace, in which we know that automatically, whatever the need is, the answer will appear. We have, not so much promises of it, but witnesses to it in such statements as, "the presence going before me to make the crooked places straight."[13] There we have the indication of an infinite, invisible presence or power that, while not tangible to senses, does go out and if necessary creates a parking space for us or finds just the hat or the dress that we need. We do not use it for that purpose, but it functions in that way in our experience.

You remember Jesus did not hesitate to call on it to produce transportation in the form of a donkey. He did not hesitate to call on it to bring forth gold out of the fish's mouth, or to multiply the loaves and fishes. But, always remember that he was not using it as a vaudeville trick, and he wasn't using it simply as a means of charity. He rebuked those who came to him continuously for those loaves and fishes and told them, "You came for more of the loaves and fishes, but why didn't you understand the miracle behind it? Then you wouldn't have needed these continuous hand-outs of loaves and fishes! I showed you the loaves and fishes and fed them to you so that you could see that there is a principle. If you could learn that principle, you would have the invisible means of life. Not by might, nor by power, but by my spirit!" In the same way, he healed the multitudes. He must have become very weary of it in the end because he said, " 'If I go not away, the Comforter will not come to you.'[14] If I go on healing all these ills of yours—oh, I can do it!—'the Father within me worketh hitherto and I work'[15]—I can do it, but where are you going to get off if you keep looking for your foundation and your healing in a man called Jesus when the man called Jesus is trying to say to you, 'the kingdom of God is within you!' "[16]

Remember, he said, "Your Father and my Father."[17] Oh, he had no copyright on it! Nor did he claim any special right to it. Very honestly, very openly he said, "Your Father and my Father" and, "Greater things will you do!"[18] We, in this age, are listening to that self-same message, the message of the infinite invisible, of that which is to the outer senses intangible, but to the spiritual consciousness, very real.

* * *

I suppose everyone in this room has experienced one healing or has known someone who has experienced metaphysical healing. Well, those healings were the outer evidences of an inner grace. Those outer healings represented somebody's developed spiritual consciousness. Never forget that every time you have ever known a headache, even a simple headache to be healed, every time you have ever witnessed a healing of something of a more serious nature, you have only witnessed the outer evidence of an inner power. In most instances that power is the consciousness of the practitioner, but it need not be so. In this day of open teaching of truth, the power is available to anyone who is willing to have it. There is no great price involved. The financial end of metaphysical teaching is not burdensome. The books on metaphysical teaching and healing are not expensive and the teachers and the practitioners do not burden people with their bills or their fees. It's a very loving ministry. In most cases those that are in it, especially those that are in it "with signs following,"[19] are not commercializing it to the extent of using it simply to make a living. That which comes to them in the form of their supply comes mostly from the love and appreciation and gratitude of those who have benefited. And it is very abundant. It comes very freely because people are grateful for health and harmony and peace but there is no demand for amounts greater than anyone can pay. Therefore it really is fulfilling Isaiah's promise, his invitation, "Come, drink of this thing; eat, without money, without price." We find it literally true that if you haven't any money, no money will be required of you. And if you have a little, the "mite" will be very happily accepted by anyone I have ever met in this work, "with signs following"–with love.

This work is like any other work. There are those attracted to it by the love of God, the love of the Christ, and naturally there are those who are attracted by the loaves and fishes. You must go within and you must find your teacher and your guidance. That which will meet your need may not meet the need of your neighbor, but if you turn within to the same spirit, the spirit of Christ in you, you will be led to your teacher and to your teaching. You will find that this whole world of truth is open to you and available to you, not only for your own personal use, but for that of the world at large.

Now, our oneness with God constitutes that presence and power of grace. In scripture we have guides along the path. Jesus himself said, "I am the way."[20] There is a way through scripture and through metaphysical writings and teachings which will lead you back to the kingdom of your own soul, where you will find your peace, your oneness, and your grace. When that day arrives, you find the demands of the outer self are lessening. You will find fewer demands being made upon you for material gratification, for human gratification, in the greater sense of love and of peace welling up from within. The secret of the inner life by grace is this: There are no yesterdays; there are no tomorrows; there is only the ever-present *now*! We have no penalty to pay for past mistakes. We are not piling up rewards for the future. We are living the fullness and completeness of life in this very minute. We can all say that right here and now because I feel it here. Now—in this minute—you are living, for you cannot live yesterday and you cannot live tomorrow. The only possible thing you can do is live here and now this minute. And of course, tomorrow in your experience will really be now also. Otherwise it won't be at all. It has to be now. It is all a continuous now, now—*now*! This minute is now. Next minute will be now. It's all—*now*!

The value of this for our spiritual purpose is this: If you are living in the fullness of your understanding at this moment, you are doing all that can be expected of you. All that we are ever required to do is to forget the past, live to the highest sense of our spiritual capacity, and leave the rest to God!

You know, we have this teaching of "karma" that is about as true a teaching as there is in all the world. Only it isn't called karma in the Christian religion, it is called, "as ye sow, so shall ye reap."[21] Now, all there is to that is the fact that what we are living this minute will manifest itself in the next minute or the next year or the next era or the next incarnation if we consider the form of the continuity of life as incarnation or reincarnation. Regardless of what we think about reincarnation, the truth is that life is eternal. And the truth is that as we are living that life—*now*—we will be living it eternally. We will be living this life in whatever consciousness we ourselves unfold. Can you understand this just for a minute? That now, this minute, is the only life you have and that right now, in this very minute, you have no past and no penalty to pay for a past? If you can agree that "I now am living in the fullness of God; I now am living in the fullness of love; I now am entertaining no animosity, no hates, no jealousies, no envies," can you imagine how much love there is at this very minute right here in this room? Love for me; love for you; love for each other; love for the truth; love of God; love of the Christ. It was only love that brought us here!

Then think how little there is here of envy, jealousy, malice, lust, greed. Then all we have to do is continue that consciousness in this minute. Continue it! Keep this love that is in your heart this very minute, this love of God that brought you here, this desire for the understanding of the Christ that led you here, this love you can feel for the message, the love that you know I must feel; think of that love and then think of the impossibility of any other quality entering consciousness! We are responsible if we go out of here and permit other thoughts to enter our consciousness. Who is responsible but our own selves? Yourself or myself. Is there any power in the world decreeing that you should hate someone or fear someone? Is there any power outside of you that can make you be lustful or greedy or jealous or

envious? Certainly not. You would have to open up
your own mind to it in the way you had to open up your
own mind to the love of God that brought you here.

A human being left to himself will never seek out
God. Never! That's why there are so few of us on this
path. There are always few on this path. There are only
a few opening their consciousness to God. This is your
responsibility. That was the import of Jesus' message:
"The kingdom of God is within you."[22] But oh, remember how he put his arms around them and said, "Jerusalem, Jerusalem![23] I would love to do so much for you! I
feel you are my little chicks! But why won't you open up
and listen to me?" Well, here is the same thing but now
your consciousness has opened itself. You didn't have to
be invited in. And it isn't only here in this class. Evidently you go wherever you feel the spiritual urge.
That's the love of God welling up in you that you can
keep all the night long. You don't have to fear who is the
president of the United States or who is the president of
Russia. That won't touch you as long as your heart is
filled every minute with love, which is God.

Living by grace means living by love. I think I have
told this here before but if I have, it will stand repetition:
I used to be puzzled by the sign up on the Christian
Science Church wall, "Divine love always has met and
always will meet every human need." How many, many
times, how many, many years I looked around and said,
"It's not doing such a good job for a lot of people around
here!" But you know, it isn't that that sign isn't true. That
sign is true. It is that we do not correctly interpret that
sign. It is really true that divine love always will meet
your human need. But, there is no divine love up in the
sky. There is no divine love going to come and operate

in you or through you or for you. The divine love which meets every human need is the divine love you express! The impersonal love you express! The impartial love you express to your enemy, the love you express to those who persecute you! You pray for your enemy and watch how that divine love will very quickly meet your human need.

There is a story told about that by one of the old Christian Science lectures: A woman had a room to rent and didn't rent it. She finally went to a practitioner to ask for help and told the practitioner how if she only had this ten dollars extra a week, all her needs would be met! Yet nobody came to rent the room in spite of the fact that she was advertising it. The practitioner told her she had gone about it in the wrong way. "You have been too concerned about what you would get, what you need! Have you ever thought what that room would do for somebody out in the world living alone, for someone who could benefit by the beauty or the harmonious furnishing of that room, by the spiritual atmosphere of your home, by the cleanliness of your home, by the morale and morality of your consciousness? Have you ever thought what would happen to a person who could move into that consciousness? Who could have the divine protection of your spiritual thought? You go home and think about what would happen through you to someone out in the world. And then see what happens." It was not long before a man came to rent the room. On his way out he saw her Christian Science books lying on her table and he asked, "Oh! Are you a Scientist?" "Yes," she said. "That's a strange thing. I am, too. And I have been carrying your ad about for a whole week and all of a sudden today the urge came to answer the ad!" You see what it was, don't you? He probably had a higher sense of love than she did and he was looking to carry love somewhere but not to someone who was just seeking ten dollars a week. He was looking for someone who was ready to express love.

Now this love which you and I express is not only for each other, for even the Scribes and the Pharisees expressed love to each other and to their families and their friends. No, this love that we are called on to express must be given to our enemies, to those who despitefully use us, as well as to those who come within the range of our friendships and our families. That is, of course, the power of love; that oneness with God. Oneness with God is the conscious expression of the qualities of God, therefore it isn't a mysterious factor; it isn't an occult factor; it isn't something you have to do in the "wilds" somewhere or out in the woods. You can do it right here in the room. You can do it in the streetcar. As long as you are looking out on this world with love, with forgiveness, and with great joy for the fact that all who open their consciousness to the presence of God will in some manner bring it forth, that is all that is necessary. It is a reality that there is within you greater capacities for joy than any you ever have known in the external world. I myself have always been a voracious reader from the time I was a child. I have read books almost as fast as they could print them. But I can tell you that today I can find just as great a joy welling up within me as I can find outside in a book. Though I still enjoy beautiful books, I also find that if I were in a place where there were no books, all that could be found in books can be found in my individual consciousness and yours.

Peace—joy—power! "My peace I give unto you: not as the world giveth!"[24] You know the peace that the world gives? Oh, that peace is money, home, automobiles, theaters, dances, good food–that is the kind of peace that you get from the world. But how about "my peace?" How about "the peace that I give you that the world cannot give you?" That is the peace we are seeking. That is the grace of God. And please believe me, it isn't outside of you to be achieved or acquired! It is already within you in the fullness, or else there is something wrong with Jesus' statement, "Lo, I am with you unto the end of the world."[25]

Now, that Christ, the presence of God, really and truly is with you, within your own being. But the world makes it very difficult for us to find that peace. For that reason we must find it within our being. We can't find it in apartment houses and not even in 50 foot ocean front homes. We have to find it within ourselves! And the same way with security. In this age you are not going to find security in your bank account. We can, though, all come together in places like this, each of us with a different background, and still we can have a feeling of warmth and love held out to us at the door, with nobody asking whether we are saints or sinners, nobody asking whether we are Jews or Gentiles, or what we have in our pockets. And you know, that's love! That same love that you find in here has to be expressed by the individual who has enough of that love to give this service to the world. You and I have to have that same degree of love in order to fulfill that sign, "Divine love has always met and always will meet every human need." Certainly it will! The love that we manifest. The love that we express!

Now, love is only one facet of God. There are many others: light–truth. Let us take truth. Now and here we are expressing truth. I am expressing truth in the sense of the words that are coming through, the words about God. You are expressing truth not only in the sense of hearing those words, but by being here. Your very presence is an expression of truth itself. You knew when you came here that there were not going to be any pink teas, there was going to be only truth. So your very presence here is an acknowledgment. It's the evidence of your own desire for truth; your own desire to *be* the truth. So now, in this very minute, when our consciousness is filled with truth, isn't it also true that it is a continuing experience, that the truth which is present as our consciousness now must be there forever? Otherwise we deny Jesus' statement, "Lo, I (truth) am with you unto the ends of the world."

Then this truth which you are accepting in your consciousness this moment is with you until the end of the world. All you have to do is consciously remember that every word that has been said here tonight, every word of truth, will be a continuing treatment or prayer in your consciousness. It's up to you. You are the master of your own experience. And the way you do it is through this "nowness." To realize that "I am with you until the end of the world," and that the Christ of God, the son of God, is the very consciousness of your being until the end of the world; and then you look out at all of your neighbors and say, "Isn't it wonderful! Right there, too, is this same truth, this same eternal life, this same love." Then you are fulfilling the two commandments from Jesus: "Love the Lord thy God with all your soul, with all your heart" and "love thy neighbor as thyself."[26] You are doing that *now*. Only you can make it a continuing experience which is a moment of grace. The wholeness of the Godhead is flowing in you and through you and it is appearing here visibly as you. Every one of you presents to me the face of God and as you look up here and look through what you think of as a human face, that is all you can see too—God shining through; the grace of God speaking.

In that now you are under divine grace. All of the time that existed before this minute is wiped out. So far as you are concerned, there are no benefits from the past because in this now you need nothing of the past. You have the fullness of the Godhead bodily—in you and through you—at this very moment! You can't want more than that! The fullness and the allness of God manifesting in you and through you and as you this very minute. And, "Lo! I am with you until the end of the world!"

This grace, this truth; do you know we are having a holy experience here this minute, right now? Can you feel that where we are the very grace is manifesting because we have had nothing here but the dedication of our own temple, the temple of our own bodies, to truth? We brought it to this room—for what purpose? For the truth. Can we withdraw that dedication? It does not lie within our possibility because "I of my own self " did not bring it here. It was the spirit of the Father within that urged it on and brought the consciousness alive and brought it to this point. And so with you. Of your own human selfhood you didn't come here. But the spirit of God, the presence of God in you lifted your consciousness to something higher and better than even good or happy humanhood, to dedicate yourself, to dedicate your bodies for this hour to truth. Your body is the temple of the living God and you dedicated it to the divine life and the divine love which are its presence and its power. How are you going to withdraw your body and take it out of the presence of God, or take God out of it?

"Lo, I am in you and you are in me, we are one in the Father." There is no drawing back. You can't turn back even for a single moment. You've got to realize from now on that you have been given the peace that passeth understanding because of your own dedication to God, because you have brought your body as a temple to be dedicated to truth, to life, to immortality, to spirituality. What more can you do? What more could I do? Nothing. Nothing more is expected of us. When we reach out only one percent to the Christ, it reaches out ninety nine percent to us—at least we are told that in scripture, and scripture has a way of proving itself true.

Now let us remember this. That at this moment we can drop our human concerns; we can drop our fear of whatever bodily conditions, or mental or financial conditions seem to beset us. That we have opened our door to God, to the Christ, to the receptivity to the "peace that passeth understanding,"[27] to the divine presence that goes before to make the crooked places straight. And that is all it takes—one little moment of dedication. One little moment of opening consciousness to this truth and realizing that what happened in this *now* is a continuing experience. It never stops—and it never will.

~9~

PRAYER OF UNDERSTANDING

THE PURPOSE OF PRAYER is the unfoldment of our own soul. I wonder if you would like to remember that? Only the Soul, the being that is illumined, finds peace, harmony, wholeness, in what we call this human experience. All of the good that we ever attain in this world is attained through the development of the soul. Those developed souls are always happy people, successful, prosperous, because they have an awareness of spiritual value. Those of whom we say, "oh, poor soul!" are usually also poor in health, poor in spirit, poor in purse.

The purpose of prayer, then, is the unfoldment of the soul. Prayer should not be a going to God for something of a material nature. I am going to speak just a little bit about the various concepts of prayer: You all are familiar with the Old Testament, the Hebrew Testament, and of the many forms of praying for good. But you also find there prayers for the destruction of the enemy. It seems strange that we should pray to a God to destroy something or someone, for who is to judge which is in the wrong and which is in the right? Those prayers are really paganistic prayers. That same form of prayer continues down through the ages. It is the most popular form of prayer today. You know how we pray for the destruction of our enemies today? As a matter of fact, we

have recently been guilty of praying for the destruction
of one nation and then joining it as an ally and praying
for the success of its arms, and soon after praying for its
destruction again. Mustn't that give God a laugh, if God
could laugh? Don't you see how foolish that must sound,
even to a human being with any degree of intelligence—all this praying for something?

On V-E Day, the day that the war ended in Europe,
a call went out from the churches to gather in the
churches the next Sunday to thank God for ending the
war. That call went out on Tuesday. How that must
seem to an intelligent being, to wait from Tuesday until
Sunday, and then to pray only in the church edifice.
Why not call on people to pray a prayer of thanksgiving
now, where we are? (Although, in this case, even that
wouldn't have been justified.)

You know, before World War II it was pretty well
known that a war was on the way, so churches were
praying for many weeks in advance that the war would
not take place, that God intervene. But evidently God
went about its spiritual business and paid no attention to
these earthly demands because the war came along on
schedule. Now, all throughout the war we had days of
prayer on which the people of this nation and other
nations were called together to church to pray for peace.
Again God went on its merry way and the war went on
its not-so-merry way. Then came the day when the
so-called enemy was out of ammunition, out of food, and
the war ended. Then we were called on to thank God
because the war was ended. You know that even if God
had ended the war, he had done a pretty bad job!
Millions of people had been made destitute. I don't
know if you can feel how foolish it is, but you will in a

minute when I tell you that while these people were in church thanking God for ending a war in Germany, the same war was going on in the Orient and God wasn't doing a thing about it. He just brought peace over here on this street, but the war on that other street He paid no attention to! Then one day He evidently decided to end that, too—just after we threw two atomic bombs!

Do you believe that? Do you believe it was necessary to thank God for ending either the European war or the Asiatic war? No! If God were due thanks it would have been for preventing such a catastrophe; for preventing such an experience. I am illustrating this mainly for the purpose of bringing to light the nature and purpose of prayer. If I can, in this small way, cause somebody to think about what kind of praying he is doing, my purpose will be achieved. Perhaps you are praying for the end of some disastrous condition about which God knows nothing. That ought to make all of us stop and think about this subject of prayer. Volcanoes go on; tornadoes go on; tidal waves go on; and God goes on. Is there a connection between God and the terrible events on earth? No. There is no connection whatsoever! In the mind of God, no such things ever take place. Well then, does that mean there is a condition apart from God? No, it doesn't, since God is omniscient and omnipresent. It cannot be that such experiences are going on; it cannot be that men and women are dying; it cannot be that men and women have died. And, it is impossible that any man or woman will die. Otherwise God is failing, and in Its main work, which is eternality and immortality.

Then prayer must have some different significance than asking God either to end a war or thanking God for ending a war, or thanking God for our victories at the other fellow's expense. All wars have not ended in favor of those who were morally right, you know. And yet all wars have resulted in deep gratitude to God for ending them.

The purpose of all this is to bring to light for a moment the question of what prayer really is; what it should be, and what degree of that we are practicing. How far are we failing in the right sense of prayer in this twentieth century even when we have received enlightenment on so many other things? Prayer can never be successful unless we know what we are praying to, or praying for—and that brings us to the subject of God. All prayers are uttered to God; all petitions are offered to God; all affirmations and denials are aimed at God. What is God? Where is God? What is the function of God? Until we rightly understand those questions we can never pray aright. If you pray and do not get your answer, it is because you pray amiss. Yet how many of us have been in metaphysical practice for years and years and years without getting an answer, and still keep on praying in the same old way? It is about time we woke up, isn't it? It's about time we acknowledged that we are praying amiss, that we do not know how to pray or to what to pray or to whom to pray or in what manner we must pray.

"By their fruits ye shall know them."[1] If we are praying correctly we are showing it forth in the degree of harmony, health, wholeness, prosperity, and success we express. And I don't mean by that that just because we have a healthy physical body or lots of money, it is a proof we are praying right. Oh, no! There are many people who know nothing of prayer who are physically healthy and materially wealthy. No, I mean that if we are praying aright, we are reaping the fruitage of the spirit. The fruits of the spirit are love, well being, peace, joy, dominion—spiritual qualities, not material things; spiritual qualities which appear to us externally as a wonderful physical universe.

So the first question that has to be answered within our consciousness is: What is God? Until that is solved, we will never know the answer to what prayer is. Strangely enough—and I am sorry about it, too—I can't tell you what God is. I doubt that anyone can. I can give you a lot of names for God, but you can find those for yourself in the Bible and in metaphysical literature. God is love; God is mind; God is soul; God is spirit; God is life eternal. But that doesn't tell you what God is. That just gives you more names for the same word—G-o-d. It just takes one word and puts in its place another, but it does not tell you what God is.

No one ever will tell you that, for that is something which is found within your own being. It is for this reason that I can say the purpose of prayer is the unfoldment of your own soul! As you go within your own mind, within your own consciousness, with the question, "What is God?" or "Father, reveal thyself!" or "Speak, Father! Thy servant heareth,"[2] as you adopt that attitude of life, you are really praying, you are really turning within and asking God to reveal itself to you. You are asking that your own soul be revealed, be brought forth, be enlarged.

Of course, God, Soul, is infinite and can't really be enlarged, can't be developed. The seeming development lies in our conscious awareness of that which already is infinite and omnipresent. But here we have poetical license so we can say "the development of the soul" or "the enlargement of the soul" without really meaning that. We do mean developing our *sense* of soul, developing our conscious awareness of the nature and character of soul, of God. It's our sense that is enlarged, not God. God is already infinite; God is already omnipresent. But the omnipresence of God is of avail in proportion only as we come into conscious awareness of that presence.

All the secrets of television and all the secrets of the jet plane have always existed in consciousness and always have been available but were of no use until someone caught the very first glimpse of the secret; caught the first awareness, and from there developed it and ultimately brought forth the secrets in their fullness. So it is with God. God is infinite. God is omnipresent. God is omniscient. God is all-wise. But God comes to our protection, to our enlightenment, only in proportion to our awareness of it. Therefore, the first step in our spiritual experience must be learning the nature of God, and in learning the nature of God, we are praying! That's real prayer. That's the highest and finest prayer there is on this plane. There is one higher prayer that is attained—when the human senses are entirely stilled and the voice of God says, "Be still and know that I am God."[3]

There are many people who make that declaration and think that when they are saying they are God, they are praying a very high prayer. That isn't true. That is atheism. That is trying to make a human being God. That's like I said the other night about developing ourselves, not through religion, but through psychology, making the human mind our God, making the human mind power. Oh, no, no, no! Those are steps on the way up. But when our human mind, when our thinking, reasoning mind, is entirely still and we hear a voice saying, "Know ye not that I am God?" then you have reached the highest prayer there is in all the world. Jesus uttered that when he said to Philip, "Hast thou been with me so long, Philip, and hast not known thou seest me, thou seest the Father that sent me?"[4] Jesus the man had already evaporated and disappeared out of his own consciousness, and all that was left there was God. Then he could say "I am He!"

So long as we are indulging our hates and enmities and fears and doubts, it is a little bit foolish going around saying "I am God." But it is a beautiful thing and a wonderful thing to develop an attitude of listening, an attitude of introspection, an attitude of inner peace, so that God can declare itself. And our God does ultimately declare itself.

Prayer and treatment in the metaphysical world are often held to be synonymous. Some of you who have read my writings know that I have made the distinction of "prayer" and "treatment" as two separate things. It is not that I am quarreling with the world or that I am trying to change the language of metaphysics. I am merely trying to use the terms as they become clear to me and to pass them on for the benefit of anyone else who can see and understand what I mean. So without trying to change any dictionary meaning and without trying to find fault with any approach to metaphysics, I say to you that, to me, the word "treatment" and the word "prayer" do not mean the same thing. To me, treatment is a declaration of truth. It is my denial of error. It may even be my understanding of the nature of God and man. It is even a declaration of the nature of law, spiritual law. It is a declaration or realization of the understanding of the nothingness of that which appears as error in any form. To me, any thought that I entertain about the nature of God or man or power or error represents treatment. However prayer, to me, is the word of God and the word of God is never uttered by the "man whose breath is in his nostrils."[5] The word of God is uttered only by God, the universal, divine, infinite wisdom and love, to the individual expression of God's being–you and me.

As individuals we are like the Prodigal Son who has gone away from home and set up a separate identity that, for the time being, calls itself Joel Goldsmith or some other name. And as long as there is a sense about me that there is a Joel Goldsmith, I must turn within to that depth of me which is God, that infinite unseen part of me which is God, that which might be called my Father. And as I turn within to It, I hear It say to me, "Oh, son, all that I have is thine! We are one. I am in you and you are in me. We are not two, we are one! That which you are thinking of as your outer self, that's only the tiny little visible part of the infinite invisible *me*. No! Don't set up that little thing out there called Joel Goldsmith and set him to worrying about his own life and his own supply and his own home. I'll take care of that! Leave that with me. Take no thought for your life, what you shall eat. That's my responsibility, the responsibility of the infinite unseen which is the creative principle of all men!"

When I hear such a message, when I receive such divine assurance within my own being, the word of God is being spoken to me. And then you ought to see the miracles that happen! When that happened to Moses, manna came from the skies, water came from the rocks. When that "still small voice" spoke to Elijah and Elisha, you know what happened! The ravens came around feeding them. The dead boy was raised. All manner of miracles took place. Why? Were Elijah and Elisha so different? Oh, no! They made their contact so that the voice of God, that still small voice and that great infinite power was able to come through. That was the difference. And I don't need to tell you what happened when the "Father that is in me" came through Jesus. It healed the multitudes; It walked on water; It disappeared through crowds; It disappeared through walls; It preached the Sermon on the Mount. Finally, It said: "I have overcome the world!"[6]

Those are the glorious things that can be done. By you or me? No. By God! By God when we have prayed sufficiently, when we have heard the "still small voice" often enough. When we have made of our outer selves something of a vacuum so that that thing could come through. You know, this is not a new message; this is the oldest message that has ever been on earth. There has never been a person of spiritual enlightenment who did not know this secret. You will find this secret in Brother Lawrence; you will find it in the Catholic saints and the Protestant saints; you will find it in the religious characters of the Hebrews and of the Hindus, you find it throughout the world: "I can of my own self do nothing[7] . . . My doctrine is not mine, but his that sent me." You hear it through Paul: "I can do all things through Christ which strengtheneth me." Never has one of these people claimed anything of himself or for himself. Never has one of them said, "My understanding is so great that I can move mountains." But every one has indicated that in the degree that he could become a state of receptivity to the divine power, It walked on the waters, It performed these miracles. That is why the true sense of humility isn't hiding your face and saying, "I am nothing." The true sense of humility is the one that recognizes God as infinite and supreme and realizes that God is pouring through, and then gives all credit and all honor to It: "Thou shalt have no other gods before me[9] . . . Cease ye from man whose breath is in his nostrils for wherein is he to be accounted of[10] . . . Put not your faith in princes."[11]

All of these sayings indicate but one thing: First, they mean that God is not afar off, It is within you and within me. But It doesn't actually exist inside physicality, does it? Then It must be within the realm, or range, of our consciousness. Ultimately we will discover that God is our very consciousness. Then, as we learn not to use this thinking, reasoning mind, as we learn to use that mind that was in Christ Jesus and allow it to be in us, we feel the divine impulse. We feel the divine energy flowing through us. We note the divine will being made manifest in our affairs. And remember what Jesus said? He had to wash the feet of the disciples in order to show them that he was a servant of God, not a master—a servant of God.

We, in our human identity, are servants of God, but servants in the sense that we allow God to use our mind and body, our soul, spirit, and life for Its glory and Its manifestation, not to set us up on high; not to bring us a million dollars so the world can say, "Hasn't he got a lot of understanding?" No! All of the good that comes to us is for the showing forth of the presence and power of God. And it is done through silence. When we learn to silence our personal will, our personal desires, when we learn, absolutely, the sense of humility, the idea of "I am here as a servant of God, I am here to show forth the glories of God and I will never be satisfied to be showing forth some disharmony and discord!" then it happens.

Now we might go back to the old question: Why did Jesus feed the multitude only a few times? Why didn't he just keep on feeding them continuously? Why didn't he set up free kitchens all over the Holy Land to operate seven days a week and save the Hebrews the hard work of agriculture, even the hard work of retailing food? He could have saved them an awful lot of work! If he just had let those loaves be multiplied every day of the week, what a nice life those people would have led! But Jesus didn't think so. He didn't think that was the function of the Messiah. He didn't think that was the function of God or of the Christ. To him, his function was to reveal God in individual consciousness so that others could "go and do likewise." Please remember that, won't you? That if somebody could bring food out of the air, unless you could see the principle behind it, you would be fed only for one meal and you would expect that fellow to do it over and over again. Finally, the rebuke would come which Jesus gave to his followers: "I fed you yesterday, and now you are back for more! Why didn't you see the miracle yesterday, so that you could do it yourself today? You weren't looking for the principle; you were just sitting out there waiting to be fed." Is it any wonder he got tired and walked away from them and went across the lake? No! It must be a horrible thing to show people healings day in and day out, to heal them of colds and grippe and flu and corns and bunions and cancers and consumption and then ten years later have them come and say, "I need another healing!"

The purpose of healing work isn't simply to make people well: it is to show forth the principle that exists as your individual consciousness! That's the purpose of healing work. I am absolutely sure that when Mrs. Eddy began her ministry, she had no idea of setting up another form of *materia medica* that people could turn to and get healed. And I am sure that the reason she published books and magazines in the days when she had no money to do it with, was to show the principle, insofar as she understood it, to the people so they could learn it for themselves. Then she expected them to go out and do likewise, and for their patients and their students to go out and do the same.

That same thing happened to the Fillmores in Kansas City. Mrs. Fillmore was a truly marvelous healer, a truly wonderful healer, one of the great healers of her day. I am sure that she never expected to sit around doing healing work all her life because she too got busy and published books and pamphlets and lessons. She did not want to hug the principle to herself and put a patent or copyright on it and say "come to me and get your healings!" She very freely did the same as Mrs. Eddy: published it in books and sent it out for you to learn and for me to learn—sent out books describing the principle.

Well, you know I think those people expected that in one or two generations the whole world would be in metaphysics and they had a right to expect it within one, two or three generations. But instead of that, what have we developed? A group of practitioners—and—a group of patients! It's laughable but it's sad too, because two thousand years ago the Master refused to set up a dynasty of healing. He said, "If I go not away, the Comforter will not come to you!"[12] He would not stick around to do the healing work! He even rebuked the disciples when they had cases that they weren't able to heal. "Why, you have been around with me two or three years, and you still haven't seen the principle? How long do you require to learn this principle?" It isn't a difficult principle. For us in the occidental world, the only difficult part of it is to learn to be still long enough to hear the still small voice. Once we make the contact, from then on it's as easy as watching the gentle rains fall in spring. What isn't easy is to raise the whole world or to heal everybody or even to heal ourselves of everything. We are dealing with a great mesmeric force in the world—call it universal belief—and it's really powerful even in its nothingness. It baffles us and it fools us, even the smartest of us. So far as I have seen, even the spiritually enlightened come under that spell once in awhile.

But that's not the point, whether or not we are demonstrating one hundred percent. Heaven knows that if we are demonstrating ninety percent of it right now we are doing a fine job! Not one to be satisfied with, but one which shows us that at least we are on the way. A principle, to be a principle, must really be absolute, mustn't it? That means when we can catch the principle in its fullness, we'll have one hundred percent healings. However, not so long ago in this world we started out flying in airplanes with a little two-lung engine and we have come now to a great big 64-cylinder engine, and some even greater. We have come from twenty miles an hour in one generation to six hundred miles an hour, and that isn't the end; we will soon go to one thousand miles an hour, or twelve hundred miles an hour. And so it is in our spiritual world.

So far as demonstration is concerned, we are still partly in the human experience. We are still a little bit over-indulgent in our food, in our love for our family and friends. As we study the New Testament, we find that we will not come into the fullness of this vision until we have overcome our love for our mother and father, our sister and brother! It sounds strange, doesn't it, for a religion of love? But it is true. The love that we have to come into is the love which God has for the spiritual universe—love impersonal and impartial. The only way we will ever know how far we are coming along the spiritual path is when we are just as ready to lend our money to a fellow down the street as we are to our own brother or sister; when we are just as ready to forgive somebody on the other side of the ocean, as we are to forgive our own wife or husband or son.

In other words, the overcoming of the human sense of love must take place and it must be replaced with a sense of divine love. Divine love is the healer. When John said, "God is love,"[13] he did not mean the counterfeit that we use for love, the kind of love that makes parents spoil their children and have them end up in jail sometimes or have them end up as selfish beings. That isn't the love we mean when we speak of God, nor is it the love that we entertain toward some person for a selfish purpose or motive. That isn't love, either. Love is that sense of being which is able to take the whole world in and say, "I really love you!" Oh, it doesn't mean that if they have not awakened to their true identity we have to open our homes and make parasites of them. It means that we can look through their human frailties and see the divine within them and hold no personal animosity. The whole demonstration lies in our ability to give up our personal sense of love and hate and fear and enmity. As we are able to do that, we are rising in spiritual consciousness and that means that we are praying aright.

True prayer is the development of the soul. True prayer is when our soul rises to such great heights that it says, "Father, forgive them; they know not what they do[14] . . . Neither do I condemn thee. Go and sin no

more."[15] That is divine love. That is spiritual consciousness and nobody can develop that for you but you. The
greatest teacher, the most spiritual master, could lift you
up a little bit toward the place where you would desire
that; a master can help you attain it; but it has to come
from within your own being! This kind "goeth not out
but by prayer and fasting."[16] Are you willing to "fast"
from personal sense, from personal desires, from personal hates, personal fears, personal enmities?

So far we haven't asked God for anything in this kind
of prayer, have we? We haven't even turned to God for
anything except the unfoldment of our own soul within
our own being. And that's the right sense of prayer. That
is the true sense of prayer. Pray always that God reveal
itself; that God unfold itself; that God disclose itself to
us, to our so-called human awareness—actually to our
individual awareness. We, as individuals, can become
aware of God. We can be as infinite as God is, to the
degree that we lose this personal sense.

The promise is, "Son all that I have is thine!"[17] But
we, as individuals, must make ourselves fitting temples
for that and the way we do it is not just by making
affirmations about God's goodness and "my" spirituality.
It isn't that. It is by turning within and letting God reveal
its own being; its own identity. You will find this: as God
fills your consciousness, so God fills what appears to us
as an outer world. The outer world is only the form of
our inner world. Our inner world is the substance; the
outer world is the form that that substance takes. Therefore, when consciousness is filled with the idea of God,
when consciousness is filled with the spirit of God, then
the outer form, the picture, the pocketbook, the health,
the wealth, the home, the home relationships, begin to
take on spiritual, harmonious form.

Now, there is another aspect of prayer. Let's not waste any time in these days ahead in praying to God to stop a war or to stop a depression. Let us not waste any time asking God to look down upon us and be merciful. It won't work. It's been tried thousands and thousands of years. Go back to Hebrew scripture and then into the Christian scripture. For many thousands of years the prayer has gone out, "Oh, God, be merciful to me, a sinner! Oh, God, be merciful! Oh, God, forgive!" Let us get this straight. There is no such God! If there were, it would have been made manifest in earthly affairs centuries before now. God is a law of love and we have to come into conscious oneness with that God or law of love in order to benefit by it.

How many people in metaphysics have tried to give this law of God to their children and found that they could not do it? Or to their brothers or sisters or mothers or fathers? It is an individual experience. You can join a Baptist church and your children will be Baptists; you can be a Catholic and your children will be Catholic. But you can't become a metaphysician and make a metaphysician of your child! I have seen too many Christian Scientists try to make their children Scientists. It works sometimes, but it works only because those children had it within their own being to desire it; to want it. They catch something that makes them follow along that path and if they haven't caught it, they throw it all over! See how many children there are past fourteen, fifteen, sixteen, seventeen, in the Sunday schools. When they get to be eighteen, nineteen, twenty, most of them have thrown it away. In later years they often return, certainly. Where else are you going to turn except to God when you get into enough trouble? But this all shows that it has to be done individually. You can't be a metaphysician of any school by inheritance. If you can have parents or Sunday school teachers or practitioners who are able to impart to children enough of this wisdom so as to awaken in them a desire for it, that is fine. But barring that, the individual must himself go to God. So for us to sit around praying for all the people of the world to be spared from war when in their hearts and souls they are plotting and planning another one, how is it going to work? Wasn't it Abraham Lincoln's old prayer, "Not that God be on my side, but that I be on God's side." That is why ninety nine percent of the prayers of the world are never answered. It isn't prayer and it is uttered to a nonexistent God ignorantly worshiped.

You are one with God as you yourself are the outlet for that love; that divine love; the love which passeth understanding; the love which is grace, gentleness, peace. God is infinite intelligence and you are one with God in proportion as you are opening your consciousness to be led by that infinite intelligence. "Not my will but Thine be done!"[18]

So you could go through all of the synonyms of God that the Bible or metaphysical literature holds, and realize how much of God you are showing forth by how you conform to those guidelines. Do you see what I mean? I hope this is clear because if it is so only in a tiny measure, a measure only so large as a grain of dust, if you can see that you have to overhaul your concept of prayer and your concept of God and you've got to begin the work of conscious "at-one-ing"—attuning—and that it's your individual job; if only as a grain of dust I can make you see that, my whole lifetime will have fulfilled itself.

If I can catch a higher concept of God than I have now so that I can feel just one bit closer to this almighty spirit which is the reality of my being, I have no other purpose in life. I know it will use itself through me for some good end. And in the same way I know right well that I can't go out on street corners and preach this. I feel very, very fortunate if the few who are drawn to me of their own at-one-ment with this type of consciousness can catch one little glimpse of what I am trying to say and what I always so poorly say and write. Someday it will be said better and written down far better than it is now but if I can bring to life only one tiny little bit of spirit that will say, "I must overhaul my idea of prayer; I must do a little higher praying and have a little higher concept of God than to believe that he began a war or that he is ever going to end one or that he is ever going to forgive anyone his sins *in* his sins," I am fulfilled.

Forgiveness is accomplished only by the forsaking of the sin. There is no other way. We can no more be forgiven than to keep on in mathematics saying 3x3 is 8 or 4x4 is 19 and expect the principle of mathematics to say, "Well, after all, you are a charitable soul so we will give you the correct answer!" It isn't done. Not with mathematics and not with music, nor with painting, art, sculpture, or writing. Those who turn to those arts and gifts must turn to them with a full openness to the principles of them. Those who turn to God must turn to God with the full openness of consciousness to it.

Does this mean that if we are indulging some sin or sickness or hate, envy or jealousy and we cannot humanly stop it, that we are damned? Oh, no! It doesn't mean that at all! As a matter of fact, I think most practitioners will say it's much easier to work with a nice healthy sinner than it is with the usual "saint." The sinner at least knows he is a sinner and he knows he isn't deriving too much good from it and he is perfectly willing to let go of it if it can be made possible for him to do so. In that spirit of emptiness, that spirit of the realization of the "nothingness" of sin, it is very easy for that person to experience grace, salvation, and healing. The person who is already sure that he is perfect just because he happens to be a pretty good human being, has no real sense of humility. None at all! The real sense of humility comes with Jesus' statement: "Why callest thou me good; there is but one good, the Father!"[19] In that sense you can say, "Well, if that is the case, then I need a lot more awareness of that Father to wipe out some of this human 'goodness'!"

In this approach to God there is no reason for a hopeless attitude. There is no reason to be afraid because, for the moment, you can't give up your hate, envy or your greed or lust. Oh, don't be afraid of those things–they won't hurt you if you have to come to a place in consciousness where you realize they are not what they are cracked up to be and you would love to be rid of them! From that point on salvation is sure. It may sometimes be slow because we have lessons to learn–but it is sure.

There must be acknowledgment; there must be an emptying out of the false ego; there must be the willingness to turn within. Then, as we feel and realize God within us, we have achieved pretty closely the ultimate of prayer: hearing the still small voice; being consciously directed in all our ways. Then, instead of all of this praying for humanity, praying to stop wars, let us forget about that for awhile and turn within for the presence of

God! See that outpicture itself, not only in our experience, but in the experience of those that are around us.
Then let the circle spread from there until ultimately it
takes in the world. That will bring peace on earth—and
only that.

~ 10 ~

SPIRITUAL LIVING

ON THE SUBJECT OF SPIRITUAL LIVING—the spiritual way of life—you will note that one of the facets that goes all the way through the subject of spiritual living is spiritual law. You cannot get away from spiritual law. First, however, a few words about spiritual living, or the spiritual way of life. It is not a way of life that will separate you from your present experience; it will not take you out of your present activity except as you progress. It may lift you up into the practice, teaching and lecturing on spiritual subjects, but be assured it will not lift you out of your life; merely will it enhance the beauties, the safety and the security of the life you now are living.

Jesus taught—and it is on his teaching that all of this is based—that you were not to leave this world, that you were to be in the world but not of it. You are to be in the world and enjoy liberty, freedom, happiness, content-ment, peace, joy, dominion. He did not say anything about going out into the wilderness and becoming an ascetic. He did not teach going apart from the world and living in the universe of our private thinking. Rather, he increased the very loaves and fishes that the people were accustomed to eating. He brought forth gold from out of the fish's mouth; the same gold that was used as cur-rency in those days.

So is it with the spiritual way of living. It is not meant that you should live in poverty, but rather that you should live in the infinite abundance—and no limit to that, either, except the limit of your own ability to accept it! There is no sin in money, no sin in wealth; the sin is in the love or hate of it. That is the only sin that has to do with money. So it is right for us to be wealthy. It is also right for us to be healthy, although mere physical health will not bring us immortality. No matter how healthy your body is according to medical standards, you have no assurance of that health tomorrow or at sixty or seventy or eighty years of age.

Now, the spiritual way of living is not so much to improve your physical health as to bring about health in the body through spiritual means and to maintain it through spiritual means. In other words, it means to change your concept from the material to the spiritual. Let me explain this for a moment. Suppose at the present time you assume that your income comes from your work. Now, the spiritual way of living doesn't interfere with your income, whether from work or from investments, or from your marriage; but the spiritual way of living prevents your believing that such a source is really the source of the supply. It may be the avenue of supply to you—but not the source. In the spiritual way of living your attachment is not to the money, the job, the investment, or to the husband, or to the wife. Your attachment is to the source of the supply, which is God, the divine consciousness of your being. In the spiritual way of living you change your belief that money "out here" or an investment "out here," is your income. You change that belief to the understanding that God, the divine consciousness of you, is your supply. Then you let the money that comes just be the added "things," just what those loaves or fishes, or the gold out of the fishes' mouths were to Jesus. You don't hold onto it; you utilize it, save it or invest it.

But whatever you do, you no longer have a fear of its absence; you no longer have concern about whether or not you will have it. Why? Because God is the source of it, and since God has no beginning nor end, does it make any difference whether you are in the prime of youth or approaching old age? If God is the source, that source will always be there. And as long as the source is there, the supply will be there. Those of you who are familiar with my pamphlet *Supply* will remember that I brought out there the fact that the oranges on the tree do not constitute supply, they constitute the effect. The supply is the life that is appearing to us as an orange tree. As long as we have the life manifesting as the orange tree, we will continue to have oranges. So what use then is there for us to horde oranges, knowing that we have this life is going on all the time producing and reproducing. So with dollars as supply. Think of them as the fruitage of supply and understand that as long as you exist you are really the law in action. You are the law of life. As long as you exist you are a law; you are your own master; a law unto your supply. You are the life of your supply; the intelligence of your supply. Therefore, your supply will be continuous. Why hasn't that been taught up to this moment? Only because of a lack of awareness.

As long as a person thinks of dollars as his supply, I tell you he will not demonstrate the law of supply. A person must make that transition to where he understands, "As long as I am alive, I myself am a law unto my supply. The dollar must appear as a result of the law which I am." Now, were I to permit my attention to leave that truth, were I to go out and think of people out here as my supply, sooner or later that supply would not be there. Sooner or later something would show me that my faith had been in "princes" and that the "princes" had failed me. We are not to put our faith "in man whose breath is in his nostrils."[1] We are not to put our faith into dollars or investments. Faith must be in the law of God, which I am. The same is true of health. As long as you consider your heart, liver, lungs or stomach, or any other part of your body, as having power or jurisdiction over your life, just that long are you in slavery or in bondage to the physical sense for existence which is birth, age, decomposition and eventually death.

Now, that vicious circle from birth to death will go on in your individual experience so long as you carry that age-old belief that your life is in your liver, your heart, your lungs and your stomach, or that your body is a governing factor of your life. The spiritual sense of life reverses that and says: "The consciousness which I am forms this body and that consciousness keeps on unfolding and unfolding until eternity. If I desire to remain on this plane for one hundred, two hundred or five hundred years, I can. It is possible to accomplish this. It is possible because life is eternal!"

In orthodox religions it is agreed that life is eternal but that the body is not eternal; in the spiritual sense of life, life and the body are one. Life is the substance and the body is the form in which that substance appears. Suppose we had a great block of mahogany and out of that block we formed a desk. Mahogany would be the substance and the desk would be the form. Then you might ask, "How long can this desk last?" Well, it can last as long as the mahogany lasts; when the mahogany comes to an end, the desk will come to an end. "Desk" is merely a name given to mahogany in that particular form. Is that clear?

Now, life is what I am! Life is what is looking out from back of my eyes. It is consciousness; It is spirit, or soul. That is why we say that the eyes are the windows of the soul. Place me right back of where I seem to be and really am—God, Spirit or Soul—*that* is consciousness. What you are seeing here is the form. This is the form in which that consciousness appears. If I can hold to that in spite of the mesmerism of world beliefs, then I can maintain myself here in this form for as long as I can hold that realization. When I turn to the mesmerism of the world belief in a life of three score years and ten, or perhaps to the human belief of being lonesome because all my friends and relatives are gone and there is a new generation around, all of these things can remove me from this realization. It is the terrible part of mesmerism that it can do this. You have to be most alert when you turn to the spiritual way of life; temptation lies on every side. It is not always a physical thing like a physical illness, but also these invisible little foxes like lonesomeness and fear, that hypnotize. We exist as consciousness, that infinite spiritual consciousness; and your body is the temple of the living God. Your body is form. Your body is form which consciousness has fashioned in order to express through the individual, that infinite form and spirit.

Judging from appearances, the church of today has failed. Its failure has become more and more pronounced and because of that it becomes necessary to be more aware of truth than we ever were before. Some

time ago Rabbi Liebman, then one of the leading rabbis
of this country, wrote a book called *Peace of Mind*.
Almost every page of that book says religion is a failure.
This book turns you to psychology; tells you that you
must learn psychological truth; tells you to turn to
psychiatry and philosophy. It is a strange thing we must
do–turn from religion to the kingdom of the human
mind, almost deifying it. And that rabbi is not the only
one. In *Omnibook Magazine* for October, 1948, there is a
condensation of the book, *A Guide to Confident Living*.
This book was written by a minister of one of our oldest
Protestant churches. Almost every page of this book,
too, says, "Turn to psychology; turn to your mind."

Think of that! Not to God! Turn to the mind to find
how to obtain a happy marriage! A man consults a
minister because he wants happiness brought into his
family. The wife comes too. She is told she should keep
her petticoat up above the hem of her dress and should
stay at home and should make her beds in the morning.
But she says, "I came for spiritual guidance and you say
these things to me; that these habits are the way to
married happiness!" Believe me, I am not saying this in
a sense of criticism but to show that here is a difference
between spiritual living and a merely improved belief. If,
in a marriage, a wife does keep her petticoat where it
belongs and her house clean and her beds made–is this
a spiritual way of living?

Not all the cleanliness or good cooking in the world,
not being a good husband, a good mother or a good
wife, will lead to spiritual living. This may be a part, yes.
If one is leading a spiritual life these things will follow
naturally. This minister telling us how to "think" our
way into success does not sound much like Jesus saying,

"Take no thought for your life!"[2] Now, psychology can make you a much better human, but that is not what I am referring to when I describe the spiritual way of living. What I have in mind is this: when you no longer believe that lands or dollars are supply, and you no longer believe that your heart, lungs, liver or body is a governing factor of your life; when you believe that the life which you are is the governing factor of your body, you are living a spiritual life.

We are told to improve our thinking. Let us suppose for a moment that for reasons beyond our control we are very sexual or sensuous in our ways of thinking, and somebody says to change our thinking. How would we go about doing that? We would have a very difficult time. If we are in the position of having sexual or sensuous thoughts it is not because we willed it that way and nobody is more eager, perhaps, than we are to change it. Or suppose we are embroiled in a poverty complex. Changing our thinking will not change our demonstration. But if once the spirit of Christ enters our consciousness, how long would sensuousness or poverty remain there? In the spiritual way of living we do not try to be better humans. We turn and try to become or to imbibe the spirit of Christ and let that spirit of Christ erase all the disease and poverty. In the case of an alcoholic you can't say, "You stop drinking and then come to me and I will give you a treatment!" If you were able to stop your poverty thinking or your sensuous thoughts or your alcohol drinking, what need would you have for metaphysics, or religion, or psychology? You would find yourself in the kingdom of heaven already.

When a practitioner becomes sufficiently clear and established in the spiritual way of life—when he no longer fears or hates error so that his consciousness is in some degree like that of Jesus who could say, "I have overcome the world,"[3]–then that practitioner brings you health of body, health of mind or of purse. In other words, it is the Christ of the practitioner's consciousness that brings about the correction. It is not one human mind telling another human mind how to be better. So, the spiritual way of living is not being merely a good human. Becoming a good human will not of itself lift us to the spiritual life. It is that state of consciousness which knows the nature of God which brings peace, joy, harmony and wholeness.

Now we come to the most important part of this whole subject. What is God? On your understanding of that hinges your whole success in obtaining the spiritual way of living. As long as we think of God as something separate and apart from our own being, we will not attain the spiritual way of living. God is divine consciousness. But because God is infinite, God is the consciousness of every individual! As we have quoted here over and over, God is "nearer than breathing, closer than hands and feet."[4] How close is that? Why, it is right here, right where I am. Where God is, I am! "I and my Father are one."[5] This consciousness which is infinity is your consciousness and mine, and therefore wherever God is, I am. If I make my bed in hell, whomever shall I fear? That is also a spiritual law. I cannot get away from God. God is the very consciousness of me and I cannot get away from my own consciousness. Yet if that is true, why are any of us ever in a state of sin, sickness, death, and limitation? Because we do not know this truth; the little prescription that Jesus gave us: "Know the truth."[6] He never said the truth will make you free, but to *know* the truth. It is your continuous knowing of the truth that makes you free.

Truth is right here in this very room. All the music, all the languages, all the skills, are right in this room; but until we let them into our consciousness we cannot be musicians, sculptors or architects. So with God. Only in the degree that you accept, really understand his word, feel and gain the conviction of God as a reality having being, the reality of your being, so you feel this oneness, this contact, only in that degree can you prove the law, the law that says that no harm can come to you; no weapon formed against you can harm you. That must sound pretty strange to people who are out getting wounded and hurt. There are lots of weapons being formed against them and they are being badly harmed—as a matter of fact, the weapons are winning out. Let's not fool ourselves.

The Bible is law; the Scripture is law—not only the Scripture that we call the Old and New Testaments. "No weapon that is formed against thee shall prosper."[7] To whom is that addressed? Only to you who accept and have the actual conviction of the presence of God. Certainly no weapon that is formed against thee can prosper for there is no place where the presence of God does not exist; from the bottom of the seas to the topmost sky is the presence of God. But, it is only the conscious awareness of God that does the trick and that is spiritual living.

From the moment that you have this conscious awareness of the presence of God, something wonderful begins to happen. You may have sat in a draft and caught cold. Once you realize the presence of God you can sit in a draft and you won't catch cold. You can violate all the germ laws when you have the conscious awareness of the presence of God. They are only beliefs—not laws. They are like fads; they change every few years. If you should ask a doctor whether he would practice medicine according to the medical books of many years ago, he would laugh at you, for today *materia medica* itself laughs at many of those things they used to believe in that generation. You become free of these world beliefs only as you individually renounce them and understand that they do not exist as law, but as beliefs. And that is the entire secret of metaphysics—where healing comes in.

We can say with the Master, "I have overcome the world."[8] All it means is that I have come into the realization that nothing of this world has power. Nothing in this world, whether in the form of thought or thing, has jurisdiction, government, or control over me. I am in this world but not of it. I can enjoy going to shows; I can enjoy dancing and the companionship of friends. One of the outstanding phases of spiritual living is joy, as well as happiness, peace and contentment. This means the ability to enjoy vacations, good trips into the mountains, or any other form of living, and yet be so untouched that if the opportunity to do these things did not arise, you would not find them necessary. You stand so completely in control of your own being and your own body that you understand that God, acting as your infinite intelligence, is a law unto all your experiences and nothing out here can enter to defile it or to make a lie.

Are you commencing to catch just a little glimpse? Do you begin to understand that spiritual living hasn't anything to do with removing your normalcy or naturalness? It won't make a saint out of you, except that you

will not be touched by the world. You can be in it, but
not touched by it. You can have all the health and wealth
in the world, and not dissipate it; you can live with all
there is in the world today and yet not miss these things
if they aren't there. So it is not ambition for health or
wealth, but it is this recognition of the presence of God as
your individual life, and then letting all the good things be
added. On top of that, it is the realization that the
thoughts and things of the world cannot enter your
consciousness to defile. They have no presence or power
over you and find no outlet through you. All that flows
out from me is love; not my love, but God's. Intelligence;
not my intelligence, but God's. This is spiritual living.

The very moment you understand that all the good
any one expresses is God showing through, you com-
mence catching glimpses of spiritual living. The moment
you think of any intelligence, any skillfulness, any virtue
or any demonstration as being an evidence of your
understanding, then your senses are warped and you are
heading for trouble. Watch out! If it were not for that
mistake, Jesus would have been spared the experience
of the crucifixion.

There is nothing good but God. There is no one
loving but God. God lives its own life individually as
you and as me and that is what constitutes our immortality. If ever you want to cut that short, just believe that
you have a life of your own and see how naturally it will
seem to come to an end. God is the life of the individual
and that is what makes immortality. The credit is God's.
The only credit to you is that when the vision came to
you, you accepted it. If you can accept the fact that God
is the only life, that is living and the only mind expressing its intelligence as you; then, any dependence on

human ties is shifting the balance to the side of materialism; to the side of limited living.

So, let's be normal and live our lives as joyously and
normally as we can and get all the joy we can from
human companionships, whether they are husband,
wife, child, parent, or friend. Let's not go up into the
stratosphere and believe that our spiritual life in any way
separates us from peace, contentment and fulfillment.
You do not break the ties of human relationships, but
you bring them to a higher level and understand that
God is the life of your husband, your child, your wife,
your friend. In this way you form a bond much closer
and more meaningful than any tie of blood or affection.

~ 11 ~

Spiritual Freedom

You know this is not the easiest subject in the world to talk about, and I approach it always with a little bit of hesitancy. Always we have been talking about the spiritual way of living and of course, the subject "spiritual freedom" is a part of the spiritual way of life. Spiritual freedom is a result of the spiritual way of living; it is one of the results, but it has to be understood in order to be demonstrated. It has to be understood in order to be lived. In our material sense of life we are in bondage to hundreds of different thoughts and things—there is no denying it. We are so apt in the metaphysical world just to say, "There is no accident in divine mind," or "There is no bondage in divine mind." Of course it is true. There isn't bondage in divine mind. It is also true that if we were living in divine mind we would not be here speaking or listening to this subject. It is only because we haven't yet reached the life of divine mind that we are interested in a way or a path to achieve it.

The term "path" or "way" is an interesting one. Jesus said: "I am the way."[1] But 600 years before Jesus, Lao Tzu's teaching in China was called "The Way." The term "way" refers to that spiritual path that gives us freedom. If we are to achieve freedom, it must be freedom from some form of bondage. Actually you know there is no freedom in spirit or soul because there isn't anything to be free of. There is only divine being.

When we talk about spiritual freedom, we are talking really about a quality or condition of being that results from our search for and attainment of truth itself. I am coming to this very, very slowly, because I am–and I know that I am–on a delicate subject. You will appreciate as I go along, how delicate it is. What I am leading up to is the fact that there is a power greater than any of the powers you are familiar with in the human sense of life and yet a power that you never will see, never hear, taste, touch or smell. It is a power that you will discern only with your spiritual senses, and if you cannot be lifted up to the point of spiritual discernment, you will never know the meaning of spiritual freedom.

That's what makes it delicate; the fact that it isn't something I can say to you intellectually that you can grasp intellectually, and then say, "Oh, I understand that!" No. You would have a much easier time with Einstein's theory of relativity than you will with the subject of spiritual freedom because there is the possibility of developing the human mind to the degree of grasping and understanding Einstein's theory, but you never can develop your human thinking, your human mind, your intellect, to the degree that you will understand spirit and spirit activity. So remember that we are discussing this from the standpoint of opening our consciousness to the recognition and the discernment of a presence and a power that you won't see. You will see the result of it in much the same way as if you planted a seed in the ground. If you were able to put a microscope over that seed and watch its full development, you never would see the life or activity producing what you can see through the microscope. In other words, you could watch the seed break open; you could watch the little formations come out; you could watch the roots take hold; you could watch the shoots come forth. But never would you see the life or the power—that which is called "nature." You never can see nature or the activity of nature. You can see only its results.

And so in this spiritual life. Even when you have attained (or are attaining) spiritual freedom, you will never see or actually witness that which is bringing it about. But as your consciousness of truth opens, as this seventh sense develops within you, then you will be able to enjoy the spiritual freedom and, in your higher moments of illumination, you will be able to see the whole of its operation. We are told in scripture that, "Yet in my flesh have I seen God."[2] It is possible while still being in what we call the human sense of life to behold God, but not to behold God with the eyes. We behold God through that seventh sense, that spiritual consciousness or spiritual discernment.

Now, let us start low down on the scale with the idea or thought of bondage to person, place and thing. The mother who is continuously in fear of what will happen to her child, who cannot let the child out of her sight, is in this bondage. She is in bondage to mother-love. She is in bondage to fear of a power apart from God, to fear that there is a power that can prevent God's protection from being made manifest. That is one form of bondage.

There is another form of bondage that says we must live in the place where we were born, in that town or city or state or country. This is a form of bondage that won't permit us to be pioneers. This form of bondage won't permit us to get up and go to live where we want to live, to build in some other place. That is a form of bondage, too.

There is another form of bondage, and that is bondage to payroll. We work so often under conditions that are not harmonious, conditions that do not make for happiness. We work for people who do not understand us, and the answer is: "Well, I need the money." In this sense of spiritual freedom, there is no denying your need for the money. The only denial is that you have to be in bondage to a particular place of employment. The bondage consists of your acceptance of the belief that you can't break free and seek employment elsewhere; that you can't seek it in some line of work where you are happier or freer. That's a form of bondage too—remaining in a place where you, of your own volition, would never remain; or remaining in some line of activity where you, if you could select, if you could choose, would not remain. That's bondage!

There is bondage to superstition. There are so many forms of superstition—not only being afraid to walk under a ladder but theological superstition, for instance. One of the great fears of people is that we will live to only three score years and ten. That's a form of bondage because when that thought grips you, you start right after your fifties to wonder how soon you will reach seventy, and how awful that is going to be!

There is the law of heredity—which isn't law, but a fear or a belief. The ancient Hebrews thought that the sins of the fathers are visited on the children unto the third and fourth generation, yet 200 years later they renounced that belief. But we here in this modern age have not accepted the renunciation; we have accepted their old superstitious belief, so we are walking around with diseases and habits due to heredity. We have accepted certain forms of limitation for ourselves because of racial or religious or national heredity. That is a form of bondage.

We meet many people in this world who are in bondage to their sins. These seem to be the most miserable of all because they cannot shake the idea. Their old religion, their old theology, has impressed on them that they have sinned against some law, usually some foolish man-made law, and that they are going to be eternally damned, not only here on earth but even unto the future kingdoms. That is a form of bondage too—a very, very acute form of it.

In the medical world we are under the bondage to the beliefs in climate, the germ theory, the vitamin theory. These are forms of bondage arising from theories built on human histories. You might say, "Isn't there some truth to them?" No, there isn't any truth to them because truth is of God and none of those theories are of God. They are facts in the human sense of life but the human sense of life is the bondage I am talking about. I am breaking down the human sense of life into these various forms but the whole human sense of life, even when it is good, is a form of bondage.

Now of course, along with that comes all of the beliefs incident to the material organism—the belief that there is life in the heart. Or that when other vital organs or functions are interfered with, our life is interfered with. Of course, right there, we are told, "Oh, no! I understand that my life isn't threatened but my body is." What I am saying is that your life isn't interfered with, nor is your body except in proportion to your own bondage to the beliefs of materiality; the beliefs that the organs and functions of the body can contain within themselves the issues of life. That's a form of bondage to the body. That has to be broken.

And we have other forms of bondage too. It really is sad that even into our enlightened experience come those beliefs for our acceptance. Too often do we accept them and demonstrate them.

With all these forms of bondage we can remember the First Commandment: "Thou shalt have no other gods but me."[3] No other power; no other presence; no other life; no other mind; no other intelligence; no other directing force but God! All of this other business is idolatry. It is placing faith and power in an effect.

Don't ever forget this: We are not on the earth. That belief is a form of superstition and a form of bondage. The earth is within us! It is a formation of the infinite consciousness which I am. It is a form of divine being which has been made, created by that universal intelligence which is really your individual consciousness. By all the laws of God, you yourself created the heavens and the earth—your consciousness which you are! And therefore they are subject unto you.

Let us be done with bondage to anything that exists in the realm of effect. We are not in bondage to our concepts of spiritual reality, nor are we in bondage to the reality itself. Our only bondage, if bondage it is, and it is a beautiful one, is to the Christ, the divine idea of government, the divine idea of infinite intelligence. And this is the only thing that we are subject unto.

Divine consciousness; universal consciousness; that which we call God, which is individual consciousness, yours and mine—that is the law of our individual being! Through that we individually are given dominion over

the things of the sea and the earth and the air and the
sky. And when you either knowingly or unknowingly
permit something in the realm of effect to be a law unto
you, you have become in bondage to it.

For the world at large there is an excuse. The world
at large has never been told that we are the law unto our
own being. The world has been taught about God
somewhere off in the skies, or a God on a cross, and has
been given the teaching that we are worms of the dust or
that we are mortals or that we are humans, subject to all
of these different influences. Since they accept that
teaching, not knowing any better, we cannot blame the
people of the world when they come under the bondage
of these material and theological beliefs. But for you and
for me, there is no excuse. We have been taught our true
identity. We have had passages of scripture called to our
attention which ordinarily are never brought to the
attention of the Christian or Jewish world. We have
been taught, for instance, that we are "joint heirs with
Christ."[4] We have been taught, "All that I have is
thine."[5] And we have been taught that this applies to you
and to me today, not merely to a Jesus Christ of some
2,000 years ago. It applies literally and unconditionally
to you and to me individually. Therefore for us there is
no excuse when we knowingly bring ourselves under
bondage to these man-made beliefs and so-called laws.

There are still many forms of bondage that we come
under through our ignorance because we haven't really
progressed far in this study and practice of truth. We are
really only at the first outer rim of the subject; we are far
from being at the center. So there probably is plenty that
we do not understand and because of that lack of
understanding we are in bondage. But, there is so much

that we do know and that we do not consciously practice that at this point it becomes necessary to remind ourselves–"How many superstitions am I accepting? How many phases of bondage am I accepting? Even with the little understanding that I have, I should be freer."

Freedom begins when we recognize that God is divine consciousness and that his consciousness is yours and mine. From that moment on I and the Father are not only one, but consciously one. It was always true of everyone that "I and the Father are one,"[6] but not having the conscious awareness of it has made it impossible for the manifestation to be made. In other words, our freedom comes not because of our relationship with God, it comes because of our conscious awareness of that relationship. Never forget that! "I and the Father are one" is the relationship between God and every individual. But that will not stop us from building jails and hospitals and insane asylums. We only benefit from our relationship with God in proportion to our conscious awareness of it.

You remember our favorite passages: "Thou wilt keep him in perfect peace whose mind is stayed on thee."[7] Stayed! And: "Pray without ceasing."[8] Those are the passages that must be brought to our remembrance over and over again so that we remind ourselves of our true identity, because in the conscious awareness of the presence of God, in the conscious awareness of our true identity, lies our freedom.

The particular idea has evolved that nothing external to my consciousness has power over me. Well, of course, in reality there *is* nothing external to consciousness. What was meant is that nothing that exists as an effect or as a concept of an effect has power over me.

Now, even what you see up here as me is not the
reality. You are seeing the universal concept of the
individualization of God. But even that concept which
you are seeing up here has no jurisdiction over you, no
government, not even for good. Nor has any effect of
God any power over you or dominion over you. In
other words, your consciousness itself is the power unto
all formation and through that knowledge it becomes the
power over every concept of every formation. Take your
lungs. They are not divine realities. God did not create
them. They are, however, universal concepts of some
divine idea, some divine faculty or activity. Then in the
understanding that the infinite divine consciousness
which I am is the law unto its spiritual creation, we are
brought to dominion over even the concept called a
heart or a stomach.

That is how a metaphysical treatment operates.
Metaphysical treatment never touches the concept called
foot or leg or stomach or head. Metaphysical treatment
is the realization of God, divine consciousness, being the
substance, law and cause of all spiritual creation. The
knowledge of that truth gives us dominion over our
concept of that spiritual creation. That sounds deep
doesn't it? It isn't so deep as it sounds. It is only because
the subject isn't an easy one.

God is spirit. Therefore, the universe is spiritual.
Now, you haven't seen that universe of God, except in
your moments of spiritual illumination. You may,
through your developed spiritual consciousness, behold
it but in the ordinary walks of life, you never come into
contact with either God or God's creation. You come in
contact with the world's concept or the race concept of
that creation, and your knowledge of the truth of God as

infinite being, the one power, and as all creation as subject to that power, gives you dominion over this world of concept. That, of course, is a subject that has to be carried out more and more and more and more until we come into the realization of what it means and why it means it and into the ability, then, to demonstrate it.

Now, when we take the first step toward spiritual freedom, we do it by consciously realizing that nothing appearing as an external world is a power over me, whether it is a heart, whether it is a brain, or whether it is a force or a bomb, or a bit of food or a germ. Our first sense of this freedom must come when we consciously accept the truth that nothing out here has power over us, except in proportion as we give it power. It of itself has no power. We, by fearing it, can give it power. Oh yes; there might be a chair back there with a white sheet thrown over it and we may assume it to be a ghost and sit here and tremble all night and die of heart failure—but not because it had any power over us! It would have power only because we, in not perceiving it as it is, through believing that something external could have power, would give it the power to govern us and control us. You say, "Well, that's true of the chair with the sheet over it but suppose it *were* a ghost?" Well, the same thing would apply. Even if there is such a thing in existence as a ghost, it can exist only as the effect of consciousness. Therefore, it cannot be a power over the consciousness that must have produced it. We ourselves impart power to these effects of the world or effects of God's creation, and only in that degree do they have power over us.

We have spoken of this before, too: that our bondage to dollars comes only from the belief that we accept dollars as power, purchasing power. Actually, the power is in our own being. The dollars are given to us as a medium of exchange, the same as streetcar transfers are. The dollars have a greater value, but they are the same thing. They are forms of exchange, but we can have as many of them as we can open our consciousness to. We must develop our freedom from the belief that the power of supply is in the dollar. Transfer that power to your own consciousness and say, "No. The power of supply is within my own consciousness, governing this world of dollars." Then, you automatically break the bondage which really is a fear.

You know the old scriptural words: "The love of money is the root of all evil."[9] The love of money, or the hate of it, or the fear of it, is the bondage, the evil. It isn't the money itself. Money is a glorious thing. It is just as glorious as fine clothing or fine transportation. Money is a beautiful thing. But the moment we give it power over us, dominion over us, we have lost our own spiritual freedom.

We could go on with this, you know, for days and days. We very often are afraid of dictatorship in world government and we are afraid of the law of this or that, instead of realizing that we ourselves constitute all the law there is. The law abides within our own consciousness. When we know that we can be free, regardless of what form of government may appear. It doesn't really make any difference. There are men in slave countries that are free. Those who have been able to accept within their own consciousness their freedom, are free. Bondage is in our own superstition, our own belief, our own acceptance of a presence and power apart from God. The very moment you can accept in your consciousness, in your thoughts, the idea that God created you free, that

God gave you dominion, in that moment the world knows your freedom and makes way for you.

Do you know that you yourself control the world's reaction to you? You do so by your own estimate of your own being. Where is bondage? In one's own belief. That is where all bondage is. If you are entertaining a sense of bondage to person, place, thing, circumstance or conditions, it is in your own being. It's in your own consciousness, and that is where you have to meet it. You have to learn that God is infinite, infinite intelligence, infinite consciousness, and that *That* is your mind. Therefore, you are equal before God. You are equal before God and man.

Christ isn't Jew and Christ isn't Christian. Christ is the divine spirit of individual being and is the spirit of God in man. Everybody has it regardless of race, religion, color, or creed. But unless you and I consciously accept it, we won't project it; if we do not consciously accept it, the fellow out there can't feel it. Out there you feel my state of consciousness and I can feel your state of consciousness. You can't miss it. Every time you go to a restaurant and are waited on by a waiter or waitress, you feel the state of consciousness of that individual. You know it for what it is. And when you go into a business place, you know the same thing. It is up to you to develop the degree of your freedom.

Now, having agreed that nothing in the external world has power over us for good or for evil, we have brought our attention and thought back to that which is within our own being. Reality. We have brought our thoughts back now so that we can turn within in meditation or communion and there find the Father within. Have you ever thought about how many times you have read in the New Testament about the Father within? Have you ever thought about how many times you have read in Paul, "I live, yet not I; Christ liveth in me"?[10] And have you ever thought how seldom you have sat down with yourself and said, "I must get acquainted with this Father within me and find what Paul was talking about." No. Most of us never find the Father within; the Christ. Those who do are usually on the inspirational or metaphysical path, but even there it really is sad to think how few ever decide to investigate and find out if what Jesus said is true: "The Father is within you."[11] Here again it is through conscious effort that you contact the Christ or the Father within your own being. Until you do, you cannot gain spiritual freedom. Spiritual freedom does not come from any statements of truth that you know or through anything you have learned with your intellect. All you can learn through the mind and the intellect is about spiritual freedom, but spiritual freedom itself is attained when you have touched the Christ of your own being—when you have actually felt the divine presence within you.

That's why I tell you again we are dealing with a very, very, deep subject. We are dealing with the reality, with that which is invisible to our outer senses and which therefore must be met with within our own consciousness, and each one has to do that for himself. There is no easy road. There is no royal way. We have help on this way in the form of spiritual literature, teachings and teachers, and they constitute the way. But the way you know is a path, and a path always goes some place. And Jesus said "I am the way."[12] The Christ is the way, the Christ is the path to lead you to the kingdom of God.

You know, the leaning on Jesus was so tremendous
that he told them very frankly that, "If I go not away, the
Comforter will not come to you."[13] It is a marvelous
thing to have practitioners and teachers, but it is a
terrible thing to have them for too long. It's a wonderful
thing to be able to lean on somebody in this spiritual
path for help, for guidance, for healing. But it's a terrible
thing to keep on leaning and leaning and leaning and
never finding your spiritual freedom.

In certain religious teachings there are masters, just as
in the ancient days Jesus was a master. But too often
people have the idea that these masters are to take over
your mind and your life and govern it and run it for you.
That's very bad business. A master is one to whom you
can go; one who has achieved some measure of spiritual
freedom, which means some measure of non-attachment
to the things and thoughts of the world. Through the
master's help and cooperation you can be lifted up into a
state of spiritual consciousness, spiritual discernment where
you yourself realize the master of your own consciousness.
The master is not a man or a woman. The master is a state
of unfolded and developed consciousness.

A man like Jesus had this master consciousness probably to the greatest degree ever known, but look what
use people are making of it. They use the name Jesus
Christ and they repeat it, as if the name of itself had a
virtue. And they say that the reason the name has virtue
is because it was the name of the master of Galilee and
therefore was imbued with his great spirit. You know, it
would be sad if that were true, but it isn't true. I doubt if
there was any Hebrew in Galilee who had a Greek name.
Jesus and Christ are both Greek names. Christ isn't even
a name. It is the savior or divine consciousness. And

Jesus wasn't Jesus Christ, but Jesus the Christ, although in his days on earth it wasn't either Jesus or the Christ. The man Jesus was Hebrew so his Aramaic name was Joshua, not Jesus. Now, if the name "Jesus Christ" were the name of a man who had attained mastership, certainly the name didn't attain mastership. It was the consciousness that attained mastership, and nothing but that consciousness will be the master unto you.

Jesus said, "If I do not leave you, the Comforter—the master—cannot come unto you." Why? Because the master is the divine state of consciousness, and one which you and I attain in some measure. Again, the degree to which we lose our hate, fear and love of that which appears as a person, place or thing, circumstance or condition; in the degree that we come non-attached to the things of this world, so that ultimately in some measure we can say, "I have overcome the world."[14] In other words, "I can use the things of the world or leave them alone; I can pick up my life or lay it down; I can enjoy good food, or get along with a sandwich." In the degree that we learn non-attachment, in that degree do we attain the master consciousness.

Now, those like Jesus Christ are a help to us; they are an inspiration; they are more than that. When we can come into the atmosphere of their individual beings or through writings or in groups, we are automatically lifted up nearer and nearer and nearer to the actual realization and demonstration of the master consciousness. The master consciousness has appeared on earth many times through many individuals. Actually, the master consciousness has appeared on earth in millions of people only not in the full degree that it appeared here in the person of Jesus Christ. From the effect of the man's life there is no doubt that he must have attained it most likely to the highest degree ever known. If not, there can only be one or two others who have attained such a degree of master consciousness. The rest of us can be very well satisfied if we attain enough of the master consciousness to be able to have dominion over our own individual experience and to be able to be of help to whose who come within range of our thoughts.

The master consciousness likewise brings itself forth in messages, in books. I am having wonderful experiences right now in hearing and in receiving letters from people who, just through reading *The Infinite Way*[15] and others of these books, are witnessing healings and improved conditions in their lives. These do not come because of the man, but because a certain state of consciousness has externalized itself in print and those who are able to catch some measure of that, are able to benefit by it. It hasn't anything to do with a man, any more than it has to do with Jesus. Jesus was that avenue who was able to say, "The Father within me doeth the work."[16] It is the state of consciousness that came through here and put those words out on paper.

I wonder if you can conceive for a minute what happens when these ideas and thoughts come through and get themselves down on paper; how completely independent they are of a person? Let me tell you of two little instances of this merely in the hope that you can catch the idea of what I mean by spiritual freedom or master consciousness.

One night I was in meditation for what I suppose was several hours. Later, about three in the morning, I was awakened and without knowing why, jumped out of bed, picked up pen and paper and started to write. Out of it came this "Nightingale of the East." It's the frontispiece of *Spiritual Interpretation of Scripture*[17] and now it's out on gift cards. Another time a song came forth that is sung as a sacred solo all over the land. The soloist at the Mother Church in Boston performed it for a recording that went all around the world. It's name is, "Truly There Is No Night There."

"I can do all things through Christ which strengtheneth me."[18] Christ performs these things through me. This consciousness goes before us to make the crooked places straight. You know that there isn't a metaphysical practitioner in the world who hasn't felt that sense or presence at some time in his healing work. Probably not with every healing, but there is no doubt, and I speak from many, many years of experience and from acquaintance with hundreds of practitioners, I have never known one who has not had that transcendental experience in which they felt the click of this super-consciousness; of this master consciousness; of reality in which they beheld the spiritual creation, even if only for one second. Sometimes it came as a light, sometimes it came in other ways and forms, but it was a "click."

Spiritual freedom, then, is a freedom that comes from grace. It does not come from taking thought; it does not come through mental effort. The taking of thought and the mental effort may lift us to a place where we can realize that freedom in power. "My thoughts are not your thoughts,"[19] said the Lord. So none of your thoughts give you your spiritual freedom, but right thinking is what may lift you to the place where the divine thought does come through.

I think you are asking the question, "How do you obtain this consciousness?" or, "How do you attain this spiritual freedom?" That's the natural question after all of this. I have given you an indication that one way, of course, is through contact with someone who has attained some measure of it; going to him or her either as practitioner or teacher, or, going to the writings which show such liberation.

But there is another way and a way that will make you independent of all this outside aid. It lies in your own development of a listening attitude. If you can practice from the minute you awaken in the morning until you sleep at night, practice the "listening ear," you will get there. I have been over this ground before, because it is the *way*. It is the highest way known to attain spiritual freedom—opening consciousness for the inflow of the Spirit.

Now, it won't flow in on you from outside somewhere. Rather, it will flow from the within you to the without. From the great depths and the great reality of your being comes this flow. That is what you come into when you close your eyes or when you open your ears; as you learn, "Speak, Father, for thy servant heareth[20] I will listen for thy voice"—any of the thoughts that will make you receptive to the great infinite power within your own being. So, instead of living out here in bondage to the world of thoughts and ideas and propaganda—*be free!*

~ 12 ~

GOD CONSCIOUSNESS

NOW, YOU HAVE FOLLOWED ALONG with me in these talks and have heard the foundation of the message, namely, that everything begins with the understanding of God, and without the knowledge of God, there is no spiritual message, there is no spiritual mission, there is no spiritual life.

The worship of God as something or someone afar off has separated man from his spiritual life throughout the ages. This worship of a distant God that must be appealed to, must be petitioned, or must be told our needs; all of this has separated us from the actual presence and power of God.

In these "latter days" we are beginning to understand that God is, as the poet said, one who hears: "Closer is he than breathing, nearer than hands and feet."[1] In other words, in confirmation of the teaching of Jesus, the kingdom of God is within you. We have learned that God is divine mind; that God is life eternal; that God is more than all this—God is the life and the mind of individual you and me. And this is where we have made our first gain over the ancients: We have not merely learned that God is principle, we have not merely learned that God is soul or consciousness, but we have learned that God is the consciousness and soul of me, the very spirit, the animating principle and law of my being.

Unless one clearly perceives this truth that, "I and the Father are one,"[2] he will not understand why it is or how it is that, "All that the Father has is mine."[3] The longer you perpetuate God as something separate and apart from yourself, the longer you will be seeking to get your allness from that God. In proportion, however, as you realize that God is closer to us than breathing, that Jesus knew what he was talking about when he said, "The kingdom of God is within you"[4] and "I and the Father are one," to that degree will you realize that all that the Father has *is* yours. Therefore you do not have to pray for it. Prayer becomes not an asking of God but a realization of the truth that that which God is and that which God has is already the fullness of your being and of mine. Prayer then becomes an eternal sense of gratitude that I and the Father being one, all that the Father has is mine and I am always about my Father's business.

In that realization comes our ability to give up fear. We have all heard what a terrible thing is fear, and you can watch its results in your own world. So the question does come, "How may I lose fear? How may I give up my fear?" There is only one way. If you know God to be an ever-present mind and soul, if you know God to be your own life, how then could you fear for your life or for your supply or for your security? The only way there is of losing fear is to know God and to know God as the very reality of your own being. It is your oneness with God, then, which constitutes your safety and your security. Your realization of your oneness with God constitutes your health, your longevity, your immortality your eternality.

In no way can we overcome fear so long as we believe that we are separated from God. There will always be something to fear in the form of an atomic bomb or a war or a germ. There will always be something in the form of economic depression that will frighten us, that will give us fear. But none of this will ever enter our consciousness after we have learned, first, that God is life eternal; second, that God is the mind that was in Christ Jesus; and third, that the very place whereon I stand is holy ground. Have you ever stopped to think of the tremendous import in that statement? "The place whereon I stand is holy ground!"[5] Why? Because God and I are both here. That is the reason it is holy ground. God is here where I am! Not two separate beings in two separate places and one trying to contact the other. But right here where I stand—God is.

As a matter of fact, the word "I" means God, doesn't it? God is the great I; the great I Am. Therefore, God is all there is of my being. God is the mind of me and the soul of me and the life of me. God is the spirit of me. God is the law and principle of me—and wherever God is, I am, for we are one and not two.

You see, in that realization, there is no fear. There is nothing to be feared because what is there to fear in our Godhood? That, of course, is the beginning of wisdom. Now, the question which naturally follows that unfoldment is: If this is true, why do we have discords? Why do we have sins and fear? Why do we have wars, unemployment, catastrophes? To begin with, the answer is: These are caused by the belief that human beings are separate and apart from God. That's the first reason for our trouble because we do not realize consciously our oneness with God. Secondly, we have not learned to apply, to utilize, the truth of being in our experience. So right here let us take up a few minutes' work on the practical application of this truth to our individual affairs.

As we learn to live in the conscious presence of God; as one learns to live consciously in the presence of God and to realize the power of God as the only power, it becomes unnecessary to take thought for our life. It becomes unnecessary to have processes of treatment. Until that day when all of this becomes so much part of our consciousness that we need no longer consciously think of it, until that day, it is wise we have some knowledge of how to go about bringing the presence of God and the power of God into our actual individual daily experience. In order to bring out this application of truth, I would like to ask that you follow me very closely in this first point, because on the understanding of this point rests the ability to follow through with the rest of it.

Ordinarily in our metaphysical practice, we start our treatment from the basis of the human scene or the human picture. If, for instance, there is a claim, a belief, in disease or an appearance of disease, we have started out with the human being who was claiming to have the disease, and we started to make him spiritual. We started by looking at the human identity and then declaring that, "You are spiritual," or "You are spirit." We started immediately to try to lift up this human being into a spiritual reality. And so, on the whole, we haven't done too well with it!

Now in our work we start from an entirely different premise. We do not start out our treatment from the standpoint of the patient or of the condition to be changed. The moment we are told, "I would like some help," or "I have a pain," or "Will you take up work for

spiritual." We never come down to the level of you or he or she or it. Our treatment starts with God and ends with God.

God, being infinite individuality, must appear as individual you and me; must appear as individual he and she; must appear as individual it. But it is always God appearing. It is always God expressing, it is always God–God–God! We are never expressing God. God is expressing its own infinite being and is expressing that infinite being in infinite form and variety, in infinite individuality, in harmony and grace and beauty. Always God is doing all of that. The treatment is always up here with God. You say, "What connection has that with you and me, and how does that 'hitch up' to the patient asking for help?" It doesn't! Who wants it to? We are not interested in seeing a sick mortal become a well mortal, or an unemployed human being become an employed human being, or a sinning mortal become reformed. That's not what we are interested in. We are interested in seeing God disclose itself and unfold and reveal itself. All we are interested in is seeing God; God appearing here and God appearing there; God appearing as infinite activity, infinite individuality, infinite personality. But always as God appearing!

No, you do not connect God with anybody called a patient. God itself couldn't do that. You know yourself that if God could connect itself up with a human being there would not be a sick human being in the world. It is only because human beings are something of which God takes no cognizance that it is possible for a human being to get sick. The human being is a part of what has been termed the "mortal scene." Jesus said of that: "My kingdom is not of this world."[6] That's why he would not

allow himself to be crowned and would not allow
himself to be made a king to set the Hebrews free. He
loved those Hebrews, he loved the people of his own
church, of his own race, of his own circle, but he would
not permit himself to go out and perform any temporal
deed. No, indeed! His mission was a spiritual mission
and his universe was a spiritual universe and of this
other he said: "My kingdom isn't of that."

So we do not bring God down to the human scene to
make the human being better. We learn to disregard the
human being and become more and more acquainted
with the divine being. Jesus said of himself, "Why callest
thou me good? There is none good but the Father in
heaven."[7] He did not even try to let God make him
good. He was satisfied for God alone to be good.

So with us in this work. We don't want to look out at
you or ask you to look up at us and say, "You are good,"
or "You've got God's goodness!" Don't do it! Look
within your own being and find the kingdom of God
within you. Find God as the very center of your being;
find God as the mind and soul and life and spirit of
you—then all the human will drop away. But you won't
die. You will make a transition from the mortal sense of
existence to the spiritual sense of existence. You will still
be right here enjoying good food; you will still be right
here enjoying beautiful scenery, wonderful sunsets, and
San Francisco climate. Yes, and loving it, too! You'll
love every part of this so-called human existence, only
you will learn it isn't human existence and that there is
not a good side and a bad side to it. You will eventually
learn that what you have been calling a human existence
is really the divine spiritual existence and that it has no
sickness or health, it has no poverty or wealth. It is all

the pouring forth of God's own being expressing itself in so many ways and so many forms and so many varieties that you can hardly keep up with the beauty and the joy of it.

Yes, in this work we start our treatment with the word "God." Forget the name and identity of the individual who asks for help. Let us learn to forget the name of the disease. As a matter of fact, in all of that disease-naming business, seventy-five per cent of the time we are naming a disease that isn't there. After all, even *materia medica* can't diagnose within fifty-five per cent of being correct. Calling disease by name is nonsense because you don't know the name of disease and if you go to the hospital for a diagnosis, you have only one chance in two of finding the right name for it. Why be concerned about whether you are naming a disease or a part of the body? I have never yet met a metaphysician, except those few who come out of *materia medica,* who knew anything about human anatomy. When the patient comes and says, "Oh, my pain is so terrible right here!" the metaphysician doesn't know whether it is the heart or whether it is just gas or whether it is just breathing or what it might be. Why worry or burden the practitioner with all the details about where the heaviness is and where it isn't when all the practitioner is called upon to know is that God is the life of the universe, and that God is the law, the principle, the being of this entire universe, whether the universe appears as man, woman, child, animal or plant. God is the life of all being!

The commonest mistake made in metaphysical practice is in trying to look at some sick or sinful human being and saying, "You are God's perfect child!" What nonsense! Let me tell you the truth. With your eyes you will never see any part of God's creation. All that you can see with your eyes and hear with your ears is a mortal dream, a false concept of reality, a human concept, that which has been called "Adam man," "fallen man," "Adam dream." All these terms make up the grand and glorious nothingness of mortal creation! So, to look at anything you can see, regardless of how beautiful it may be and call it "spiritual" is to lose the whole demonstration of spirituality.

There is another little thing, too, for which I am grateful to Mrs. Eddy from whose original teachings I came to this work. This is her statement: "It is sometimes beautiful but it is always erroneous." Nothing is truer than that! This universe is sometimes beautiful; in the human scene there is probably nothing more beautiful than a majestic mountain, endless valley or flowing stream, a well proportioned human form, a piece of sculpture, perhaps a painting. But regardless of how beautiful it is, it is not spiritual. To look at it and call it spiritual is nonsense. This will not bring forth spiritual demonstration.

Spiritual demonstration lies in your ability to start with the word "God." From there you can do anything you like. You can say "God life mind divine love divine wisdom." Use any term you want so long as you start with God. See God as manifesting, expressing, revealing, disclosing, unfolding its own being in all of its infinite beauty and intelligence and permanence and grandeur. Since God is infinite, there is nothing else but God. All that is ever expressing harmony and peace and joy is God.

Now, you can't have God *and* something else— therefore it is only God. It is only God that is unfolding and disclosing itself as individual you and me. But even when it is individual you and me, it is still God disclosing its own being, manifesting, expressing its own being, and in all of its health and all of its permanence and in all of its glory.

That's treatment! After awhile, when it becomes second nature to start with the word God, you don't have to do it any more. After it becomes second nature, you just look out on the universe and all you can see is God showing itself forth. You don't see the human scene. You really don't. Even when in your practice you are dealing with sick and sinning human beings apparently coming in and out of your office, you really are not aware of them as human. All you are aware of is that little glimpse you get from the eyes which is the soul shining through and that soul is God.

That's why it is a very difficult thing for a practitioner to like one patient better than another. There is only one thing that makes the difference to a practitioner between one patient and another. There are those who give some indication that what they are seeking is God and the mysteries of God, and these bring forth a closer kinship and with these we spend more time. Those who come and continuously cry about their little problems as if that were the main issue of life instead of merely stating them and saying, "Show me the principle of healing," those are the ones who say, "Oh! this practitioner is partial!" or "Why does he give so much time to that one and so little time to this one?"

This is the answer. The practitioner or the teacher on the spiritual path who really has attained some measure of the understanding and love of God, simply can't take too much time talking about the problems of humanity.

The problems are merely an opportunity to bring forth the principle of God. Therefore, when you find the practitioner or teacher giving more time to one patient than another, just make up your mind that the one getting that attention is the one most eager for the unfoldment and revelation of God. He brings his problem into the discussion only as a basis from which to work–you may say, as an "excuse" to get to the subject of God.

Problems at this particular stage of development are more or less necessary. How few people would seek God without some deep problem to bring to God! It is sad but it is true, and I am not saying this in a critical or condemnatory sense. I can't afford to. I came to this work only because of a problem that would not yield. If I had had a quick healing I would have been off about my business having a good time. No! Only because one problem after another piled up and because as fast as one was solved another one came, did I find I had to stick to it or sink. Of course by sticking to it I finally caught a glimpse of what this truth is and I can't get away from it. I wouldn't want to, either!

Please remember this: While your problems are, and may be, stepping stones, don't let them be your whole existence. Just use them as an excuse to come to an understanding of your relationship to God and of how to utilize this understanding to work out the problems.

Right now we are at the point where we no longer use spiritual treatment to change a material circumstance. I want you to remember that statement because it is the most important one that I am making here today. We are at the point of spiritual development where we no longer use a spiritual truth with which to make a material demonstration.

That's a shock, isn't it? When so many times we have been trying to demonstrate a parking space down the street, or a new automobile, or a hat or a dress! We are entitled to the parking space and the automobile and the hat and the dress. Let's not be concerned about that. We are entitled to it and we are entitled to it on the highest level of demonstration obtainable, but we are entitled to it only as an added thing; only as a result of seeking the kingdom of God and finding it. We are not entitled to go to God and say, "I need a new pair of shoes and have to meet my rent."

We do have the right to go to God and find in God our spiritual wholeness and to let God interpret that to us as shoes or rent or parking space or automobile or books to be published or anything else. Never, never forget that. It isn't right to go to God and ask him to give me an idea I need to write a book, either. But it is right that as I turn to God and there learn to commune with that spiritual essence, some truth will come forth that is worthy of being written down and worthy of somebody else's reading and benefiting by it. That's an "added thing," too.

If you will learn to let your human picture unfold itself of its own accord through the development of your spiritual consciousness so that all of your good humanhood becomes an added thing, you will be living and working and having your being in accord with the law of God. If you let yourself be tempted to use this truth to demonstrate a loaf of bread, sure enough you will fail! You will not make your demonstration. If you do, it will merely be on the mortal, material or mental level and it will not lead to your spiritual development and unfoldment.

It is probably necessary for us to go through the mental stages of metaphysical work. I am in no position to know or to judge. I have never been able to understand the mental approach, and haven't been able to use affirmations or denials, so I do not know whether or not they are ever necessary. I am certainly ready to admit those stages may be necessary. But in admitting that, I would go only so far as to say that these are necessary only as a step leading from the material up through the mental, up further into the spiritual.

All those who are here, all those who have been led to come day after day, night after night, to these talks of mine, have been led only because of their readiness to leave the atmosphere of improving a human; to leave the state of consciousness of using a spiritual truth to make humanhood better. The Master truthfully said, "My sheep hear my voice."[8] I expect that only those who are attracted by the particular state of consciousness that I show forth in my talks or writings can understand and receive and respond to this.

I say very, very honestly to every one else: "Find your teacher. Do not make the effort to follow someone because your friends and relatives follow him. Do not make the mistake of following a teaching because your friends or relatives are following it. Your demonstration is to go to the kingdom of God within your own being and to pray that you be shown your teacher and your teaching. Then be fair with it. Stay with it. Follow it. If the time ever comes when you outgrow it, be satisfied and willing to outgrow it. But stay with that which God reveals to you until God reveals another step."

Keep your thoughts high and then you will find it easy for your human experience to unfold harmoniously. Do not let your demonstrations come through hard work. Have them come through natural spiritualization of thought, through developing your consciousness on higher and higher spiritual levels. Have always at hand a word, a sentence, a paragraph of metaphysical reading matter to keep thought on high levels.

The willingness to have God appear as consciousness; to voice truth as we understand it; to discipline ourselves to complete reliance on the within; to overcome our hate, fear or love of the world of effect, these lead to God's expressing itself as our individual being. God-consciousness follows the dedication of ourselves to the word and works of God.

~ 13 ~

God Is Not Mocked

It has become more and more clear to me that the real purpose of spiritual teaching is not merely making the demonstration of daily living, daily harmony, even peace and health, in the human way. There is a higher sense to life than making the organs of the body a little healthier, or making physical life last a few years longer, or increasing one's income by ten dollars a week, or even a thousand dollars a week.

Realize that life is spirit; therefore our individual expression of that life must be spiritual, and our entire existence can show forth the harmonies and perfections of spirit, and not merely physical health and wealth. This is the message.

Now, one of the scriptural passages that opens to us a great deal of this thought is the one we are using as the basis for tonight's talk. Let me read a line from the book of Galatians, chapter six: "Be not deceived, God is not mocked; for whatsoever a man soweth, that shall he also reap. For he that soweth to his flesh shall of the flesh reap corruption; but he that soweth to the spirit shall of the spirit reap life everlasting."[1] Be not deceived; God is not mocked. If you look out at the human world, I am sure you will contend that God is mocked. When you see the sin, the disease, the wars, the depressions, it is an impossibility to believe this verse, "God is not mocked." Surely, God has never planned such scenes as we witness in the human world for its creation. Therefore, if we were to judge by the human experience, we would have to agree that God is mocked.

We are told that God said: "I have no pleasure in the death of him that dieth,"[2] yet not only are the highways filled with death every day, but we send out the flower of youth to make sure they get killed off even faster than we would normally do it in traffic! Yes! In the human scene, God *is* mocked.

Anyone who has ever spent any amount of time in spiritual healing work, any measure of time with people suffering with cancer and consumption, will agree that God is mocked. Yet, we have scriptural authority for the statement that God is not mocked. But we also have this passage telling us that if we sow, we shall reap. If we sow to the flesh, we shall reap of the flesh; if we sow to the spirit, we shall reap of the spirit. It is in that passage that we have the answer to this whole problem of human sin, disease and death.

God is not mocked while we are sowing to the spirit, while we are living the life of the spirit, while we are living in oneness with God, in attunement or at-one-ment with God, while our thought is on the spiritual way of living, on the spiritual pleasures of life, on the spiritual business and activity of life; then God is not mocked, in that those who are sowing to the spirit reap spiritual treasure.

In the same way God is not mocked when we turn from God, when we turn from the spiritual way of living. Then we pay the penalty of that desertion; and in that also, God is not mocked, since it is not possible to reap the good of God while violating the laws of God. In Oriental philosophy this comes under the heading of karma, or reaping the result tomorrow of our acts of today, or reaping the results of our former acts today. In philosophy, we call this cause and effect. Here in scriptural language we have: "Whatsoever a man soweth, that shall he also reap." All of this would make it appear as if it were true that we can experience both good and evil, that we can choose to do good and receive good, and that we can choose to do evil and reap evil. Here, of course, it becomes necessary to turn to our metaphysical revelations, the revelations of ancient scripture, as well as to the more modern Bible teachings, and learn that the spiritual life is the only life and the only real life. Therefore, the only cause being God or Spirit, the only effect actually is spiritual–good. This, then, merely means that as long as we live in accord with the principle of Spirit, which is our original life, our original and only real existence, we are reaping the fruitage of that harmonious and perfect existence.

However, at some point or other there sprang up in human belief this sense of an existence apart from God. Somewhere the story of the Prodigal Son was set in motion and we came to believe that we were something or someone separate and apart from God and there we have this idea of sowing to the flesh and reaping corruption. In other words, as long as we accept the material code of life, as long as we accept the doctrine of finiteness and limitation, we in our way, and actually in belief only, reap that very state of existence; whereas, by turning and re-turning to our original demonstration of spiritual existence, we again become aligned with all that is good, all that is spiritual, and all that is harmonious.

Many people who have had the benefit of metaphysical help in any of its schools, and then found they were not receiving their healings, have discovered that they were trying to bring the law of Spirit or God into the mortal or material sense of existence. In other words, they were trying to patch up what has been called this "Adam dream." They tried to improve a mortal concept of life, instead of turning from it to the spiritual life.

Right there the question comes up as to how may we know that we are sowing to the fleshly existence, or how may we turn from it to the spiritual sense of life, to the spiritual consciousness of life? All of us, from birth, have been living in the material sense of existence. This material sense of existence is made up of catering to the personal I, trying to earn a living for the I, trying to gain something, acquire something, achieve something. Now, all of that is the limited or finite sense of existence. That is what we were born into as human beings; that is what we must now turn from in order to sow to the spirit. The spiritual sense of life is the direct opposite of that. The spiritual sense of existence declares that "I and the Father are one."[3] It declares that all that the Father has is mine. Therefore, instead of my being a receiving station, instead of my having to demonstrate or get or achieve health or harmony or success or wealth, I become that point in consciousness through which God manifests itself to the world.

There is where we sow to the spirit and reap of the spirit. Setting oneself up as someone who deserves something, is worthy of something, who is something of oneself–that is where we are sowing to this finite, limited sense, and where we reap corruption. We reap the daily chances of living well in the prosperous or boom days and living poorly in depressions, of being healthy in our youth and then starting to deteriorate somewhere in our middle years.

All of that is dissolved in the universal or impersonal the moment any one of us begins to realize that we have no demonstration to make; God is the only one who has a demonstration to make and God's demonstration consists of expressing itself as individual you and me. The moment we put the government on its shoulder, the moment we drop the responsibility from our own being and really realize that God is our life, God is our soul, and that the responsibility for our success or failure, the responsibility for our achievement, the responsibility for our work in life, is on the shoulder of the principle that brought us into manifestation–that moment we begin to live the spiritual life.

God is not mocked. That is almost like saying those who live in glass houses shouldn't throw stones. In other words, God, being the omnipresent reality of our being–the all-knowing, ever-present mind, ever aware of our existence–is certainly not mocked, since we cannot violate the laws of life, of God, and not meet the fate of that violation. Therefore, those of us who live in glass houses mustn't throw stones for fear that we ourselves will be the ones who are hurt.

Let us learn this minute to reverse the human picture. Luckily it can be done very quickly, or it can take quite a long time. It really depends on how tenacious we are in our determination to perpetuate the I that is Joel or Bill or Mary, how determined we are to have our own personal way in this existence. Now, it is true that those who live to that personal sense of existence oftentimes achieve that which they are seeking–personal health, personal success, personal wealth–but in most cases it proves to be Dead Sea fruit, because after it has been achieved, it is discovered that this is not it. Somehow those who turn to the spiritual sense of existence seem to have found happiness or peace or security, yet to have achieved it without doing so at someone else's expense.

It is possible in this age to duplicate the miracles of the Master in feeding and healing the multitudes the moment we begin to start, not from our personal powers or our personal wealth, but from the infinity and omnipresence of God. God is a word that has many meanings. It means many things to many people. Each one must determine for himself what God is to him, but let us for a moment agree that God is the creative principle of the universe, the infinite wisdom of the universe, the great law. Then is it possible to see that this law, this infinity, can pour itself through you or through me in the same manner that it poured itself through the Master? Actually it appears as you and as me.

There is only one law; there is only one principle. It remains for each one of us to permit that law or principle to use us, instead of our attempting to use the law. That is, of course, one of the great differences between the finite sense of life and the infinite. In the human picture, too often we try to use a spiritual law. We try to use an infinite power for some personal good. The law really works the other way. This law uses us. Probably in scriptural language that would be something like saying that "whatsoever ye do, do all to the glory of God."[4] In other words, we are not doing it at all; God is doing it through us or as us for its own glory.

Let no one mistake the mission of the Master and believe that in healing multitudes or feeding multitudes he was building up a great glory for himself. Had that been his idea, he would not have been presenting a principle which we could use. Had the purpose been for the glorification of a man named Jesus, there would have been no principle, no rule, or no law to be made manifest in our individual experience, since with the departure of Jesus there would have been no one to use or show forth this law. On the contrary, the Master said, "If I go not away, the Comforter will not come unto you."[5] In other words, if you persist in turning to this person called Jesus, if you persist in believing there is some personal power that I have and that I can use for your good, you never will learn the principle or be able to experience its good in your life.

So today, if anyone believes for a moment that any of this metaphysical truth is for the glory of any individual, or that its purpose is to glorify or to show the great powers of saintliness of any individual, one is entirely missing the mark. The whole purpose of spiritual truth is to show forth the great principle that God is the universal life, and the universal power; that God is ever available; that God is here for the manifestation of its own power and its own glory. Certainly that leaves any one of us out as personal demonstrators, as people with personal healing powers, or enriching powers. There is no such person on earth, and there never has been. The only power is God manifested as individual being, and then manifested only through the understanding and apprehension of this divine idea.

In the degree that we are able to open our consciousness and let that consciousness take possession of us, in that degree do we show forth the harmony, the health, the joy, and the peace which is of God and not of man.

The moment we realize that God, this great divine I, is really the I that I am, we have begun to see the universality of God, of good, of spirit, of life eternal. The moment we have stopped thinking out upon life from the finite sense of ourselves as human beings subject to all of the moral laws, all of the material laws, and begin to realize that the I of me is God—the I, the infinite consciousness, is God—in that moment we have lost the finiteness; we have lost the sense of separateness from God that has driven us out into the world as prodigals; and we begin to retrace our steps back to the Father's house, there to be vested with the purple robe and the jeweled ring.

I am going back to Galatians for a minute: "Brethren, if a man be overtaken in a fault, ye which are spiritual, restore such a one in the spirit of meekness . . . Bear ye one another's burdens, and so fulfill the law of Christ. For if a man think himself to be something, when he is nothing, he deceiveth himself."[6]

Again, you who are spiritual, you who have realized even in a measure, that God is the creative source or principle or life of your being, the moment you begin to realize that, you share in that understanding by beginning to know that truth about everyone in the universe. You bear your neighbor's burden, not by paying his rent for him, nor by sitting and sympathizing in his illnesses. You bear his burden—and actually you bear it away from him—in the degree that "ye which are spiritual," you who have begun to realize the spiritual nature of your being, begin to share that with your neighbor in the understanding that we are all children of the one Father; that we are all offspring of the same spirit; that whatever is a law unto one, must be the law unto all spiritual being.

"Let him that is taught in the word communicate unto him that teacheth in all good things . . . As we have therefore opportunity, let us do good unto all men, especially unto them who are of the household of faith."[7]

Now, ordinarily we think of that as meaning that we can help only those who are of our faith, of our church, or our spiritual or metaphysical teaching and we probably have learned to leave the other fellow strictly outside. This will not do. While we do not go about preaching the Gospel in the sense of proselytizing, in the sense of forcing metaphysics or the spiritual life on those who for some reason are not ready for it, or are not desirous of it—at least not in the way we wish to present it—nevertheless, it becomes our duty the moment we realize one iota of spiritual truth, to know that it is the truth about all of God's creation; to leave no one outside.

It is true that we can go a step further with those who are of the household of faith. Wherever an individual shows an interest in a metaphysical or a spiritual teaching, we can go so far as to talk to him about it, or to offer him writings on it, or offer him help, individual healing help. Or, we can go the limit, depending on his readiness to receive it. Therefore, we might say that we do go further with those who show their interest in our teaching. But that does not absolve us from our major duty of realizing God as the universal principle, and leaving no one outside of its fold.

Now right here I am going to come to the Master's teaching, or that part of his teaching which I have been emphasizing for the past week or two: the two commandments which he gave. The first one is the old Hebrew commandment, "Thou shalt have no other gods before me,"[8] and the second is the one which he added to that: "Love thy neighbor as thyself."[9] Now, in this first commandment, we have, of course, the entire secret of demonstration, and that is the realization of God as the one and only power. There is where we come back to our original premise—God, truth, is not mocked. If you understand God as truth, and then realize that this truth which is God is the I Am of your being and of mine, then that truth will not be mocked; you will not be dragged through sin, disease, lack and limitation. Or, if these temptations do come nigh unto you, they will be quickly and easily removed.

God, truth, is not mocked! If you abide in this truth of your being, if you begin to accept for yourself the fact that God is the one and only power and that this God is your mind and your life, your own consciousness, then you have the ever presence and availability of eternal life and eternal and infinite supply! Truth, then, is really not mocked. We show forth in a measure the infinite harmony of God, and we do it through grace. Not by taking thought, but through grace. The moment we realize that: "I am of my own self nothing; I can of mine own self do nothing and be nothing; but the infinite nature and character of God, the infinite allness which is God, is forever pouring itself through as my individual being; is ever appearing here on earth as my individual being, the word made flesh, and that I can meet any and every demand made upon me, not as if I were of myself something, but because the infinity of God pours through as all those who turn to it!" In that moment you and I begin to experience that peace of mind, that security which is of God.

We do that in even greater degree the moment we fulfill the second commandment: "Love thy neighbor as

*it does for

thyself." That of course, is exemplified in this sixth
chapter of Galatians. To love our neighbor as ourselves
means, first of all, to recognize God as the universal
principle and, therefore, to realize that whatever we
have declared to be the truth of our own being is the
truth of all men's being, whether or not they, at the
moment, know it or realize it or are demonstrating it. To
love our neighbor means to un-see him as male or
female, as white or black, as Jew or Gentile, as German,
Japanese or Russian or American or British; and to see
through that exterior to the life which is God, to the
mind and the soul which is God. And when we do, there
begins to come through the first realization of a miracle.
Follow this for a few minutes with me.

We are living today in an age when anything can
happen and a lot is going to happen. We are living in a
human age of uncertainty, of unrest and of danger. If
there is any hope for the world, that hope will have to
come through those of spiritual illumination. It is not
going to come through any human doctrine. It is not
going to come through an atomic bomb, or an Atlantic
Pact. How can it? All of those things mean death and
destruction, not only to a so called enemy, but as we
have seen now, this defense sword is a double edged
sword. As the Master so clearly told us, "All they that
take the sword shall perish with the sword."[10] And if you
don't think that that is a spiritual law, go back to your
history books and read the stories of the nations of the
world in different eras. One after another has disappeared even in spite of their many victories in the field
of arms; one nation becomes victorious on the field of
battle, but in its turn is defeated and goes down. Does
anyone in this room actually believe that the Atlantic

Pact or the Western Coalition or the atomic bomb is going to save the peace? If he does, he is a poor historian, and an even poorer student of spiritual truth.

The one way in which peace is going to come to the world is through the illumined thoughts of those individuals who turn to the spirit for its fruitage. Somewhere, sometime, this spiritual evolution will begin. Probably the first public statement about it, or at least widely known public statement, came through Steinmetz, the electrical wizard, who left as his last message to the world, that in this age spiritual power would come to the fore and be recognized as the great power; that we would make more advance in this age in the spiritual world, in spiritual knowledge, than has ever been attained before. Since that time, many have come to this same light.

There may be another war, and there may not. We are not here to prophesy about the human picture. There may be found a way of ending this threatened war even by human means. But at best, it will be a temporary thing, since, judging in the same way we have judged history in the past, or as they say they judge horse racing now, you have to go back and see what the past performance was. The past performance is that we have had wars since the beginning of recorded time and that we are still having them. And there is no sign that they have come to an end. However, at no time in the world's history has the spiritual awareness been made as manifest among men as it is today. At all periods in the world's history, there have been men in the priesthood and in the ministry who have known spiritual power, who have known their true identity, and who have been able for themselves and for some others, to bring this spiritual power into concrete manifestation. Today, however, throughout the world there are people like you and like me, people who make up the average man in the street, who have some little glimpse of what spiritual power can do. Nearly everyone here, nearly everyone to whom I speak, has had some proof of the power of the spirit. He has had healing either of the body, of the purse, or of morals. Nearly all of our audiences have seen, in some measure, what the spirit can do in individual experience. Now the time has come through our greater awareness to accept the responsibility of world thinking, of universal thinking, of beginning now to know that God is not mocked even on a national or international scale; that the law of God does operate.

We are to utilize our understanding, to permit this spirit or law of God to operate through or as our consciousness. I have seen this worked out practically. I have seen this worked out so that I can say definitely that it works in proportion to our faithfulness to it. We who individually accept this great revelation of Christianity, or universal truth, or the omnipresence of the Christ—that is, of the omnipotence and presence of the spirit of God in men—must each day recognize that this truth, this Christ, this spiritual light, is present wherever an individual raises his thought to God. All over the world people are lifting themselves, lifting their thoughts to invoke help from God. It is true that some of them are thinking of this God as the Gentleman up on a cloud; others are thinking of this God as Jesus Christ of Nazareth. Others are thinking of God in some other form but what their idea of God is, is not important, since it is only a concept. You know there are very few people on earth, and there have been very few in all the history of the world, who actually knew God, who actually knew what God is. Men entertain concepts. You have your concept of God and others have their concepts of God. Those who have achieved the actual awareness of God have come to see, "I am he." And there have been few of those in the world's history.

Now, regardless of one's concept of God, this is included in the consciousness—that God is present, and that God is available as a help, whatever the emergency may be. You have all read stories of aviators in the war, as well as of other soldiers in the war, who in times of danger lifted their thought to God. It may have been a Hebrew God, or a Methodist God, or a Catholic God, but they lifted their thought to God and they found omnipresent, immediate help.

Now, it is the person who is living the spiritual life that can make that experience a more universal one. In other words, every time, every day, that we consciously realize Christ as an ever-present principle of light, life, as an ever-present help wherever an individual raises his thought to God, we make Christ's truth available to individuals somewhere on earth. You do not know what person, in what minute, may be lifting himself into this realization of God and finding himself tuned in on your beam. It would not be too important if that merely resulted in saving his individual life or sense of life or bringing some personal benefit to him. But the real benefit is that as we make Christ available to all those on earth who lift their thought to any concept of God, we bring the universality of Christ into manifestation, and we bring the day nearer when Christ will be present at the bargaining tables of the world, at the business tables of the world.

Many men have proved this omnipresence of this Christ power at conferences with labor leaders, with unions. Many men have proved this presence in the banking house, in the business house. But, it takes the recognition of it to bring it into concrete manifestation. Usually it takes the realization of one calling himself a metaphysician, or one on the spiritual path, one who is so completely loving his neighbor as himself as to be willing at some part of each day to realize Christ as omnipresent wherever men lift their thought to God.

Every time there is a metaphysical lecture of any nature, somebody or other, and sometimes whole groups of people, are realizing the presence of the healing Christ for the purpose of realizing the presence and the power of God. The result of that is that at most if not all metaphysical lectures and services, someone or more than one goes away healed of some sin, of some disease, of some lack or limitation. Somebody's realization of the omnipresence of God has freed someone in that audience. Sometimes the lecturer alone carries that work of spiritual realization. Sometimes committees are appointed to help in that work of spiritual realization. As a matter of fact, every metaphysician every day of the week should be realizing the omnipresence of the Christ, not only at metaphysical lectures but wherever men gather on earth—in gambling dives, in prisons, in the hospitals—everywhere on earth.

If you love your neighbor as yourself, you will make the effort to realize Christ, Christ presence, Christ power, at any place and at any time that any individual anywhere lifts his thought for the hand of God. The hand of God is not "shortened that it cannot save,"[11] and God is omnipresent. Why, then, are there these disasters in the world? Not because God is not omnipresent, but because the omnipresence of God was not realized. We might just as well say, "music," as "omnipresence"; why can't I play the piano since I'd love to? Just because I haven't realized the presence of music as an activity in my own consciousness. You will all agree, especially those who are musically inclined, that there is music in my consciousness but I haven't realized it, to bring it forth. So, not only is music present and mathematics present, but you may be assured that God is also very present as my consciousness and yours, as the very activity of my being and yours. But it takes your recognition and mine to bring it into awareness.

Isn't that the secret of metaphysical healing? When you call on a practitioner, what takes place? The practitioner realizes God as your life, as your mind, as your soul. The practitioner realizes God as the substance of your body, as what appears as the organs and functions of your body. The practitioner realizes God as the wisdom of your being, as even your receptivity to truth. Now, all the practitioner has been doing is realizing Christ's omnipresence and omnipotence in your experience. Well, isn't it only one more step to realize Christ, omnipresent and omnipotent, as the experience of every individual on earth, and therefore make it available to all those who reach out? After all, we are not supposed to have a monopoly on God and the Christ. I said today that there was a time when the availability of the Christ was for the Hebrews alone. Those days are passed. Paul, I think, ended that for his particular time when he made this Christ truth available to all men, and said they didn't necessarily have to become Hebrews in order to become Christians.

We today have to realize that we do not have to become a Christian Scientist or a Truth student or a Unity student in order to have God and the Christ available to you. Let us get over that idea that only metaphysicians can have the benefit of the grace of God. Let us learn to love our neighbor as ourselves. Oh, yes, especially those of the "household of faith,"[12] but let's not confine it to those of the household of faith. Let us realize Christ, Universal Principle, Divine Love, ever available to all men wherever thought is lifted to God. Then we make God available through grace, not through taking thought, not by learning metaphysics, not by making affirmations and denials. But wherever an individual is, and whatever concept of God he lifts himself to, there let him find grace, there let him find the "peace of God, which passeth all understanding,"[13] because of your and my realization of omnipresence.

That, then, must be our contribution to the world. We cannot go out into the world and say to it: "Let's give up war." We haven't yet proven that we ourselves can give up individual warfare to enough degree to tell the world to give up its sense of war. There will be plenty of time when we have learned to pay all of our bills without being sued, when we have learned to settle our affairs without suing the other fellow, when we have learned to settle all our human existence without quarrels. Then will be the time for us to go out and tell the world: "Let's not have any more wars. Let's abide by the teaching of the Master." But until that day comes, we do not have to sit idly by, watching the world destroy itself. Oh, no! Just as one individual in Galilee gave forth this teaching for the entire Western world and left it here—intact—for all those to accept who will, so we today can repeat that

teaching, and we can reinstate it in our individual experience, and show the fruitage of it by our experience. We
ourselves can live by grace, or at least we can make a
start. We can pray daily. We can pray without ceasing.
And, we can make our prayer the realization of spiritual
existence. We can begin first of all by realizing that
instead of this individual having to be at the standpoint of
receiving good, this individual stands at the point of
expressing good, of sharing good, of bestowing good—not
in and of itself, but by the grace of God, which is the law
of life of this being. In other words, when you and I begin
to reverse ourselves, instead of using truth for some
benefit for ourselves, we let truth use us, so that it becomes us—God itself made visible, the word made flesh.

You know, no one realizes any better than I do that
what I have said in regard to reversing our position is
the biggest thing that ever can be said, and the most
difficult to demonstrate. I am not a bit fooled by the
simplicity of the words, or by the fact that they sound so
simple because they are one and two syllable words. I
am not fooled into believing that what I have said is an
easy thing to achieve. But I have learned that it is
necessary to achieve and to accomplish just that, whether it is easy or whether it is difficult. The Master did not
set before us an easy task. He said that "strait is the gate,
and narrow is the way, and few there be that find it."[14]
Indeed, there are few! Most of us still want to use God,
truth, to improve some human situation in our experience, instead of coming to that place in consciousness
where we say, "Speak Father, Thy servant heareth."[15]
Or, "Use me; let me be that place in consciousness
through which God flows to all those seeking God; not
seeking my personal power, but seeking God; let me be

the vehicle or the avenue through which God pours itself into expression for all men to utilize and receive, until they themselves learn that all that I am, they are, too; all that Christ is, I am—I in God and God in me. All one. Children of God, and if children, heirs, and if heirs, joint heirs with Christ in God."

You see, you break through this personality that is so willing to do for one and not for another. When once you see through that human frame before you and see that God is pouring itself forth as individual you and me, that only God is pouring itself forth as individual you and me, that is sowing to the spirit. When I see you as human beings, or if I see myself as a human being with a demonstration to make, I am sowing to the flesh and I will ultimately reap the corruption of the flesh.

But God is the "you" of you. God is the life and the mind and the spirit. God is the reality of your being and all there is to you is God. When you realize this, then you are sowing to the spirit and you must reap spiritually. When I realize this, then I am beholding you as you are. You know, when we awaken, we shall see Him as He is. We don't have to die to awaken. We don't have to become like Him. We can do our dying daily right here and now; if only a little bit of us drops off each day, if in only a small way we realize that we have no demonstration to make, that we don't have to take thought as to what we shall eat or what we shall drink or wherewithal we shall be clothed. All we have to do is to relax and to realize that the heavenly Father, which is right here and now, knoweth that we have need of these things and that it is His good pleasure to give us the kingdom.

I wonder if you really believe me when I tell you that at that moment when you relax your conscious thinking in the sense of dropping responsibilities and actually accepting the truth that God knows, your whole life changes. You never again have to take a thought up here in your head. You never again have to plan or think or plot. You never again have to barge around mentally or physically to achieve some good. Your good appears each day as it is needed, as it is necessary. It appears in the form of money; it appears in the form of friends or relatives, companions, husband, wife, home. It appears in any and every form necessary to your present experience, but it appears without your taking thought.

Now, watch this carefully. If your thought is on a demonstration of a thing or a person or a place, you are sowing to the flesh. You are taking thought for things and that is a violation of the Christ teaching. The moment you have desire for a person, a place, a thing— any form of good—you are violating the Christly teaching. You are not supposed to take thought for things or persons. Your whole mind must be not on the form in which God appears, but on God itself as the reality of your being, as the Infinite Consciousness of your being. And then, in that realization, you drop your human thinking for the person, place, or thing, and you let person, place, or thing appear to you in their order. It may not be the person, place, or thing you have been thinking about, but it will be a very satisfying person, place, and thing.

In my writings you will notice all the way through the reference to Luke 12: 22-32, that marvelous passage of the Master in which he tells his disciples to "Take no thought for what they shall eat or what they shall drink or wherewithal they shall be clothed." He called their attention to the "lilies of the field" and to the birds; and he ends with, "Your Father knoweth that ye have need of these things; and it is your Father's good pleasure to give you the kingdom."

One day I suddenly realized the meaning of that particular passage, that message to the disciples. I saw that sowing to the flesh meant trying to achieve something in the manifest realm—even good things like good positions, good dollars or lots of dollars, or good companions. I realized that it was on that point that we wrecked our ship of life. It was on that very point that we went overboard, namely this attempt on our part to decide what person, place or thing we desired, and then trying to use the law of God to get it. In that passage I found the answer to my whole life's problems. I saw that as I took no thought for those things, but kept all of my thought—as the old Hebrew prophet said: "Thou wilt keep him in perfect peace whose mind is stayed on thee"[16]—as I kept my attention centered on God and the things of God, as I tried to realize within my own being the spiritual nature of life, all of a sudden I found it wasn't necessary to take thought about these things of daily living; they always found a way of getting to my table or my desk a little before I knew that I needed them. I still find, that that principle works, and it is not necessary for me to think about who is going to do this, or when, or how it is to be accomplished—or why. I find that as long as I abide in my meditation, as long as I abide in this realization of God, and then do every human thing to the best of my ability as it is presented to me to do, that seems to be sufficient for the experience I am having at the present time.

~ 14 ~

IMMANUEL

Make a joyful noise unto the Lord, all ye lands.
Serve the Lord with gladness: come before his
    presence with singing.

Know ye that the Lord he is God!
    It is he that hath made us, and not we ourselves;
    we are his people, and the sheep of his pasture.

Enter into his gates with thanksgiving,
    and unto his courts with praise:
    be thankful unto him, and bless his name.

For the Lord is good; his mercy is everlasting;
    and his truth endureth to all generations.

Psalm 100

"KNOW YE THAT THE LORD HE IS GOD: it is he that hath
made us, and not we ourselves." Let us take that for our
guiding light of this moment. Let us try to realize in this
moment that it is he that has made us, not we ourselves.
To begin with, just to be reminded of that fact should be
a healing influence. Immediately, whatever of sin or
disease or discord is floating anywhere in or around our
thought, mind, body, should really begin to fade out
with that realization: "It is he that hath made us and not
we ourselves." That places the responsibility on his

shoulder, does it not? That places the responsibility for our health, our wealth, our peace, safety and security, upon him, upon it, upon God, upon this creative principle, whatever it is that in your thought is God.

To each one of us God has a different significance. To each one of us the word God means something different. But all of that is not important. What is important is that we recognize that there is a creative principle, a causative power, and that it created us, and not we ourselves.

Of course, we have confirmation of this in the New Testament: "Now are we the sons of God."[1] Again it must be clear that God is the causative or creative principle of our being. Once we are able to accept that, how restful it is to realize that that which God creates, God must maintain and sustain. God must be the law unto it; not only the law-giver, but the law itself. God must be the life of that which God creates, and if God is the life of your being, then your being is eternal and immortal. So even to accept for a moment the belief or fear of death, of passing on, of leaving this plane of consciousness, is really a sin against the Holy Ghost. Remember, we must honor God; we dishonor God when we forget that it is he that has created us, and not we ourselves.

In my work the Scriptures play a greater and greater part as the inner meaning of Scripture unfolds and reveals itself to me. Merely as a religious book the Bible is not too important; there were too many years when none of it really made sense to me. It is only since the years in which spiritual realization has come that I am able to see the meaning of Scripture. It does not mean making affirmations or quoting scripture, but accepting these statements, analyzing them, pondering them, and getting from within the real meaning or essence of the word.

"We are his people, and the sheep of his pasture." Naturally, in those old Hebrew days when sheep and pasture were the common form of life, when everyone had pastures and everyone had sheep, it was understood that these sheep had to be cared for even as Moses cared for sheep on the hills of Midian. The teaching of God as a sheep-tender became embodied in Hebrew literature as "That which careth for his flock."[2] Naturally, all of that is only symbolic, but it does bring to our thought, to our awareness, this sense of a very loving principle, a very loving power, and an ever-watchful one that watches this being and body of ours, even as the sheep tender guards his charges, his sheep, and gives them pasturage. In that way then, we are to realize that "It is he that hath made us, and not we ourselves." We are the creation of this great God, this great principle, and we are the sheep of his pasture. We are to realize that we are under his supervision, under the divine guardianship of an infinitely wise and an all-loving principle which we call God, or Father-Mother.

We come here to "enter into his gates with thanksgiving, and into his courts with praise," to "be thankful unto him, and bless his name." All through Scripture you find such passages as: "In all thy ways acknowledge him, and he shall direct thy paths;"[3] "Thou wilt keep him in perfect peace, whose mind is stayed on thee;"[4] "Pray without ceasing."[5]

In all of these and in hundreds of other passages, we find the teaching, not only of these ancient Hebrews, but from the time of the Master on up through the Christian era, we find the same teaching of the necessity of acknowledging God in all our ways, acknowledging God first as the creative principle of our own being; acknowledging God as the source of our supply; acknowledging God with praise and with thanksgiving for all of the good which we must experience in our spiritual life.

Now there is no other way to pray without ceasing than continuously to acknowledge this infinite power, this infinite presence, this great keeper of the pasture—the universe—and all of God's creation which includes men and women upon the earth.

For a moment I am going to call your attention to three words or terms. The first is the Hebrew word "Immanuel" or "God with us." The second is the Chinese term "Tao," the third is "Christ." All these terms mean the same thing. They mean the presence and power of God with us—*in* us. They mean the actual realization, the actual feeling of divine presence. When the Hebrew spoke of Immanuel or God with us, he meant it literally in that sense—an actual feeling of the divine presence with us, not off somewhere, but actually with us. This Immanuel interpreted itself in human terms of a pillar of cloud: "The pillar of the cloud by day, and the pillar of fire by night."[6] It interpreted itself to the Hebrews as manna falling from the skies and as water coming from the rock. It interpreted itself to the Hebrew prophets as food brought by the widow or by the ravens.

Always, Immanuel, or God-with-us, appears to us in a form necessary for us or to us at that particular moment. When Lao Tzu used the word Tao he meant the "Word" or the "Presence" and always that word is associated with becoming "flesh." Always the word becomes flesh and dwells among us. This word, or Tao, which in my language today is the "Infinite Invisible," that great Infinite Invisible, becomes visible and tangible in the form necessary to your experience and mine. That great infinite invisible Word becomes flesh in the sense of becoming visible or tangible as the health of our body, or the wealth of our pocketbook or the happiness of our home, or security from the dangers of the world.

Remember this: there is a word, Immanuel, meaning God ever-present with us and becoming visible and tangible in the form necessary to our unfoldment and experience; and there is this other word—Tao—meaning the self-same thing, meaning the Word or Infinite Invisible becoming manifest as the experience of the moment, as the harmony of the moment. And then, in our latter-day language, we find the same thing written—"the Christ."

Now, no one has given us a better understanding of this than our friend Paul, in saying, "I live; yet not I, but Christ liveth in me,"[7] and, "I can do all things through Christ, which strengtheneth me."[8] This term, the Christ, is again the Word, the Infinite Invisible, the Tao or Immanuel. But remember that the Christ is ever-present, living with us, within us, and appears to us as food with which to feed the multitudes where seemingly there is no such food, or appearing as the "peace, be still"[9] to the waves, to the wild waves of the ocean.

If Christ be not present in your consciousness and mine, then Christianity is a failure and a fraud. If Christ be not present awaiting our recognition, we have no hope in the world. Human experience from birth to death is nothing more nor less than chance and change. Only the presence of Immanuel, only the presence of God with us, only the presence of the Christ, can transform human experience into a spiritual revelation. If you live without this sense of God's presence, without this sense of Christ imminent, then all you have is a physical body beginning to deteriorate almost before you reach thirty years of age, and continuing that deterioration until the end.

Once, however, Christ becomes a divine reality in consciousness, an ever-present feeling, from then on the body becomes the temple of the living God, that which it originally was intended to be, and that which in reality it is—the temple of the living God. Then, there is no such thing as age, change, decomposition or death, not even in passing on, not even in transition.

Never let us forget that. Death itself is a failure. Death is an enemy. True, according to Scripture, it is the last enemy that will be overcome, but it is an enemy, and let no one welcome it; let no one look upon it as a wonderful demonstration for a release from human fears or human sins or human disease. Death, or passing on, is none of those things. It is failure to realize our true identity as "children of God," and if children, then heirs—heirs of God and "joint heirs with Christ" to all of the immortality and eternality of existence.

Does that mean we are to live here on this plane forever? The answer is, yes, if you so desire! However, when we leave grammar school for high school, or high school for college, it is merely the transition from one state of consciousness to a higher one. In the same way, if we become aware of our Christhood to such a degree that we manifest health and strength and vitality in the body, then should the time ever come when a "call" comes, when a realization comes that there is a greater work to be done, a higher work to be done, we may leave this plane of consciousness and go forth into the higher work on higher levels of consciousness.

But let no one for a moment believe that dying out of this body through disease is the way to a greater unfoldment of God consciousness. It is not true. We may leave this plane of existence; we may walk out of this body, or at least appear to walk out of it; we may rise to a higher and higher degree of consciousness, since certainly this level of consciousness called the earth is not the first or the last. But we do not go from one to another through failure—and death is failure, since it is the last enemy.

The way to overcome disease, the way to overcome that which the world calls age and decomposition, is through the conscious recognition of the great truth of being. Here we find, "For the Lord is good; his mercy is everlasting; and his truth endureth to all generations." Well, we start with this: "For the Lord is good." If the Lord or the law of God, or this infinite Christ is good, it cannot for a moment forsake us, can it? It cannot for a moment leave us without divine care, protection and spiritual unfoldment. Since the Lord is good, our experience, even in what we call the human picture, must be good, or else we have taken ourselves out from under the care of this Lord who is good.

But watch this: "His mercy is everlasting." Does that allow us, even for one moment, to deteriorate or decompose or die? His mercy is everlasting. It must be just as merciful, just as powerful, just as loving when we are one hundred years of age as when we are one hundred days of age. Then is it not our acceptance of a universal belief that would make us believe that God is less merciful and that good is less everlasting because of the passage of what we call time?

And now watch this: "And his truth endureth to all generations." What is his truth? On the understanding of that hinges our entire demonstration of life. What is his truth? Now you may hold onto your seats while I tell you: I Am. "I" am truth! I am life eternal! I am the resurrection and the life! And this truth which I am—and I am his truth—this truth is infinite, omnipresent, eternal. There is no separation and no point of division between God and God's truth which I am. Truth isn't something that I know; truth isn't something that I possess. Truth is something that I am. "I am the way, the truth, and the life."[10] "I and my Father are one."[11] And, "He that seeth me seeth him that sent me."[12]

Let us remember this: I am the truth which endureth to all generations. Who said that I am man or woman or child or person? Who said that? The Master asked that very question: "Whom do men say that I, the son of man, am?"[13] And the foolish answered him saying that he was this man or that man or some reborn one, but that wasn't the answer. The answer finally came: "Thou art the Christ, the son of the living God."[14] Then we are told that Peter did not know that intellectually. That had not been given to him just by reading it in a book, but rather the Father within him had disclosed this to Peter. The Father within, spiritual consciousness—the divine wisdom, the spiritual wisdom of the age—revealed, unto that one consciousness prepared for it, that "I am the Christ, the son of the living God!"

Oh, it has been construed in orthodox religion that Peter's recognition applied only to one man in one particular period of time. If that had been true, truth would not be everlasting or eternal throughout all generations. Truth would have stood there on the shores of Galilee for only a brief thirty-three years, or even a more brief three years of spiritual ministry.

Oh, no! We recognize truth given by the Master as a universal truth, as being the truth about you and about me, the truth about all who have been on earth or are on earth or who will be on earth, unto the end of time. And actually, no one has left the earth, and no one is going to come to earth, since again Scripture tells us that he that came down from heaven and he that went up to heaven were one and the same—and always that one and the same—I Am. I am the very living truth of God, and I am infinite and eternal and omnipresent. I live throughout all time. "Lo! I am with you always, even unto the end of the world."[15]

This *I* that we are talking about, which might appear up here as Joel Goldsmith, and out there as Joe You, or Mary You—this *I* is not a person. It is an absolute presence of God. It is the absolute allness of God, merely appearing as individual you and individual me. It is again, the "Word made flesh."[16] It is the Word itself made flesh and dwelling among us as you and as me. Only as we accept this unfoldment, this revelation, this teaching of the Master, will we come into our own heritage of life eternal—and not only ours. We will bring it forth for all those who are able to accept the truth of the universality of God.

It is always a great joy to me when I read the writings that come forth either from my pen or my tongue, and realize that in all of them is this constant return to the universality of God or truth, and that in all of these writings there is complete freedom from the necessity of believing that one church differs from another, or one land differs from another, or one people differs from another, so far as their spiritual identity is concerned. Whether one chooses to continue in the path of the

Judaic church and belief, or the Christian church and belief, or Hindu or Muhammadan; or whether one chooses to belong to one or the other of the metaphysical movements, is of no concern at all in the demonstration of this universal truth. This truth is just as available to one as to another, and it is just as available outside the church as in it.

This revelation was never meant to be the property of a person or an institution or of an organization or of a church. It was to be a revelation of the truth of being, and the purpose of any organization is to set forth that teaching, making it available to all who wish, or who are prepared to receive it. Organization has no other function, but certainly in this age organization has a function, and that is to set forth the universality of this great truth.

That is why it always gives me so much joy to speak the word "Immanuel" of the Hebrews, the word "Tao" of the Chinese, and the term "the Christ" of our Christian age. To me, all of these words mean something like a cloud that I can almost feel behind me from the shoulders on up, arching itself over my head. Always I have that sense or presence of that protecting influence, of that divine influence, of that inner guidance that comes from that cloud around my shoulders. Not a cloud in the sense of a shutting out, but a cloud rather in the sense of a light foam, something upon which one can almost lean back and feel, really—a supporting cloud.

That, to me, is Immanuel, Tao, the Christ. That, to me, is God-with-me. It is my assurance that I am never alone. It is my conscious awareness of the presence and of the power of God. And therefore I can sense it as it goes before me to make the crooked places straight, as it goes before me to prepare every step of the way for that which is to come.

Whether we are in the business world, the religious world, or the world of the home, none of that is of any account, really, in the plan of this presence. This presence is a guide to us, not only in religious work, but in the business world, and in the household. Wherever we are at this particular moment we are because of our readiness for that particular step. Once we have acknowledged the presence of this Christ, once we have acknowledged or felt the presence of this influence in our experience, it may well be that our next step will be on a higher one away from whatever we are doing at the present moment.

The thing for us to remember is that it is not spiritual to desire to be in some other place, or to be doing some other work. That really is a form or acknowledgment of failure where we are. We are where we are because of our developed or undeveloped state of consciousness. We will never be in any other place or any other position than where we are, except through the development and unfoldment of our spiritual consciousness. Therefore, instead of looking back with regret, instead of looking forward with wishes, desirous to be somewhere else and doing something else, let us again get back on spiritual ground. Let us here and now, at this very moment, begin to acknowledge that the place whereon I stand is holy ground.

Now, understand me. If you are not in a good human place, it doesn't mean that the evil human place is holy ground. On the other hand, if you are occupying the very best human place there is on earth, do not believe that even that is holy ground. Holy ground has nothing to do with where you humanly appear to be. It is that place where you are in divine consciousness; that place where you recognize yourself as being the son of God, the offspring of God, the very I that I am. The moment you make that recognition you are on holy ground, you are in and of holy spiritual consciousness. Then pay no attention to the human place whereon you stand. Pay no attention to the human position you occupy, and don't be glorified or happy if it happens to be on some spiritual platform, because that is of as little consequence as being on the street-car conductor's platform in the human scene.

What counts is, where do I stand spiritually? Where do I stand in consciousness? Now, if I stand on this great truth that I am the truth, if I stand on this great place–God consciousness–then I can say that the place whereon I stand is holy ground. From that spiritual standpoint, I can make the next declarations that all that the Father has is mine, and all that God is, I am.

Again, do not look on me humanly, and never permit anyone to look at you humanly to see how close to that divine idea you are. The picture will be very disappointing. Even the Master recognized that in his great remarks: "Why callest thou me good? There is none good but one, that is God."[17] "I can of mine own self do nothing."[18] "If I bear witness of myself, my witness is not true."[19] "My doctrine is not mine, but his that sent me."[20]

Always, if you are looking at yourself or another through finite, human eyes, you will not be satisfied with the picture that you see. You have all heard the great spiritual lights of this age criticized and condemned and I am sure that you have all read that every spiritual life from the Master all the way back to Moses was likewise

judged, criticized and condemned from the human standpoint. And who are we to say that in their human experience there may not have been things that could be criticized, judged or condemned?

However, our function now is not to judge according to the appearance. Our function is not to look at each other humanly and see how far we have come or how far we have failed. Our attitude is that of the practitioner when he is called to the penitentiary to give help perhaps to a deep-dyed criminal. The practitioner does not look at that individual and judge from appearances and start saying: "If you were just a good human, what wonderful things God could do through you!" No. The practitioner looks right through the human appearance and says: "Rise, son of God! There is healing in this realization of your true identity, for you are the living Christ. You are the one true son of God!"

Now, we have the same thing when a practitioner sits beside the bedside of one who is supposed to be dying. Can the practitioner look at that individual, judge by appearances, and then say: "Thou art life eternal; thou art the truth of God"? No. Only through the developed spiritual sense can the practitioner perceive that which is appearing outwardly as a sick or a sinful human being is actually the very presence of God itself.

In that same way we turn our gaze away from what we appear humanly to be. We turn our gaze away from what our neighbor appears to be, and we begin with these great and wonderful truths: "The place whereon I stand is holy ground; all that the Father hath is mine; all that God is, I am." And, as we learn to abide in these truths and to live in that consciousness and to judge only after spiritual appearances, then gradually we form and

develop, manifest and express, this spiritual intuition, this spiritual insight, which becomes the light of the world. Then, as we go forward in and as that light, everyone within range of our being, everyone within range of our experience, feels some degree of attraction toward us. Then we find that it isn't toward us at all, it is toward the light which we have become through this great spiritual revelation.

Only in this way are we able to help others in the world. Only in this way are we able to raise up the level of consciousness so that it begins to perceive that "I am he," and that all that the Father has is mine unto eternity, forever and forever, without any trace of age or decomposition or disease. In the light of this truth, then, it isn't we mortals who ever understand or achieve health, it is the I that I am, the divine reality of my being, which is the health of my body, the health of my being, and the health of all those who come to me for assistance.

As we begin, even in a very slight measure, to realize that health is a property of God, a quality of God, and an activity of God—in fact, that health is the natural state of eternal life, and that eternal life is the life of my being and of yours—then in that degree do we bring forth what appears to the world as bodily health. It appears to the world as a heart that measures 72 beats to the minute, or a digestion that is perfect, an elimination that is free. It is none of these things. It is really and truly Christ itself, the divine harmony and presence of God, visible to the world as harmonious you and harmonious me.

> The Lord is my shepherd; I shall not want.
> He maketh me to lie down in green pastures: he
> leadeth me beside the still waters.

He restoreth my soul: he leadeth me in the paths of
righteousness for his name's sake.
Yea, though I walk through the valley of the shadow
of death, I will fear no evil: for thou
Art with me; thy rod and thy staff they comfort me.
Thou preparest a table before me in the presence of
mine enemies: thou anointest my head
With oil; my cup runneth over.
Surely goodness and mercy shall follow me all the
days of my life: and I will dwell in the
House of the Lord forever.

                                                  Psalm 23

I will live in the consciousness of God. And if I live in
the consciousness of God, I will not only live forever,
but I will be divinely and spiritually fed. I will be
spiritually guided and governed and directed.

But remember the price. I must live in the consciousness of God. I must acknowledge him in *all* my ways. I
must recognize God to be the source and foundation of
my whole existence. I must recognize God to be the
guiding light, the infinite harmony of my individual
experience. I must pray without ceasing.

In doing all this I am becoming obedient to the first
Commandment: "Thou shalt have no other gods before
me."[21] That one God means one power, one presence,
one life eternal. As I acknowledge no other power, as I
acknowledge that sin, disease, lack and limitation are not
powers but shadows of belief, without presence, without
power, without jurisdiction, without government or
control—as a matter of fact, without entity or identity—I
am likewise seeing God, understanding God as the great
universal principle of all existence. From that I pass on
to the second great Commandment which Jesus gave,
"Love thy neighbor as thyself."[22]

When you begin and when I begin to understand that every word that has been spoken here tonight, that every word that appears in Scripture, is a universal Word and is, therefore, the truth about all being, and that any other appearance, whether appearing as enemies or friends, is the illusion of sense, then we are loving our neighbors as ourselves. "I and my Father are one" is the universal truth about all beings; then we are loving our neighbors as ourselves.

~ 15 ~

UNIVERSALITY OF GOD

IN THE BOOK OF JOHN, just before the twelfth chapter, we have the Master raising Lazarus from the dead. When Chapter twelve opens the Master is coming to Bethany and there, a supper is prepared for him. The supper is prepared by Mary, the sister of Lazarus, and Lazarus himself is at that supper. Of course, this little town is very much excited about all of these experiences–Lazarus being raised from the dead; Lazarus even eating supper after having been dead and in the tomb. We, of course, might imagine that this was an occasion for rejoicing and for everybody to be happy and celebrating. But that is only because we are apt to think too quickly and to believe that the whole world wants truth, that the whole world wants this evidence of the dead being raised to life and sinners being reformed. In this experience there were two of these events: one the raising of the dead, and the other, Mary Magdalene kissing the feet of the Master, pouring oil upon him–a sinner reformed.

But the "world" as a world does not like these things, and more especially the Church that cannot produce such healings, dares not like them, and here we find the first murmurings of resentment and discontent, rising to greater heights and here the Master realizes that trouble lies ahead.

We are in Chapter twelve beginning with verse 23:
Jesus says, "The hour is come, that the Son of Man
should be glorified. Verily, verily, I say unto you; except
a corn (kernel) of wheat fall into the ground and die, it
abideth alone: but if it die, it bringeth forth much fruit."[1]

Now, here, just for a moment, we have the principle,
the very principle itself, on which my own unfoldment
is based. Everything that you are reading in my writings,
all that you will gather from my classes, is based on that
very statement that unless the seed "fall into the ground
and die," it does not bear fruit. Translating that into our
language of today, it means this: that unless we die to
our humanhood, we cannot be re-born of the spirit; we
cannot bring forth spiritual fruit while continuing to live
as human beings.

Ordinarily in our metaphysical work, and I go back
to my own entrance into the metaphysical field where I
came for healing and enlightenment, the idea with me
then was, "I am a human being, one who knows nothing
of God, and I am sick. My desire is to be a human being
who knows something about God, and who is well."
And that was the extent or the height of my purpose or
intent when I took up the study of Christian Science.
Since then I have met thousands of people in the metaphysical movements, and I have no hesitancy in saying
that for the most part that was their intent—to bring a
sickness to metaphysics, and come out well; to bring a
poverty-stricken purse to the study of truth, and have it
prosper. In most cases—and this is the tragedy—people
seem intent on staying on that level of demonstration; to
want all of the good human things of life and to be freed
of all the discordant human things of life, and continue
merrily on this human way to the age of three score

years and ten, or a few beyond, and then pass on as, ordinarily, mortals do.

For years and years that seemed to be my understanding of the purpose of metaphysics in this age. It was only as the years went on, that I realized that we were only *materia medica* in another form; that we were merely people who healed rheumatism, or consumption, or cancer, or arthritis, but with a different method than the doctors used. We prayed, or we knew the truth, or we did a daily lesson, or we did something of that kind, and ultimately found that our sinful habit had left us, or our disease had left us, or perhaps our supply had grown a little greater. In place of fifty dollars a week, sometimes we earned one hundred dollars and I have known men who even became millionaires, merely through the study and application of truth.

Wonderful as it is to be a healthy human, wonderful as it is to be a wealthy human, if one has enough intelligence to know what to do with the wealth after he gets it, that still is not the goal for those seeking spiritual illumination. There still remain the age old questions: "What is truth? What is God? What is the son of God? What is it to live the spiritual life?"

It is very evident that had the Master just gone on healing sick people or feeding poor people, that he would have come to his end and been celebrated as a great philanthropist and healer. Evidently though, he was carrying his particular work further than that because he was able to reveal to them: "Except a corn of wheat fall into the ground and die, it abideth alone: but if it die, it bringeth forth much fruit." And he followed it up with this verse: "He that loveth his life shall lose it; and he that hateth his life in this world shall keep it unto life eternal."[2]

There you have the answer to the secret of spiritual living. If you attempt to hold on, through your metaphysical work and your metaphysical practice, to the humanhood into which you were born; if you merely think of your metaphysical work and your spiritual work as a means for becoming a better or healthier or wealthier human, in the end you will find that you will lose your life. In other words, you will come to the same end that all humanity comes to—that is, the grave. Some come to it early in life, some in middle years, and some in very late years; but you know that humanity all comes to the grave. And in coming to the grave they come to a place where they are merely making a transition into a denser state of humanhood than the one they had left. For them, death or passing on, is not an advanced step or a progressive step.

Too often in metaphysics, when someone passes on, we hear, "Ah, yes! But now they are free!" That isn't true. It is true only if one passes on while on the progressive, upward spiritual step. Then even if one does succumb, through some human error in the form of accident or disease, even that one failure to demonstrate, will not prevent him from very quickly re-establishing himself on the upward spiritual path. For such as this one, passing on may actually be a release from mortality. The person who really is on the upward spiritual path, even though he fails in one particular demonstration, even though he fails to achieve this one particular healing and passes on from the disease or the accident, even that will not be a barrier to the ascending soul, to the ascending consciousness. It will be only a temporary stopping place, quickly overcome. He will pick up and then that which is often said about those who have passed will become true: "He knows the truth and he is released and is really free."

Those who have been using truth merely for some personal end have not yet caught the first glimpse of what the Master meant when he gave us this great teaching, a teaching so great that one could take those two verses and probably write a set of books on them; those books would have to show what really can't be said in just a few moments–that even good humanhood, or healthy humanhood, is not spiritual life.

Spiritual living is something that does not find any counterpart in the human scale. Spiritual living is entirely a different realm, as different as electricity is from gas, or gas is from whale oil. There are different fields, different levels of consciousness, different types of power. And so, material living and mental living are two strata of one thing, and that one thing is materiality.

But spiritual living is an entirely different universe! Jesus puts it in very strong words, doesn't he? "He that hateth his life in this world shall keep it unto life eternal."[3] Well, it doesn't really mean hate in our sense of the word "hate," but it does mean he who recognizes that any degree of human living is not the spiritual life; he who is willing to see the human sense of existence fade out of his consciousness so that the spiritual sense of life can come in. He then is ready to be raised into the realization of the Christ.

This teaching of the Master does not mean that we are to succumb to death and then find life eternal. To succumb to death means to get more deeply into death, mortality, materiality. No; it means to begin to die daily, now and here, to those things which we have heretofore considered objects of demonstration. In other words, let us stop being concerned over whether or not the body is complaining of something at the moment and being satisfied when the body says, "Oh, I feel much better" or, "I am entirely well!" Let us not be satisfied just because our income has jumped up to one hundred dollars or one thousand dollars per week, or some sum that completely satisfies our every need. Let us not be satisfied, since that is death to our spiritual development.

Our work should be the realization of spirit and spiritual living. Certainly, we will still appear to the world as normal human beings. We will still be so many feet tall and so many inches wide (we hope!); we will still enjoy our food and drink and our automobiles, but the heart will not be in these things. These will just be the "added things," the comfortable things of daily existence. Therein lies the entire difference between hating this life and being willing to die out of this life and finding life eternal. Just that one difference, wherein we accept all the human good as the added things of demonstration, but not the objects of demonstration.

"Now is my soul troubled; and what shall I say?" This is still the Master speaking: "Now is my soul troubled; and what shall I say? Father, save me from this hour: but for this cause came I unto this hour."[4] Surely he can't ask to be saved from it, since that is the purpose of his whole demonstration. But then he follows with: "Father, glorify thy name."[5] That's the secret! "Father glorify thy name." Show forth the glory, the health, the harmony, the eternality of thy being *as* me, as my experience! Not glorify me; not glorify Jesus; not show forth how healthy or wealthy Joel can be, but glorify the name of God, the nature and character of God, by showing forth all that God is, all the harmony, all the perfection, all the eternality and immortality which is of God—show that forth as my individual being!

This spiritual practice does not show forth the wonderful understanding of the practitioner, but rather the harmony of God made evident as your individual health and wealth. Every healing from this basis shows forth the infinite nature and character of God made evident as your individual experience. And so your health, then, is really the perfection of God made manifest individually as the health of your body. Do you see the difference between that, and your or my having a healthy body or a great understanding? Oh, we haven't got a great understanding. There is no such thing as a great understanding. God alone is infinite perfection, and all we can do is show forth the perfection which is God. Whether we show it forth as understanding, or as health, or as wealth, it is still the activity of God being made manifest—the Word becoming flesh and dwelling among us. Do you see all that?

"Lean not unto thine own understanding. In all thy ways acknowledge him, and he shall direct thy paths."[6] Always realize that we are not showing forth the understanding of a man. We are showing forth the spirit, the eternal life which is God, expressed as our individual being. Jesus, then, could not say to the Father, "Save me from this hour,"[7] because it was for this very purpose that he had come to this hour. I hope you are going to make a study of chapter twelve of the Book of John, and catch the great picture of Jesus showing forth, not his understanding, not his demonstration, but showing forth that all that is of the Father is made evident as Jesus' individual being. And to what purpose? That we might learn the principle and go and do likewise.

And what is this principle he has been showing forth to us up to now? That we must die daily. Or, in old Scriptural language, hate our human sense of life. In other words, not to cater to it, nor desire that it be made a little healthier, or dragged out a few more years. But rather, that in turning away from the physical sense of life, we may achieve the spiritual consciousness of life, which is life eternal.

"Then came there a voice from heaven, saying, I have both glorified it and will glorify it again."[8] I, God. I, the very life of your being, always glorifies itself by showing itself forth as your perfect life. "The people therefore, that stood by, and heard it, said that it thundered: others said, An angel spake to him."[9] Of course, that is our individual awareness, isn't it? Sometimes we hear it as if it were the still, small voice just whispering in our ear; sometimes it thunders; and at other times it is a sensing.

Somebody called me very early this morning for help. I was sitting at my machine dictating, and just for a moment I closed my eyes, which is my usual listening attitude, and it really seemed as if God were whispering. It was a voice that said, "Your thinking can't change anything." I had such a sense of release that that ended it. "Your thinking can't change anything." That's how it comes. Just a still, small voice, but it can thunder in our ears, too.

"Jesus answered and said, This voice came not because of me, but for your sakes."[10] Surely you know that! The Master himself knew that the physical sense of life is not life eternal when he stood at the grave of Lazarus and said that it was not for his sake, but for the people's sake that he said his prayer to God that Lazarus come forth. He didn't need any prayer to God; he didn't need even a command for Lazarus to come forth. So far as he was concerned, life is and always has been eternal and eternally manifested. So it was just a little hocus-pocus for the people, for the public, to let them think that the dead was coming to life—in their language—because at that time he couldn't tell them that Lazarus had never died. They probably wouldn't have thought it a miracle.

You remember the story, I am sure, about the man who called the practitioner for help for his wife. She had a wonderful instantaneous healing. The next day he went to give the practitioner a hundred dollar check, saying, "That was wonderful, wonderful work you did for my wife, so I brought you one hundred dollars." The practitioner said, "I didn't do it; God did it." "Oh," said the husband, "I am glad you told me!" Then he tore up the check. Sometimes you see, it is better to put it in plain English!

Now, here is a strange thing, strange if it has not been a somewhat similar experience of one's own, that even the people who saw Lazarus raised from the dead, even those who had been fed in the wilderness, even the multitudes who were healed, didn't believe at this particular point. They were all willing to walk away. The moment the test came, the trial came, the minute there was something not quite regular, even those who had benefited by this healing work were willing to walk away.

Now, don't think for a moment that this applies only to the people of that age. No, it applies to the people of this age, as well. At all times when you enter upon this work as a practitioner or teacher or lecturer, remember this: You are presenting Christ, Christ living, Christ omnipresent, in Christian language; Immanuel, in Hebrew language; Tao, in Chinese language. You are presenting the idea of the very imminence of God. And therefore no one can build you up, since you had nothing to do with it, except to become aware of it, and then become willing to share it. Those who do permit themselves to be built up, to develop into personalities, end up on the cross. There is no way to prevent this because that is the nature of human experience.

We should not be here, as we shall see later, to glorify the personal self, since the personal self, whether by taking thought or by any other means, can of itself do nothing. "I can do all things through Christ."[11] That is true. And Jesus said, "I can of mine own self do nothing."[12] He knew that it was the Father within who did the work. Paul recognized that same thing. Every mystic, every person of spiritual insight, has come to learn that Christ, or God, the presence of God, the infinite, the power, the realization of God, can make water come from the rocks; it can make manna come from the skies; it can multiply the loaves and fishes; but no man of himself can do those things. All power is given to us through God, through this Christ.

So here we have those people deserting the Master. Strangely enough, Isaiah, gave this very prophecy. He said: "He hath blinded their eyes and hardened their heart; that they should not see with their eyes, nor understand with their heart, and be converted, and I should heal them."[13] All those still anchored in the desire for improved humanhood will want their eyes closed, will not want to see this Christ that takes away what appears to the world as ease in matter. Even though it is only a temporary stripping bare, it is so comfortable to go on in this good, healthy, wealthy, human way. So always—and I am only saying this because it shows forth a principle with which we work in this world—humanhood will want to turn itself from the Christ.

Then of course, there were those among the chief rulers also, who "believed on him, but because of the Pharisees they did not confess him."[14] Why did they not confess him? "Lest they should be put out of the synagogue: For they loved the praise of men more than the praise of God."[15] Isn't it a miracle how history repeats itself through all of the ages? But that has a deeper significance, too. It means, actually, that until we come to that place of hating that human sense of life, we also want not so much the praise of men, as the demonstrations of men. Probably we want them for praise; probably some men like to have it said that their metaphysical understanding has brought them a Cadillac instead of a Ford; or perhaps they like to have it said that their metaphysics has given them this healthy body. And so they in that way, would rather have the praise of men than to forget the Cadillac or the healthy body and seek the realization of God.

"For they loved the praise of men more than the praise of God." Watch yourself on that point. Not that you are in danger of wanting the praise of men, but re-translate it, or re-interpret it, and see occasionally, if you are wanting something of men more than something of God; if you aren't wanting a little more of the human comforts rather than that spiritual life which transforms the entire being. On that point, you see, hinges our spiritual demonstration.

"What went ye out for to see?"[16] What is it that you are seeking? Watch that. Is it human good in one form or another? Is it human comfort of one form or another? Is it anything of human nature? If so, there are many paths, there are many ways of achieving it, but this isn't one of them. This spiritual path is a path that may not for the moment, give us all of the human demonstrations we are seeking. But, when we have achieved an awareness of the Christ, a recognition and an acknowledgment and the attainment of the Christ, then all of these things are added—and truly in a greater degree than ever we thought possible when we were trying to demonstrate "things."

Now, Jesus cried and said, "He that believeth on me, believeth not on me, but on him that sent me. And he that seeth me seeth him that sent me."[17] That sounds like a paradox, doesn't it? It sounds like a mystery, but it isn't. There again it is as clear as a bell. If you are thinking of the human, then, of course, you are missing the mark in praising Jesus or believing on the name of Jesus. Missing the mark entirely. And he says so here: "Believeth not on me, but on him that sent me. He that seeth me seeth him that sent me."

The very moment that you begin to see that it isn't a person, it's a principle—God being made evident to you as an individual—you can then, if you like, believe on any individual because that individual is the showing forth of all that God is. "He that seeth me seeth him that sent me." That is, if you are not looking too sharply at this body. But if you are looking at "me," then you are seeing the Father that sent me.

Always differentiate between looking at a man, or looking at a body, and thinking you are seeing me. You are seeing me only when you look behind the eyes, and there see the light that is being made manifest as individual being. When you do this, you are seeing the Father that sent me. Then you won't believe on me as Joel, but you will believe on *Me:* The Word, the life, made manifest as your own individual being, since this universal principle not only appears as Joel, but as John, Bill, and as Mary.

I am come a light into the world, that whosoever believeth on me should not abide in darkness.

And if any man hear my words, and believe not, I judge him not: for I came not to judge the world, but to save the world.

He that rejecteth me, and receiveth not my words, hath one that judgeth him: the word that I have spoken, the same shall judge him in the last day.

John 12:46-48

Remember? God is not mocked! Truth is not mocked! Truth is the judgment. You can't mock truth any more than you can mock the principle of mathematics. You just go fooling around with 2 x 2 is 5 and see what will happen to you. And there won't be any personal judgment upon you, either. But the very principle of mathematics itself will take a toll of all those 2 x 2's that come out to 5. I know that from experience. I am one of those check book operators who gets 2 x 2 are 5. But I don't get away with it! No! God is not mocked. This principle is not mocked. But it isn't a man who judges. It's the principle itself that takes its toll on us.

And now, listen. "For I have not spoken of myself."[18] It sounded above as though he were speaking of himself: "He that seeth me seeth him that sent me."[19] It would seem for a moment, if we did not already know, that he was speaking of himself. We knew better all the time, but now he actually says: "I, of myself, cannot do this, but the Father, he doeth this."

For I have not spoken of myself; but the Father which sent
me, he gave me a commandment, what I should say, and
what I should speak.

And I know that his commandment is life everlasting:
whatsoever I speak therefore, even as the Father said unto
me, so I speak.

John 12:49-50

In other words, truth revealing itself as this individual
being and through this individual being, presents to you
the bread of life. You take it or you leave it. But in
making the decision—and the decision isn't a difficult
one—it's just whether we are to use truth for some
personal purpose in life, or whether we are to develop a
consciousness in which we permit truth to use us, in
which we permit the Father to speak through us, or as
us. That's the difference. And that's the difference in
demonstration.

"In my Father's house are many mansions."[20] In this
God-consciousness there are many states and stages of
consciousness, many states and stages of awareness,
many stages of demonstration. It does not lie with you or
with me to complain if our progress is slow, because if
we do, some day when the progress is too fast, we will
also complain that we are being pushed ahead too fast
and made to do and say things the world is not ready
for. And it would seem then as if we would cry out,
"Father, Father, hold me back. This is too much for me.
This 'meat' is too strong."

Let us not complain at this period if we seem to be
slow in going forward. Let us not complain later when
the going gets rough and the impulse from within, the
drive from within, is so terrific that it doesn't let us have
much sleep at night, or much rest by day, even if we

have to take it out in pounding the pavements or going up into the hills.

All of these things come to those who have embarked on the spiritual path. It is the old story being relived. "Ye have not chosen me, but I have chosen you."[21] When that call comes, when God takes possession of our consciousness, we are compelled, then, to take forward steps that oftentimes we wish we didn't have to take. We are compelled to say things and to do things, to act things, that we know right well outwardly may be misunderstood. That's not for us to say any more than it was for the Master to pray to the Father that this hour be removed, when this was the hour for which he came.

Except a corn of wheat fall into the ground and die, it abideth alone; but if it die, it bringeth forth much fruit.

John 12:24.

~ 16 ~

WHOLENESS OF SPIRIT

As LONG AS WE ARE SPEAKING TODAY, not about the parts of the spirit, but about the wholeness of the spirit, I want to sum up the entire subject by bringing forth, as much as I can, the subject of "the Christ." You will remember that we have used the term "the Christ," as the Christian term for the presence of God; and the Hebrew word "Immanuel," meaning the same thing. And we also referred to the Chinese word, "Tao," meaning the same thing. So we gained a sense of universality in this subject of the spirit of God, or presence of God, or what we in the Christian world term "the Christ." It is necessary that we understand the universality of the Christ, otherwise we get back into orthodox religion in which one church is better or nearer the kingdom of God than another church, or that belonging to this group or this sect or this organization in some way entitles us to benefits of God which our less fortunate brothers do not have.

Now, in our enlightened state, that is really ridiculous. As a matter of fact, it isn't even honest, although the people who teach it are sincere in believing it since they were taught it as children when they had no defense against it. You know the old saying that if you are given a child up to five years of age, the world can take over after that because you have already indoctrinated the child with whatever teaching you wanted him to have. Anything that can be taught a child still in its earlier years, can, of course, be accepted by him with all sincerity and honesty even though it is the most vicious lie.

There isn't any teaching in the world more harmful or more destructive to one's own soul than the belief that the Christ knows anything about a church or a religion or a creed or a sect or any particular group. It is sinful to believe that the Christ is not available to saint and to sinner—please remember that. The most difficult thing for people to believe is that the church did not teach them correctly when it taught them that they must be good in order to get the benefit of God.

You do not have to be good in order to get the benefits of God. Scripture tells us that, "His rain falls on the just and on the unjust."[1] And you will remember that the Master exemplified this by his willingness to heal the woman taken in adultery and the boy born blind—undoubtedly through some claim of syphilis on the part of the parents. In no wise did the Master distinguish between saint and sinner, except of course to caution the sinner to "sin no more,"[2] because once someone does receive the benefits of God, that which would cause him to sin should be eliminated. In other words, this teaching does not encourage anyone to sin. It merely reveals that the Christ is ready and omnipresent wherever you may be, whether you are in sin or in disease or in lack or in prison—no matter where you are—to lift you out of it. And of course, the activity of the Christ which would lift you out of those conditions would so change your consciousness that you could never imagine yourself getting back into that same state of sin or disease, lack or limitation or prison.

We are well aware of the fact that if we had a few hundred thousand dollars worth of bills, of actual currency, we would be able to grasp the value of them and understand what could be done with them. In the same way we are able, through material sense when we have a healthy body, to understand it and know it and enjoy it. But now with this term—the Christ—we come to a different state of consciousness. We come to that which is invisible and intangible to the human sense. It is much like Job speaking of God who, "hangeth the earth upon nothing."[3] Will you remember that? God "hangeth the earth upon nothing." Now, you have all seen pictures of the earth whirling around in space with nothing holding it up (although at one time we believed there had to be a man with broad shoulders to hold it up, and from that we have the symbol of Atlas). To human sense it is impossible that this earth is swinging in space with nothing holding it up, yet that is what we are asked to believe.

In the same way, a doctor can well understand his ability to remove a pimple or a growth. He can well understand his ability to remove germs from the blood with medicine. But it is a very difficult thing for a doctor to believe that one can sit in a hotel room in San Francisco and remove impurities of blood from somebody in Chicago! That, of course, is impossible for material sense to conceive, since material sense is built on that which we call time, space, height, width, and depth. The moment you take a person out of the realm of height, width, depth, time and space, you are leaving him high and dry, because that is all that material sense is composed of, and that is all that it can understand. Now, we are asking ourselves to accept this truth, that there is something that exists that is not included in time or space, that has neither height, width nor depth, and yet is so real that it can provide food for multitudes–actual fish, actual loaves of bread; that it can provide healings for multitudes of any form of sin and disease, that it actually can take a person out of poverty and raise him into affluence.

Well, that's the story of Aladdin's lamp isn't it? It exists in the realm of that which is not tangible to sense, and in that case of the story of Aladdin it is called wishing. Now, we have gone further than wishing, we have gone further than desiring. We have gone to this place in consciousness where we accept as real, as omnipresent, as all-powerful, that which we can never see, hear, taste, touch, or smell. Isn't that a wonderful state of consciousness? You either are in a realm of insane belief, or you have touched some great reality that the world doesn't know.

The Christ is the spirit of God appearing as your individual consciousness. The Christ is an ever-present power and a reality, and even though it exists as that which can never become tangible to the five physical senses, It appears tangibly as food, as transportation, as homes, as companionship. Let us prove this for a moment with the Master. You remember the scene? He is talking to the woman at the well of Samaria. He has asked for water. The conversation has gone along to the place where she is made to wonder how he could produce water, since he has no bucket. And then he tells her that if she knew who he was, she would know that he could give her water that would be a wellspring of eternal life; and "whosoever drinketh of that water that I shall give him shall never thirst."[4] Well, of course he was talking to her about the infinite, invisible principle which would appear tangibly as water or as inspiration or as spiritual awareness, which it did, because she immediately recognized him as the Christ.

We go along in that same scene with the disciples offering to bring meat to the Master because he had probably missed his lunch hour. And again, we have the answer: "I have meat to eat that ye know not of."[5] Well, did he actually have what we call meat? No. he had this "meat" of the spirit, this sense of the Christ, this awareness of the omnipresence of good; and he knew that even if he missed his luncheon and many more meals, that he still would be fed and fed tangibly, and that he wouldn't be hungry.

There again you have the infinite invisible, this Christ which is intangible to human sense but which appears visibly as meat, as sustenance, as rest. It is this very spirit which enables those on the spiritual path to eat less food than they did while they were wholly in the material sense of life; it enables them to sleep fewer hours than were required when they were living wholly in the body and depending on its functions. In other words, this spirit feeds the very body with what the world would call food, and yet it is an invisible food. It also supplies the body with rest, even while the body is not lying on a bed or lying in unconsciousness. One can be wholly conscious and about his work and receive the same rest that others receive in sleep upon a bed—probably an even higher sense of rest.

The only thing necessary in order to receive this visible expression of an invisible substance is your own ability to discern Christ where a human being seems to be. Now humanly, we look out through the eyes and we see men and women, we see children and adults, and we see white and black. But when this spiritual sense is discerned, the only things we are consciously aware of are children of God, or the very presence of God. There is no division in one's thought about whether it is male or female or whether it is young or old. There is the realization of all, "one in Christ." That is part of the subject of "spiritual wholeness." Spiritual wholeness is the ability to realize—not separateness; not separate men and women; not separate people with separate interests—but the one, the same, divine love made manifest as individual being, individual you and me.

We do not lose our individuality. We gain more individuality. The more of God that appears through us, the greater the degree of what the world calls individuality. Sometimes it is called personality. Every quality attached to a person as personality should be understood as some phase or facet of God shining through, and not as some personal quality of that individual.

Jesus told us that, "I speak not of myself,"[6] and: "He that seeth me seeth him that sent me."[7] Therefore, he wasn't raising himself up to Fatherhood. He was showing that the Fatherhood was all, and was eliminating that which was personal self. But he didn't do it by blurring his face or his speech, or making his tones monotonous or deadly. I doubt if the Master could have said those marvelous words of his in any deadly monotone. There is such power, such force, in his message that I doubt if it could be delivered in any "milk-soppy" way. Let us agree on this then, that the individuality of God is infinite and that it appears infinitely, and that if you or I show forth any qualities that the world calls desirable, let us at least give God credit for being the source and foundation and reality of whatever those qualities may be. Above all things, let us not hide our personality or our individuality, but let us realize once and for all that it is the infinite, invisible God appearing outwardly to the world as whatever qualities of character or qualities of appearance we may have.

Now, we have come to this point where we are facing a practical world. We are facing a world in which there are banks, money, and bills to be paid; and at our present time, there is the space between your home and downtown, or your home and your office, and that space must be traveled with cars or automobiles or trains or airplanes or ships. We are in the practical world where food must be paid for, and all of the rest of the practical experiences must continue to go forward, since we are not to leave the world. Jesus did not say that we should be taken out of the world, but that we should be left in the world; *in* the world, though not of it. Now, in the world we must conform to the ways of the world, at least in the sense of eating, drinking and sleeping and paying for the drinking and eating and sleeping, and all the rest of these things that go with us. Therefore, we will engage in all of the activities that the world engages in—commerce, art, industry, healing work, publishing work, printing work—all of the practical things of life. But we will do it with this distinction from the world: We will not look to our own cleverness, our own education or experience or inheritance. We will look to the Christ, the infinite, invisible spirit within us, to lead us in every rightful way and direct us in just the activities which we should perform at this given moment.

In other words, if I am to appear in this place, on this platform, at this time, there must be an inner guidance to bring me here. When I am here as the result of that inner guidance, of that divine wisdom, I find those out here who are ready and prepared for this particular mission. If I left that infinite invisible out of my calculations, I might have recourse to some of the world's ways, like advertising, and have ten times more people present than are here now. That way, though, I might have only one-tenth of the number of people capable, able, and willing to receive and respond to this message. But with Christ, which is my consciousness and your consciousness—with that Christ, recognized, acknowledged, and always listened to—that Christ, operating in and through and as your consciousness and mine, brings those of us together who have this in common; namely, that we are all of the same path, we are all of one mind in one place, seeking the same unfoldment. Now, we may have come from widely different backgrounds. We are Jews and Protestants and Catholics here, and we may also be Muslims and Hindus and Chinese, Confucians or Taoists. But regardless of what our backgrounds may have been, we have progressed out of that background and we are here together at this moment, of one mind and of one spirit and of one intelligence, and with the ability to understand and receive this particular message.

The same truth applies to your own experience. It has been the Christ operating as your consciousness that has led you step by step to this hour in this room; but also remember that that infinite invisible in you will continue to operate, will continue to lead you as much further as you can go—if necessary, to the fullness of the Christ mind.

Don't forget that teachers and teachings are only temporary things. They are but temporary points of consciousness on the way. We come to the place where we find that the mind that was in Christ Jesus is our own individual mind. Then we ourselves have really become a teaching and a teacher. The Christ is still with us. Every spiritual message is received directly from the Christ. Does that mean from a man who lived in Galilee two thousand years ago? No! Jesus Christ himself said, "Before Abraham was, I am."[8] The Jesus Christ that taught in Galilee was teaching two thousand years before that and is teaching today. That state of consciousness appears and reappears throughout history. At one time you might call it Moses, another time Krishna, another time Jesus Christ, at still another time any one of our modern metaphysical teachers. It is a state of consciousness expressing itself through a vehicle we call Joel right now, but it would be expressing itself if there were no Joel here. Your own state of consciousness has prepared you for the receptivity of this message at this time, so that nothing could keep it from you. In the same way, the mind which was in Christ Jesus, which existed before Abraham, and probably was made manifest to the world as Abraham, Isaac, Jacob, Isaiah, Elisha, Elijah, Jesus Christ, Paul, John, that state of consciousness is your individual consciousness awaiting your acknowledgment of it, or your acknowledgment of its wholeness. You acknowledge it in part every day, since if you have a headache or a little rheumatism or a cold you turn within yourself and you expect a healing through it. And of course if the claim is a little more severe or serious in the world sense, you call on a practitioner. You don't expect that practitioner's flesh and blood to do anything for you. You know that it is his degree of unfolded consciousness. It is probably a degree of consciousness higher or more unfolded than your own, although it is still the Christ consciousness; it is merely that the individual called the practitioner has unfolded a greater sense of it and you look to him for the healing of the more serious things.

Ultimately that state of consciousness unfolds within you until you can handle a claim regardless of its name or nature or degree, and that makes you a practitioner, and ultimately a teacher. All this time, only one thing has been doing it. The mind that was in Christ Jesus—and it was doing it in proportion to your degree of unfoldment of it. It is possible to walk on the water, actually, physically. It is possible to walk through the wall, actually, physically. But it takes a higher degree of this unfolded consciousness than we have attained here. We have attained a mighty measure of that Christ consciousness; we have witnessed tremendous unfoldment of it, since you know as well as I do that the metaphysical world is performing healings that only could have been believed in the time of the Master. And you know that it is that same mind that manifested itself in Galilee that is performing the healing work today; only that mind appears as your practitioner or mine, as your teacher or mine.

The Christ, then, this Immanuel, this presence of God, is the mind which was in Christ Jesus; and as it fed the multitudes then, it will feed the multitudes now. But you and I must begin in an individual way. We must each day give recognition and acknowledgment to this Christ, even though it is invisible, even though we can't see it, hear it, taste it, touch it, or smell it. We must give the recognition that "I am never alone. The Father is always with me. The Christ is omnipresent, and it goes

before me and acts within me as protection, as coun-
selor, and as mighty warrior when necessary. It is all
things to me in all my ways. It is the reality, the actual
force of being. It is a mighty power." Therefore, I can
return to Scripture and say, "Not by might, nor by
power, but by my spirit."[9] I can return to Scripture and
say again that this is the same power which Moses
recognized when he said, "Fear ye not, stand still, and
see the salvation of the Lord."[10] It is the same power
which we recognize when we are called upon for help
and hear the still, small voice say, "Don't battle the
disease; don't battle that sin; the battle is not yours, but
God's." The spirit of God in you, this Christ, is the
master of all situations. It is the dispeller of the illusions
of sense, regardless of whether the illusion appears as
sin, disease or death, or whether it appears as a sinful
person, a diseased person or a dead person. The one
thing that dispels the illusion is this very presence of
God, which we recognize more in the stillness and in
quietness than we do in mental jugglery.

Only when the human senses are very still can we
become aware of the still small voice; only when we
have learned to refrain from battling an error which has
no real existence; only when we have acknowledged
that regardless of the sin or the disease before us, it
really doesn't exist as that, since God is infinite good and
can never be responsible for that which appears as these
erroneous pictures. Once we've recognized that, and I
call that the nature of error, when we have recognized
the nature of error to be nothing but pictures, mental
pictures, illusions, mirages, suggestions, coming to us
either for acceptance or rejection. When we have come
to that point, we have come to the point of the Christ,

which recognizes there is no need to fight, there is no need to go running from door to door looking for a position, there is no need to spend a thousand dollars advertising for work, for customers. "Stand still, and see the salvation of the Lord!"[11]

If divine wisdom reveals to us the need for human footsteps, we may take them but we will find that in taking them, we are not taking them hit or miss. We are not spending days and days knocking at doors; we are led quickly to the right place at the right time, even to the right advertisement. We do take human footsteps, but we take those human footsteps under divine guidance; then we have less of them to take, and we have no foot sores with them!

Let me make this clear. Even if you were to accept what I have said today as being true, that still would be only the first step in your development, and then your unfoldment. This consciousness must develop in one and unfold in one. "I have meat to eat that ye know not of."[12] Yet the declaration that I have it never brought it into existence. It was practicing it, relying on it, trusting it, even in what seemed very adverse circumstances, sometimes even in events that took time to solve. Yet the standing on the truth gradually brought the light, the sense of all-presence, of omnipresence, of a Christ presence, of an actual thing that I can feel right here. And that comes through devotion to this work.

It really becomes necessary for us to make the decision whether we are to serve God or Mammon; whether we are to serve the human sense of existence and battle it out on that level and be successful, or whether we shall learn to find a rest from mental and physical struggling and let this Christ take possession.

We never take possession of it. We never use truth. We never use God. We never use spirit. It is the spirit that touches us, transforms us, and then picks us up and does for us and through us and as us, all that is to be done. The great mistake is in believing you can be a human being and have a great big knowledge of the spirit. It can never be that way at all.

In the degree that you are still a human being, in that degree you are lacking the understanding of spirit. It is when we die daily to the human sense of power, to the human sense of intellect, to the human sense of understanding, and become imbued with the spirit, that then we go out and become active. And of course, once we are touched by the spirit, it is impossible to be lazy anymore—mentally lazy or physically lazy. It will not give us rest; it will not give us peace while we are trying to do nothing! This is an actual opening of consciousness to the presence and power of the Christ, until it—the spirit—touches us and makes us new again. When it does, the new life begins.

~ 17 ~

GOD, OMNIPRESENT
AND THE ONLY POWER

ORIGINALLY WE CAME TO THE STUDY OF TRUTH for our own good. Most of us have come to this work because of some sin or disease or lack in our experiences. Probably some of you came seeking only God. But I think the experience of most practitioners is that they find that most come to this truth seeking for release from the cares and the ills of the world. I came that way. Most of the people I know have come that way. For awhile it is a very satisfying experience to learn that physical ills can be met through prayer or treatment, through spiritual power.

It is a very thrilling thing to experience a healing, especially if *materia medica* has said that the disease is serious or fatal. Some of these healing experiences will never be forgotten by those who have had them. After the First World War, I was given the very pleasant news that I had less than three months to live, and there was nothing that *materia medica* could do to save me. There was no known healing agency, no known cure for my trouble. As a matter of fact, in all the years that have passed since then, they still have no cure for that particular disease. In three months, though, I was completely healed, so completely healed that there has never been a sign or trace of the trouble in all the years since 1921! I have had many other healings of that nature through spirit, and I have also witnessed thousands of healings. Many minor claims, true, but some very major ones also, according to *materia medica.*

I don't have to rehearse all that for most of you, because probably everyone here has had some similar experience, either with disease or with sin. I have told this before, I don't know whether in these talks or not, but certainly in classes, that in 1928, just as I was sitting with a practitioner, all of the smoking habit, drinking habit, and card playing habit disappeared. These were not great vices, but errors according to our spiritual way of living. All of these disappeared in that one two-hour experience, never to return. It was in that experience in 1928 that not only did healing of smoking and drinking and card playing and a few other minor human errors take place, but illumination came, a lifting of consciousness above what we might call the earth plane. And let me state that never in all the years that have gone by since, have I completely come down to earth again! Yet I have had many problems during that time—many. But as I have found out, all of them were in relationship to my own development.

I turn this into a testimonial meeting for one purpose only and that is to illustrate the beginning of my work, as it is illustrative of the experiences of most of you. It is a typical case. It is typical of most of those who come into the metaphysical world, whether through Christian Science, as I originally came, or Unity, New Thought or any of the other metaphysical approaches.

As the years unfolded, I began to find a dropping away, a lessening of satisfaction in my ordinary work.

Soon after that illumination in 1928, I started to practice, and by 1930 I was professionally in the work. At first it was a thrill to sit down with sick people and see them lifted back into health. At first it was a thrill to be called out into a home where someone was dying, to sit with him awhile and then greet him in the office a few days later. Yes, it was a thrill. In those first days it was an experience that came frequently, because in my youthful innocence I didn't know how it was done. That made it simpler and easier to accomplish. It was just necessary to sit quietly, to be at peace, to feel the presence of the spirit, and then the next thing to hear, "I feel wonderful!"

For awhile, as I say, that was a thrill. Then came the realization, "I wonder what I am doing in this work? I wonder if I am becoming a doctor? I wonder if I am here just to stop people's headaches or colds or flu or cancer? And *why*? What is so wonderful about stopping somebody's pain or setting him free from some ill so he can go back to his regular human ways of living? After all, to keep on at this rate is merely to give people a few years of non-pain, where they may have had pain, or a few more years of experience here on earth." I remember it came to me one time that all I was doing was helping people to change the dates on their tombstones!

Then this new unfoldment came to me and began to bring about these healings not merely for the sake of the healing, but as part of spiritual regeneration. In other words, my thought and activity centered more on opening the consciousness of people to the realization of the presence of God and the power of God and the ever-availability of God. I found, then, a greater sense of peace and joy in my work. The healings took place, but no longer were these associated, at least in my thought, with just turning pain into ease, or disease into health, or lack into abundance. Now it seemed to me I was more nearly fulfilling the mission of the Master when he specifically said, "Take no thought for your life."[1] He gave us the wonderful messages that it is the Father's good pleasure to give us the kingdom, that in seeking the kingdom of God, all these things would be added unto us. There would be no use going after them, no use trying to demonstrate, no use trying to achieve them or accomplish them, since they were going to be added without any effort—if we found the kingdom of God.

In working along that line, the next thing that posed itself was this: Is this spiritual power something that can be utilized only for the benefit of an individual, or is it something that can be made available to the world? And it was while studying the life and works of Buddha, that great light dawned in my thought. It was when I came to that passage in which Buddha told of his desire to do something after he realized that there were sin, disease and death in the world. He indicated that at no point did it come to him to think about healing people. At no point did it enter his thought that it would be a nice thing to cure people of their sins or diseases. The only thing that registered with him was: "Is there a principle that will eliminate sin, disease and death from the world?"

That's tremendous, do you know it? Is there a principle that will eliminate sin, disease and death from the world? Not, is there a principle or law that will cure this one or that one, or fail to cure this one or that one, but, is there a principle which, if we understand its operation, would absolutely take sin, disease and death from the world? From that moment on, that became my prayer, my meditation. From that moment on, I sought a principle which, when understood, would not only cure some person, but would actually take sin and disease out of the world.

Well it will take the work of the next few generations to find out whether such a principle has been re-discovered. Buddha did discover that principle. Without question he found it. His illumination revealed the principle that there is no sin, disease or death; that these are not realities, but are mere beliefs in human thought, which, when recognized, are made to disappear. Buddha did wonderful healing work, and so did his disciples, until his work was organized. That ended this great work.

Now, whether or not that principle has been re-discovered, whether or not that principle will work to rule sin, disease and death out of human consciousness, time will tell. But this point we have now come to; this is really a new place in our individual experience. There are conditions in the world today, and there always have been, which promise evil and destruction to the world. It doesn't matter whether one believes that the New Deal might do it, or whether Socialism or Communism might do it, or whether an atomic bomb might do it. That is not important. The point is that any of these or all of these are, at the present time, suspect; that people throughout the world are beginning to fear them. There is great fear in the world. You don't have to know a great many people to find out how great that fear is. Fear of another war; fear of atomic warfare; fear of germ warfare.

With all of this fear in the world, there has also come the opposite side of the picture. We are beginning to hear people talk of a spiritual power with which to overcome the atom bomb or the next war or the next depression. We are beginning to read in print that nothing will stop this coming catastrophe except spiritual power. We know that even people who are not interested in metaphysics, who know nothing about metaphysics, are talking about spiritual power being a possibility–as a matter of fact, being the only possibility–of preventing these horrible, feared affairs in the world.

Now it is a wonderful thing to read all this about spiritual power. It is a wonderful thing to be told that in this age we will make a greater advance in spiritual power and spiritual understanding than ever before. It is a marvelous thing to read in print that more and more people are turning to spiritual thought, to spiritual power. But, have you ever stopped to think that no one has told us what this spiritual power is and how we are to utilize it? That's the question. This thing of reading that spiritual power might do it, or that spiritual power can do it, is a beautiful thing. But what is spiritual power? How do you go about using spiritual power to overcome the effects of atomic warfare, or prevent it? How would you go about bringing spiritual power to bear on problems? What is the spiritual power? How does it operate? And who is to do the operating?

Now, before we get to that point where spiritual power really does these wonderful things, some of us will have to know a lot more than we know now about spiritual power and how to bring it into our experience. So, back again to those healings which have taken place in our experience. These have come about through this spiritual power. If something has been healed in the metaphysical world, it has been healed through spiritual power. The spiritual power was brought into experience by the practitioner most of the time, though occasionally by the student. Mostly, as you know, the practitioner did the work and the patient just said, "Thank you, that was beautiful!"

Sometimes an individual has been able to work out his own problems. Usually when that happens, he ultimately becomes a practitioner himself. Now, what was the spiritual power that was brought into action to heal a disease or overcome a sin? We could start with the statement that it was the power of God, but that would be just as mystifying as saying it was spiritual power. It would be true; it is a true statement; it is the power of God. But there again, what is the power of God, and how does it operate? I want this to be clear to all of us: Spiritual power, is a power that is based on the realization of the allness of God, and actually is the realization of the unreality of that which has appeared as the power of disease, or the power of sin. There is where spiritual power becomes evident as healing.

Any church in the world will tell you that God is all, or that God is everything, that God is all-power. And yet those statements have not healed diseases in the orthodox church except in those rare instances where the minister himself may have been of a very spiritual nature and through his own nature, not through the teaching of the church, not through declaring God to be all, caught some degree of the Christ. Minister, rabbi, priest–some individual–had caught some degree of the Christ, and it did the healing.

It was only when the metaphysical world came into being that healing could take place, not just hit or miss, not just when some spiritually developed soul came along and performed healings, but with real regularity as the result of a principle or rule or law. The principle of healing is based on the allness of God, but the allness of God is never brought into actual demonstration except in proportion as an individual comes to know and realize the nothingness, the lack of power, in what appears as sin or disease. To the human senses disease is very real. As a matter of fact, some forms of it can actually be seen under a microscope and some forms do not even require a microscope because you can see them with the unaided eye. And yet spiritual power reveals that there isn't a bit of power in that disease, that the power exists not in the disease itself, but in the universal belief or fear about the disease.

Now, if a single healing has ever taken place in the history of the world—and of course you all know that there have been millions of such healings—through the realization of the non-power of that which appears as infection or contagion or germ, if even one case was actually healed through that awareness, then a principle is thus discovered, and that principle is the non-power, the unreality of all that would appear to sense in the form of what we call error, sin or disease. That is the spiritual power.

Now, if that is true, and I am one who believes it so firmly that I spend my life living only for that purpose, then it becomes necessary that each one of us in some measure and in some degree realize too, that whatever forces are in operation in this world that claim to have the power to produce evil, to produce death, lack or limitation, are not powers. It becomes necessary for us to know that the human thought throughout the world that plots and plans these things, either consciously or ignorantly, is not power. And don't forget this: There are more men and more women plotting and planning the destruction of human society ignorantly than there are those doing it viciously. Don't forget that. It isn't always some schemer sitting in a room plotting that the world has to fear. They are so few, and their power in and of itself so little, even from the human standpoint, that they are not the ones to be feared. It is really the ignorant dupes of those people, the ignorant do-gooders who become the tools of these, who encircle the globe and ultimately bring about these evil conditions.

In the human experience they are as powerful as infection and contagion are in the realm of disease. In other words, nobody here, nobody well grounded in metaphysics, would ever declare that infection and contagion aren't serious threats in the human world, when believed in by the human world. All one has to do is think back to the flu epidemic or to the "virus X" epidemic or to the polio epidemics to know that in the human world, these human beliefs operate as law and act to produce their own image and likeness in disease. But if a metaphysical treatment has proven that these infections and contagion are not power, then it is our duty next to prove that the very thoughts, the very beliefs of a political nature, of a governmental nature, of an economic nature, which would threaten to be as disastrous as an epidemic, are likewise not a power.

I should like to tell you of the experience of New York State when its legislature was debating the legalization of the Christian Science practice. A doctor addressed the legislature and said that if this form of practice were legalized, in one generation all of civilization would be wiped out, every human would disappear off the face of the earth. And he proved it! He had the

figures with him; he had all of his papers; he proved
mathematically that he was correct because one person
would get this infection or contagious disease and
neglect it through Christian Science treatment, and that
neglect would cause some member of his or her family
to contract the disease; then, of course, the neighbor
would come down with it, and then the person across
the street, and then the children in the schoolhouse on
the corner; and so, mathematically, following the
numbers he gave, it was easy to see that in just one
generation there would be no people left on earth. Well
of course, that gave the attorney for the Christian
Scientists the opportunity to suggest that a postponement
in the case be declared, to see if this really worked out
that way. I believe it was a year later when they met.
They found that so far, New York State at least was not
being wiped out through infection or contagion despite
the neglect that the people were experiencing. The bill
passed, and ever since then Christian Science practice
has been legalized in that state.

Similar experiences took place in other states. In
Massachusetts a doctor claimed that if they could prove
the healing of one case of leprosy he would have no
objection to the legalizing of metaphysical practice.
They brought forth a doctor, a physician from St. Louis,
Missouri, who had been condemned by his own associ-
ates and declared ill of leprosy, and who was on his way
to the leper colony in Louisiana. That man had five days
between the time he received the diagnosis and the time
he had to leave his home, and in those five days he was
healed through metaphysical treatment–Christian
Science treatment. He came as a witness to the legislature in Massachusetts and brought with him all the

evidence, all the diagnoses of these physicians, and also their statements of his cure. After that, such practice was legalized in Massachusetts.

I am rehearsing this for one purpose: to show that the things that the world calls dangerous—infection and contagion, when the human world believes in the power of infection and contagion—can be nullified and overcome through spiritual power; and, that spiritual power is the recognition and realization of the fact that that which claims power, or that for which power is claimed by the medical world, actually isn't power.

Now, everyone in this room who has witnessed a healing of contagious or infectious disease is a witness to the fact that the infection or the contagion is not power. Most women in metaphysics have at one time or other burned themselves in their kitchens and have proved the painlessness of it and the healing of it, so that they are living witnesses to the fact that the laws of matter are not laws. Those laws are beliefs and they are nullified the moment "one with God," "one with truth," comes along and realizes that that which is appearing as sin or disease, infection or contagion, is not law, is not power.

It follows that when we talk of spiritual power, we are talking about power of a consciousness imbued with the truth that only that which emanates from God is power, that only that which emanates from divine mind or divine love or divine principle of the universe is power. That which men set up as power isn't power at all. It isn't even law. It operates as such and it acts as such, but "one with God is a majority." One in this truth is a majority. So, when a practitioner imbued, inspired with this truth—the truth of the nature of error, the truth that error in and of itself, whether appearing as this form or as that, is not power, is not cause, can't produce anything, and that only our reaction to it gives it the power—such a practitioner is imbued with spiritual power.

It isn't enough to know that God is all and that God is love. It isn't enough to go around singing hymns of praise about God and to God. As long as there is a belief in our thought that God is some mysterious power that is going to cure disease or heal or reform sinners, or that God is going to overcome some form of error, we are not imbued with spiritual power.

Spiritual power is the realization that God alone, good alone, spirit alone, is power; and that anything that appears in the form of human experience isn't power at all! Nobody can have this power until he realizes that. Now, once we have utilized this spiritual power, this understanding of the nothingness of what appears as error; once we have realized it in the healing of a cold or a headache or a corn or a bunion, and have gone on further and further and further until we actually have seen cancers healed, tuberculosis healed, tumors healed, until we have seen entire sections of communities actually healed of all things (in the flu epidemic we saw practitioners go out and heal whole neighborhoods, even though the people were not metaphysicians), not until we have come to that point do we have the right to go to others and say, "What about national or international evils?"

The atomic bomb can't throw itself. A war can't declare itself. A panic can't happen of itself. A depression can't come of itself. It takes the thoughts of men to produce those experiences. The questions that we come to are: "Is human thought power? Is human thought capable of such evil?" The answer is: "Yes! Yes, it definitely is—just as germs are capable of spreading diseases." That is *until* "one with God" comes along to become a majority. This "one" understands that human thinking, whether individual or collective, is not power.

You know, it is an interesting thing to watch some of the metaphysical healing work, especially that part which approaches the field of psychosomatic medicine in which power is given to the human thought. Here are recognized such teachings that resentment causes rheumatism, jealousy causes cancer, and so on. At one time it was sincerely believed that this was true—this teaching had wide circulation. As a matter of fact it was a great part of the original Christian Science teaching until Mrs. Eddy recognized the nothingness of it and wrote her students telling them to return to her all documents that had psychosomatic "lists" in them. (This teaching, though, has been perpetuated in a portion of the Christian Science movement but you can easily discover whether healing work is done by the practitioners who apply such techniques.)

Wherever in this work you find people of a developed spiritual consciousness, you will find people who have come to the recognition that human thought is an avenue of awareness, but it *isn't* a power. You can't sit there—all of you put together—and change this button on my coat into a diamond! (If you can, I would appreciate your doing it!) And all of the world put together couldn't sit down and malpractice one person into sickness—unless that person wanted to give up his sovereignty of thought and say, "Yes, Yes! I give my body over to you! Go ahead and make me sick! I believe you have power over me." Yes, you might malpractice that person. But you couldn't malpractice the person who knows the

spiritual truth that God gave man dominion over the sea
and over the air and over the water and over all the
things in and on and above the earth. Whoever knows
that one truth is free of malpractice; whoever knows his
own God-given dominion, is free.

Why, the New Testament is full of "All that I have is
thine."[2] Jesus' whole prayer was that the Father should
glorify him with *his* glory. Can you imagine being
glorified with that, and then someone giving you a
headache by thinking you were sick? Or wishing you
were sick? Let's be through with that nonsense! The
human mind is an avenue of awareness. Through my
human thinking I can become aware that you are here,
but I can't with my human thinking bring you here. No
treatment ever known would bring anybody here except
the true treatment of the omnipresence of God. That isn't
bringing somebody in; it is realizing he is already here.

Over and over I call attention to that great prayer the
Hebrew prophet offered when his servant thought that
the enemy was too strong for them. He prayed and said:
"Open his eyes, that he may see!" And when the servant's eyes were opened, he saw that "the mountain was
full of horses and chariots of fire."[3] That prayer didn't
put those warriors there; thinking didn't do it. Oh, no!
Through the inspired consciousness of the prophet it was
evident that they were already there, because of God's
omnipresence. That's what put them there. God's
omnipresence. So with us. The inspired prayer, the
inspired thought, of any individual will open his eyes to
the truth of the omnipresence of God appearing as
dominion and life and truth and love, soul, spirit, purity.
But I promise you that none of that thinking will ever
bring the devil there. Nor ever feel that there is a devil

there, since in God's infinite being there is no such thing as a power of evil.

Now again, I am but using this as an illustration for the greater. Can we, through knowing this truth of God's omnipotence, of good's omnipotence–the omnipotence and omnipresence of spirit, soul and mind–can we be one with God and be such a majority that we can nullify all the vicious and ignorant human thought, so that it will not operate as the experience of the people of the world? Each time now that you read about spiritual power doing that, don't put it out of your mind saying, "I hope that's true" or "I wish that were true" or "I believe that is true." Utilize that spiritual power. We here are a very, very small group; all the metaphysicians in the world are a very small group but they may be great enough to overcome this belief that human thought is a power if they can get back to the real truth of being that the mind of God alone is power.

I have seen more healings through realizing that human thought was not power than I ever have through any other form of treatment I have ever known. I have studied these works. I have been in it long enough to know what the different teachings are, and certainly have investigated enough; and I can still see, after more than nineteen years, more work brought successfully forward through knowing that human thought wasn't power, that human hatred wasn't power, and that jealousy, envy, malice, resentment, couldn't create anything. Whether that hatred was in your thought toward someone else or in someone else's thought directed toward you, it could have no power.

When we begin to catch the tiniest glimpse of that truth we are ready for the experience of the Christ.

Never doubt this for a minute—Christ is a reality! Christ is an experience that any one of us can have, and can have at will, at any moment, any day, any week. Christ governs and controls our individual experience in proportion as we are able and ready to accept this great truth of God's omnipotence and omnipresence, the realization that all that masquerades as human thought, human will, human desire, lust, greed, animosity, is not power. These are shadows of a belief without anything to sustain them but our own fear of them, our own acceptance of them, as power.

What is this Christ that we may enjoy, which, if we prove it individually, we may ultimately hope to prove it collectively? Christ must be made to live in your experience and in mine. Christ is reality, but Christ must be made manifest through your *conscious* desire, through your *conscious* effort, through the *conscious* activity of your daily being.

You know, the great mystery is that God is the mind and consciousness of individual me; God is your mind and mine; God is your consciousness and mine. We don't have to go up here on a cloud for God. We don't have to contact God or get "at one" with God. God is right here where I am standing. "The place whereon thou standest is holy ground."[4] "I and my Father are one."[5] "He that seeth me seeth him that sent me."[6] Right here. "Whither shall I go from thy spirit? . . . If I make my bed in hell, behold, thou art there."[7]

Right here and now, God is the mind of me, the soul of me, and the consciousness of me. Without this understanding, we have no hope of bringing forth the Christ into our experience, since we will be looking for it where it doesn't exist—out here, separate and apart from our own being. If we come to that knowledge even intellectually, that Scripture is true and that God *is* love, but that God is not love out there; that God is the love that is expressed *here,* where I am; that God *is* mind, but not a divine mind somewhere out there; that God is the divine mind of my being and yours right here, then we have taken the first step toward the demonstration of Christ.

Christ is that state of consciousness, your consciousness and mine, where the hate and the fear and love of error has been removed. If, in the tiniest degree you can lose your fear of error—whether it is the fear of human thought or human emotion; whether it is the fear of somebody else's wrong thinking or your own wrong thinking; whether it is the fear of universal mortal thinking or whether it is the fear of infection or contagion or lack or limitation—if in a measure fear can be removed from your consciousness, in that degree your consciousness is Christ consciousness.

Of course, when we attain the fullness of Christ, that is when we can walk on water because we no longer have a fear of sinking or a fear of losing our lives. The only reason we don't walk on water now is the belief that we have a life and we can lose it if we sink into the water. Once we have lost the idea that we have a life of our own and really come into the realization that God is our life, we will walk on water too.

However, we are not really thinking of that point. We are thinking only of this point: that in the measure that we lose our fear of this world, in the measure that we are able to repeat the Master's words to Pilate, when we can say to our particular Pilate—whether it be sin, disease, lack, limitation, lonesomeness—"Thou couldest have no power at all against me, except it were given thee from above,"[8] then in that measure we are developing our sense of Christ.

Christ, being our very own consciousness, appears to us in tangible form. When you go back to Scripture, you will find that the ravens fed the prophet Elijah and that later the widow fed him; you will find that Moses drew manna out of the skies and water out of the rocks; you will find that Jesus fed the multitudes with a few loaves and fishes and he told Peter he would find his tax money in the mouth of a fish. What are these demonstrations? They are the consciousness of Christ appearing in tangible form. They are the very consciousness of the Master appearing outwardly as form, or as the form of the moment as it did with Colonel Rickenbacker when he was lost at sea and "his" Christ appeared as birds on his head, or as fish jumping out of the water into the life-raft. He had no fishing line, he had no gun to shoot with, but the fish came to him and the birds came to him. Why? Because of his realization of this great truth. He realized this great truth, that all he had to do was to sit still and fold his hands and know that his good would flow to him. Out of where? Out of the skies? Out of the air? No. Out of his consciousness!

You see, our good comes from the depths of our own consciousness. And if we haven't got any depths to our own consciousness, it doesn't come. Probably a lot of it stays away from us because we don't know that it comes from the depths of our own consciousness. We are waiting for it to come from outside, we may even think it is going to come from the practitioner or from our teacher. No, it isn't. It is going to come from the depths of our own consciousness. Once we realize God as our consciousness, we can expect anything to flow outside, anything that we need at the moment. Out of that consciousness comes our safety and our security. Out of our own consciousness we find ourselves with God, in the secret place of the most high. We find that consciousness comes as the 91st Psalm or, let's put it the other way: the 91st Psalm is our own consciousness: "He that dwelleth in the secret place of the most High"[9]; he that dwelleth in spiritual consciousness; he that dwelleth in the consciousness of Christ, of good; he that dwelleth in the consciousness of the truth that Pilate isn't a power.

Always remember that when you read about spiritual power you are not reading about a power that somebody else is generating to protect you. You are reading about a power inherent in your own consciousness, which as you recognize it, will come forth as your 91st Psalm and your 23rd Psalm. Never forget this. The only reason the world is in trouble is because it has accepted the belief that God is up there in the sky. The only reason the world is in trouble is because the world hasn't accepted the teaching of the Master that the kingdom of God is within you. It is looking everywhere else in the world for the kingdom of God, but "within you." As I have said before, they sent Bibles with steel plates in them to the boys at the front. They were looking for safety and security in the steel plates, not in the Word; relying on materials and on material power. The same material force and power that you look for to save you one day, you are expecting to use to destroy the other fellow the next day. It will not work. If we are looking for our safety and our security and our peace of world in any human document or in any human form or in a human power, we are looking for it in that thing which has heretofore destroyed the world. And how can we expect that thing to save the world?

There is only one place of safety; there is only one place of security, and that is spiritual power. Spiritual power is the power of your individual consciousness once you realize that human thinking, human planning, human scheming, isn't power and that it cannot get any further than the minds of those that are planning it and plotting it. In other worlds, human power can only destroy itself.

Now, let us be agreed on this. Let us be agreed that somewhere in the world there must be those who are prepared to go one step higher in their metaphysical work, one step above just using it to heal their own bodies or to increase their own income. Somewhere in the world there must be those who are willing to listen to the Master when he says: "He that findeth his life shall lose it: and he that loseth his life for my sake shall find it."[10] Let us understand that if we are merely trying to preserve that thing we call our human sense of life, we are merely preserving that which will ultimately go no matter what. We are not preserving it, we are pickling it for a while, that is all! No, there is only one sense of preservation and that is the one that comes to us through the realization that life is God, God is life—indestructible, and that all this human ignorance of truth cannot destroy that which is God.

As our fears are erased, as our consciousness opens more and more, the Christ appears. The Christ is this spiritual consciousness which appears as manna, which appears as water coming from the rocks, which appears as healing the multitudes, feeding the multitudes. Christ will appear in whatever form is necessary to our unfoldment and demonstration; but Christ is your consciousness and my consciousness when that consciousness has given up its fear for itself and for the world; when it has given up the belief that human thought has power; that hate, envy, jealousy, malice, can produce something, even disease or war.

What difference does it make whether you credit the human mind with the effect of disease in your body, or whether you believe that the human mind can bring about a war? It is a belief in the power of the human mind and the human mind has that power in the human world until one with God comes along, until one in the truth comes along—and we have to be that one, we of the metaphysical world.

Do you know that only the metaphysicians of the world have this truth of God's allness, the understanding of the nothingness of sin, disease, death, lack and limitation? Everybody else in the world prepares for it; everybody else in the world has hymns for it and prayers for it. The metaphysician knows that there is no such thing as death. (Oh, he fools himself every once in a while by saying, "Oh, you just pass on," which is twisting words around and that is disqualifying a real revelation.) Do you know that metaphysics is a real revelation? It is the revelation of an infinite presence and an infinite power; but it tells you what that presence and what that power is. It's your consciousness! It isn't a far off God. It is the kingdom within you.

Spiritual power is the realization of this truth. You have to become conscious of this truth yourself in order for it to work for you. It isn't any different than your checking account. Your checking account is dead; it can't move; it can't write itself out; it can't spend itself out. Unless you yourself have a conscious awareness of that checking account–the amount and its purpose and power and extent–it is of no use to you. The money in your pocket is of no use to you except in proportion to your conscious awareness of it, of its value, and of its presence.

So it is with God. God is omnipresent and God is omnipotent. God is all-power; God is all-in-all. But tell that to the people in the hospitals and the graveyards and in the insane asylums. See what good that knowledge is to them. The allness of God is made manifest to us only in the degree of our consciousness of that truth. That is why we have practitioners and workers in metaphysical work. They are the same people you and I are, the only difference is that they have gained a greater conscious awareness of God's allness and error's nothingness. That is all that makes practitioners. Just think: if a practitioner were to get frightened at some patient's pain or some patient's appearance of disease, or some patient's appearance of sin, there would never be a healing. It is only in proportion as the practitioner doesn't get frightened–and how can a practitioner help but get frightened in the face of these things, except for his knowledge that what is appearing as a horrible condition is illusion, not reality, not power, not cause and not effect?

Well, we have to carry that out into this world and the world's problems. We are dealing now with human thought–vicious human thought on one hand, and ignorant human thought on the other hand. Add it all together and it is still human thought and, as human thought, it has power only to the world that accepts human thought as power. But it becomes null and void when it hits up against truth, the truth of God's order, of love's order, of life's order, of intelligence's order. And when it does that, it is touching the Christ of your being. Then Christ appears as safety, as security, as peace.

Perhaps I haven't answered my own opening thought: Does this or does this not settle the fate of the world? Time will tell that. One thing we know. The acceptance, the realization of this truth in *your* consciousness will operate as the Christ of *your* experience regardless of what happens in the world. You will be kept free of danger, of discord, of destruction. And that's not a selfish thing because in doing that for yourself, it may follow that you are doing it for a friend or a relative. Doing it for a friend or relative, you do not know how far it may go and how it may reach out to the peace tables of the world, the political tables of the world, and settle the affairs that come up around those tables.

This we do know, and this too is revelation. If this world were destroyed, if humanity were wiped out, if civilizations were wiped out, a remnant would remain. That remnant would be those of Christ consciousness; they will never be destroyed. The sons of God are never destroyed, they can't be. Spiritual consciousness can't be shot; spiritual consciousness can't be buried in a tomb. Therefore, if you and I—one, two, a dozen, a thousand in the world—have developed some degree of spiritual consciousness, we will certainly be spared the experience of destruction and a new civilization can be built upon the spirituality that remains in your thought and mine. Whether or not we are able to promise that by the devotion of our spiritual life we can save the world, at least we can save ourselves; and by doing that, we may save the basis of the new civilization. Even that is something to work for.

Let me show you just one more thing: Reality is never destroyed. God, the one life of the world, will never be wiped out. And that life which is your individual life and mine, and the life of millions we have never heard of, will never be wiped out. Because even if humanity appears to be wiped out, not one individual soul will die. Not one individual consciousness will die. As a matter of fact, there has never been a death since the beginning of recorded history, since there has never been but one life in heaven or on earth. And that life is God. It is indestructible, whether it appears as your life or mine, or whether it appears as the life of Jesus Christ, or the tree outside. Life is indestructible because life is God and any appearance to the contrary is automatically wiped out as an individual here and there realizes that truth.

We prove, not the immortality of God—we don't need any proof of that—but the immortality of your life and mine and your body and mine. You must remember that when Jesus Christ came out of the tomb, he came out with his very self-same body, the very same body that had been crucified. It was never put into a grave and it never will be, regardless of any appearance to the contrary. With God, one with this truth is a saving presence.

God is the very consciousness of my being and of yours. And that Christ appears tangibly as whatever form is necessary to our experience—food, clothing, transportation, immortality, eternality or whatever is needed. Christ appears as that form. Remember that, will you not? Christ is your very own consciousness!

~ 18 ~

GOD, THE OMNIPRESENT REALITY

TONIGHT LET US TALK ON FREEDOM IN CHRIST—that is, freedom of health in Christ and freedom of purse in Christ. These are so different from freedom in the body or freedom in the pocketbook. To be free in health in Christ is far different from being free in health in the body and yet health in Christ manifests itself as physical freedom. Freedom in Christ is where we are not tightened up in the body or feel that our health is in the body or our wealth or our happiness or any part of our so-called human experience. It is where the freedom is a Christly one.

Now, we can just completely relax and realize ourselves as a state of receptivity to the Christ. We are a state of receptivity to the Christ. Nothing can intrude and *it* will start in. I will speak audibly for a while and then go into the silence, and you will be meditating while I speak for just a few minutes.

We are receptive to the Christ. Christ is imparting itself eternally as our very consciousness. Consciousness is the embodiment of all that is, and all that is good, since God made all that was made and we are the embodiment of that good. We are in the state of receptivity as that infinite being is expressing itself. We, as individual consciousness, are responsive only to the

279

Christ. Nothing can enter this consciousness to defile or make it a lie. There is only one consciousness and that is God, and that is our individual consciousness. As we meditate on this truth of receptivity to the Christ, we will find that Christ pours itself forth as our individual consciousness.

"Glorify thou me . . ."[1] I would never think of getting on a platform or going into a class without hours, literally hours, of this meditation, in which I realize myself as a state of receptivity to the Christ, to God, spirit, since no matter where I would stand, whether talking, lecturing, or teaching, no one could possibly have any interest in anything that I humanly could say. It isn't possible that anybody on earth could have a message of importance on a spiritual subject that would be a personal one, or that would be of the intellect. Everything that can be known intellectually has been written for so many generations that it really couldn't be of any more interest to anyone except to read the great things that have already been written.

In presenting an idea of truth today, no one would want to present it except that it was the spirit itself that was doing the work. This is equally true in whatever work you are engaged. It doesn't make any difference whether it is a truth message or whether it is selling or buying; it doesn't make any difference whether it is manufacturing. None of that makes any difference. The thing that counts is whether what we are doing is animated by the spirit, whether or not it carries with it this life and vitality of the soul.

If whatever we are doing carries with it this spiritual spark, it will prosper, it will succeed, it will make glad, it will make happy, it will satisfy. It will be of good report.

Spirit always satisfies. Spirit always fulfills itself. Spirit always completes itself in success, and remember, that it is not what work we are doing, but whether we are doing it from our own limited sense of self, or whether there is a spirit permeating the activity and carrying it out.

This morning in our classwork we brought in the incident in Scripture of the Prophet Elijah. The Hebrews had been persecuted to the point that they were even killing their own prophets, and one, Elijah, had been driven out into the wilderness. There he had the wonderful experience of being fed by the ravens, being fed by a widow, and being taken care of in other mysterious and miraculous ways. Mysterious and miraculous only to human sense. In the understanding of the Christ it was perfectly normal and natural that wherever he should appear all that he required would be there with him, whether of food or of clothing or of protection. However, there must have come into his thought some doubt as to his ultimate mission or success, since we have that wonderful scene in which the still, small voice reveals itself, telling him that God had saved out a remnant of those who had not bowed their knees to Baal. Here, then, was a man with a holy message and nothing to do with it; no place to give it; no one to share it with. In that moment of seeming failure and discouragement, the voice told him that there was a remnant ready to receive his message. Then the rest of the story unfolds within his consciousness and leaves with us a principle for our work.

Regardless of what we may be doing, there is a remnant of those to provide our audience or congregation, our ministry or customers or patients or clients. No matter what our activity may be, as long as it reflects God qualities, as long as we introduce into our work the divine idea of service, beauty, harmony, joy, peace, satisfaction, perfection—good in any form—as long as our work partakes of the nature of the activity of mind, intelligence, truth; as long as those qualities and only those qualities are present in our work, in our activity, in our service, in our labor, then we, too, can know that there has been a remnant saved out for us.

In order to find our freedom from lack and limitation, in order to find our freedom from discord, our work is to find this freedom in Christ; and freedom in Christ means to be imbued with this spirit, to have all that we do imbued with the activity of the soul. It goes back to the Master's teaching, "I can of mine own self do nothing."[2] Or Paul: "I live; yet not I, but Christ liveth in me."[3] When we embody in our work this idea of the spirit performing all that we are called upon to do, when we open our consciousness to receptivity of the Christ so that it animates all of our activities, so that it gives us wisdom, guidance, direction, what the world calls hunches, this leads us into the right path, into doing the right thing at the right time. Then we are finding our freedom in Christ. You might say that there are lots of people who have been successful in business without any thought of the spirit or of Christ, and that is true. They have done it with hard work too, and usually ended up with difficulties, either physical, mental, moral, or financial, because the world of human mind is such that no matter how great it becomes, it comes to a breaking point and an end. Only when the spirit animates our so-called human activities can they be perfect and eternal. The moment we accept the fact that our mind and soul and body are animated by the divine presence, then we, too, can say, "I live; yet not I, but Christ liveth in me." The divine presence goes before us to make the crooked places straight.

Health, too. Certainly there is such a thing as physical health. There are people who have never known a pain or an illness in their entire lives, but that doesn't mean they are healthy. That means only that for the moment, for that day, that year, or for that ten years or twenty or thirty or fifty years, they are enjoying a sense of bodily health; a sense of bodily health that may change at any moment and become disease or death. That is the history of the human world. It is only when we find our health in the spirit, when we realize that spirit is the health of the body, that spirit is the health of the mind, that spirit is the animating principle of all of our activities—it is only then that we are looking for our health in God instead of our health in the body; and then we find it. When we find it, we have a better sense of health and of youth and vitality than we knew even when it was a healthy physical body.

We are dealing with one spiritual universe and one spiritual body, but we are dealing also with the world's false concept of that spiritual universe and spiritual body. Your body is a spiritual body, it is a temple of the living God. God made all that was made. We can only understand that God is individual consciousness when we can really understand that God formed the body.

You could prove that very quickly, by agreeing on this: If we were to decide that for the next twelve months we would keep our thoughts high in God, we would keep our consciousness on the level of Christ, of truth, of spirit, I am sure that you would agree that at the end of a year when you looked in a mirror, there would be a different look on your face and probably even a different appearance to the body. It would even be a much finer form. Now let's change that and agree that for the next twelve months we dissipate just as hard as we know how and then look at ourselves in the mirror at the end of that year and see if the body and the face don't show forth great changes.

In other words: The state of consciousness that we maintain is shown forth in the body that we present to the world. Our consciousness then, has formed and forms the body. Carry it through for ten years and you will see that actually a consciousness begun today can create an entirely new body in ten years. You would not recognize your own body ten years from now if you were to go along for those next ten years, living, moving and having your being in God-consciousness, and in order to understand that, just reverse it and see if you can't imagine what you would look like ten years from now if you went on a ten-year dissipation. You know right well what you would look like; and the opposite of that is true, too. Your identity as Christ consciousness maintained for a period one, two, ten years, would transform the entire mind and soul and body of your own being.

In the same way you would transform the body of your business. You would transform the body of your home life. Everything concerned with you would be changed in just a few years if you would maintain consciousness on the Christ level. Do everything as out from the Christ. Always be a witness to the fact that Christ is the animating principle of your mind, your body, and your business, and watch what takes place. If you can understand it, if you can watch the transformation that takes place, if you follow it, you will see that it actually is your own consciousness that formed your body in the beginning. Even before you were conceived, it was your own consciousness that formed your body, and that is why it looks like you and not like the next fellow.

Now, this consciousness is God, and there is where the point of demarcation comes in. We have accepted the universal belief that this consciousness is a personal one, personal to us, and therefore our business and our family were all limited to that personal consciousness, to that consciousness of our original education or environment or experience.

The longer you hold to the belief that your body and your business and your health and your marriage show forth your personal consciousness, the longer you will experience limitation in all of those directions. When, however, you give up that belief for the actual truth that God alone is consciousness, that God is individual consciousness, then your body, your business, your health, your wealth, your home and your family will show forth, not the results of your personal, limited, finite consciousness, but of the infinite consciousness that we call God. That is where you bring the transformation into your experience.

All of us have accepted the universal belief at some time or other and to some degree or other, that we are showing forth the fruitage of our education or lack of it, our home environment or lack of it, our past business experience or lack of it. And as long as we continue on in that strain, everything, every part of our existence, will show forth limitation.

Begin at any moment of your career that you want—this minute if you like—to agree with all revealed metaphysics, that God is divine consciousness and that this is the consciousness of individual being, and that your daily experience is the outpicturing, the outflowing, of the divine consciousness that is God—and then watch the miracles that take place in your experience.

The questions are often asked, "What is our goal on the spiritual path? What is it we are seeking?" Oh, there are many answers, because the answer depends upon what stage of our pathway we are when the question is asked of us. At first we may say, "Well, I am trying to get rid of a disease," or "I am looking for a bigger opportunity in life," or "I want a better relationship in my home." But, as we advance further and further on this path, the answers change. We begin to realize that that which we are seeking is God; that which we are seeking is the peace that passeth understanding; that which we are seeking is life eternal!

You know it is all right when we are in the twenties and thirties to say, "I just want health and money," but by the time we reach the forties and fifties, we are beginning to think about life eternal because the human span seems to be drawing to a close and we don't like it. Well, I don't! I never did! I never did! I have always had an interest in tomorrow morning's newspaper, and I hope I always will. The world may be better tomorrow than it was today, and I'd like to see it. And it might be worse, but I don't believe it! But even if it is, I'd like to see it, I want to be there!

So I have an interest—personal if you will—in the subject of life eternal. I have an interest in the subject of immortality. Now at one stage of this quest, my idea of immortality was like that of many others. I thought of it as many more years. In other words, longevity. I thought that if I could live to a hundred or a hundred and fifty, I would be showing more and more immortality. I know better now. I have come to see this: that immortality or eternality is a present possibility. Not only is it a present possibility, it is a present reality, only we are not yet fully aware of it.

Just as the consciousness that I am produced and formed my body before it was in the womb, just so the consciousness that I am will be forming my body and my experience unto eternity. Now, watch this—it has deep meaning: "Before Abraham was, I am[4] . . . I will be with you unto the end of the world."[5] Now think of the word "I." Just say "I," and remember that that I existed before Abraham, and that I will exist unto the end of the world. Then you will begin to achieve, not merely believe, but achieve, a measure of immortality expressed. The secret is in the word "I." That I is independent of body. That I is not encased in body at all. That I is a universal thing which merely appears here as body. It looks to you out there, looking up here as though I am body. But I am not body at all! What you are looking at is not I, it isn't even me. What you are looking at is my body. I am back here, invisible to the eyes, and that I of me is God, that I of you is God, but it is God individually appearing as you and as me, because God is infinite. Since God is infinite, God must be infinitely expressed, and God infinitely expresses itself as your individual life and mine. That is why that I that was before Abraham was, is the I that I am, and the I that you are.

Some of you, I am sure, have had some experience (probably some of you have had great experience) in the mystical side of life, that side in which you consciously touch your oneness with God. Now those who have had any degree of that experience have had some awareness of their pre-existence. They know exactly, not only that they lived before their birth, but sometimes even how they lived and where they lived, and they remember some of the experiences that took place before what we call human existence. Just in that same way, in the mystic illumination, they realize they are infinite and at the same time they are individual, and always they are God. Always they are God, manifesting itself in an infinite variety of form.

Yes, your experience and mine is determined by our own consciousness, and is determined by whether or not we accept the human sense of our consciousness, or whether we accept God as our consciousness. If I were to accept my own education, experience, or environment as my consciousness, I assure you I would never get on a platform to talk because my background, my human background, does not include that which would be necessary for this work. All that is part of this platform or teaching work is part of the divine consciousness; it never was a part of my human consciousness. I never learned it anywhere. It is God and it has come forth from God. It manifests itself as truth and it comes out only because of a receptivity to that consciousness. By opening consciousness and permitting God to speak, it speaks. That cannot come from my mentality, my experience, or my environment, because none of those include any of this work that has been going forth from me since I have been in this public ministry.

That same thing applies to you in your work. Whatever you may be doing, if you are looking to your own

experience, your own environment, your own education, you will be limited, not only as to what you are
doing, but as to the fruitage that comes from what you
are doing. The moment, however, that you open your
consciousness to this idea that God manifests itself in its
infinity, that you open your individual consciousness to
the divine ideas and mind and life and spirit and soul of
truth, you are no longer limited. Then you hear that still,
small voice that Elijah heard, telling him that God had
saved out a remnant of those who had not bowed their
knees to Baal. God will save out a remnant for you in
your work.

In other words, God, the source, the very divine idea,
has provided those to utilize those ideas. If you are sure
that your work carries with it some activity of divine
grace, beauty, holiness, harmony, service, intelligence,
love—any of these qualities—then it comes from God.
The whole activity, the whole idea comes from God.
Then the government is upon his shoulder, and God
itself must provide what we may call customers or
students or whomever we need to fulfill our experience.

Our purpose, then, in being on this path is not merely
to give us more bodily health, longevity, length of years,
nor to bring in more dollars to our business; but our
purpose in being on this path is the expansion of consciousness to where we realize that consciousness to be
God. Or rather, we recognize God to be our individual
consciousness and therefore, infinite Good flows out
from it.

That is our real mission in this work. If only you can
die daily to the belief, to limited human belief, and if
only you can be reborn in and of this spirit—in the
realization of the fact that I am never limited to a human

mind or a human experience or a human consciousness, but that God is my consciousness–then it may flow through in an entirely new life, flow forth in new work, new activity. Or it may increase and prosper the one in which you now are engaged.

Spirit knows no limitation. Spirit just pours itself through. It comes flowing through in such a wild, rushing manner, you just can't believe it when it begins! We are beholders. It is almost as though we were watching God work over our shoulder. It is almost as though we were just watching the activity of God and wondering at its munificence, at its beauty, at its bounty.

There was a time when I used to come to the office in the morning and just say, "Here I am, Father. I wonder what is going to come across this desk today," and then just watch it unfold. Some of the things that unfolded across that desk weren't believable then, and they are not believable now and I am sure it is just the same in your own experience.

The moment you watch God unfold itself as your experience, I can tell you you've got a treat coming. You will be shocked, you will be surprised and astounded to see the infinite ways in which good can appear to us. I am not talking merely about dollars. Dollars are really the least part of our experience. They are abundant enough for all our needs, but that is the least part of the thing. It's the beauty, it's the vision, it's the broadness. Those are the things that astonish me!

Do you follow what I mean? Have I explained that point? That your consciousness, when you know God to be your consciousness, is infinite, and infinite things flow forth from it. We are in this work, we are on the spiritual path, for just one purpose: to die daily to the Joel that was, and to be reborn to the Joel of God; to die daily to the limited, finite sense of myself that I have always entertained, and be reborn of the spirit; to realize spirit as my true identity; to realize spirit—and then watch and see how it unfolds. Then you may be surprised to see a business man become a religious teacher. You may be more than surprised to see a school teacher become a painter, or a poet, or a musician. Anything can happen when the spirit is free—when we are free in the spirit.

I started off with "freedom in Christ" and that is what I meant, exactly. Freedom in Christ. In Christ I am infinite; in Christ I am that point of consciousness through which all of God shows itself forth. Only in Christ can that be; only as Christ can that be. Not as person, not as limited self, not as somebody with a human history. None of that. But only as I turn from that and find my freedom through the realization that God is individual consciousness, and that God is pouring itself forth as my individual daily experience.

Now, in one of our classes, the theme that ran all the way through was, "My conscious oneness with God constitutes my oneness with all spiritual being and idea." In another class the idea unfolded that "God, the divine consciousness, was unfolding, revealing, disclosing itself, as my individual being." Put those two together and you can see that if God is appearing as my individual consciousness, then automatically that oneness constitutes my at-one-ment with every spiritual idea and being, whether that would appear as a person, place, thing, circumstance or condition, since the consciousness which is God must be all-inclusive. It must include every idea, every person, every activity, every thought, every formation.

Then I, as this infinite consciousness, must embody
and embrace within my own being every right idea and
that must continuously flow forth as my daily experience. Now if this was true about me and not true about
you, then of course the entire mission and message of
the Master would be for nothing, for then we would be
at the place where we would be worshiping a man
again—an individual. But the message and the mission of
the Master is that this is a universal law. He refers to it
as "your Father" and "my Father." In all things then,
there is only one Father, and that is our universal
creative principle appearing as you and as me.

This consciousness which is God is that consciousness
which formed your body before it was in the womb.
That is what I meant. Not just you as a finite limited
person building a body for yourself. But the God, the
divine consciousness, has built the body for you, and this
body is his, regardless of how terrible it might look to
our eyesight at this moment. If you could see this body
through spiritual discernment, you would see it in its
infinite perfection and in its eternal and immortal
growth.

Never forget this. This very body which you so
finitely see when you look in the mirror, that looks to
you as if it needed so much correction and improvement, this very body is the temple of the living God,
only you are looking at it through the old Joel eyes
instead of through the new Joel eyes, the first Adam
eyes, instead of the last Adam eyes. Begin, when you
look into the mirror, to close your eyes and look. Then
you will see the body as it really is.

Every person who has ever been responsible for a
spiritual healing has had the experience of knowing the

spiritual man and spiritual body, since spiritual healings cannot take place in any other way. It is only as you close your eyes, figuratively speaking, to the human scene that this little inner spot within, this spiritual corner of your being, comes into play, and all of a sudden it realizes God manifest. It realizes the meaning of spiritual man and spiritual universe, spiritual being and body; and then a healing takes place, whether it is your own, or a patient's or a relative's or a friend's.

Never for a moment think that spiritual healing is accomplished in any other way. It isn't. Spiritual healing is accomplished through spiritual discernment. And what is it that you are spiritually discerning? The temple of God, "the temple not made with hands, eternal in the heavens."[6] That temple is you; that temple is your body; that temple is your business; that temple is your home; that temple is your universe; and it is a temple not made with hands, not made with thoughts; but it is the creation and the emanation of the divine consciousness of your individual being the moment you acknowledge God to be your consciousness.

Well, we could come right down to brass tacks and say then that the unfoldment of your own experience is up to you, that you yourself are responsible for it. We could be charitable and say that when you are ignorant of this truth, your experience is limited and finite and sickly and sinful and coarse, because you are ignorant of God as your consciousness appearing as your daily experience. But from the time that you enter the world of metaphysics, more especially the moment that you enter the consciousness of those who are at some period spiritually illumined, you will have no more excuse for finiteness and limitation in your experience. You then must accept your responsibility and agree that from that moment on, what you are next year is determined by what you will accept of truth this year and that your demonstration is your individual problem. You, yourself, can take the limitation off your experience–oh, in a measure only, because this comes bit by bit–and you can begin to unfold spiritually from the moment you agree that God is "my" individual consciousness; and God, as my consciousness, unfolds, reveals, manifests itself as my individual body and business and home and daily experience.

From the moment that you draw on God as your consciousness, you are drawing on infinity, and you are bringing forth infinitely. The first step on this path is, of course, the intellectual agreement that this is true, but that intellectual agreement will not carry you very far. From that point on there has to be a specific action, a specific activity on your part, and the reason is this: Nothing happens to us except as the activity of consciousness, as our own individual consciousness. In other words, if you just slide by each day without some new conscious mental activity, then you can't expect anything different next year than this year. If you are to bring something new into your world during this next year, you have to begin with this moment and continue some conscious activity of consciousness with each new moment. There is no such thing as sitting by and saying, "Well, I am going to let consciousness do it; let God do it." Yes, you *are* going to let consciousness do it, and consciousness will do it, but only in proportion to your conscious cooperation.

Now the first step in this conscious activity of opening consciousness to this truth is learning to take not less than three periods of every single day for a moment of what you might call silent prayer or meditation. Three times a day at least, and ultimately four and five and six. Sit down for one minute or two or three, it doesn't matter how short a time or how long a time you give to it–the idea is that some conscious activity takes place which we might describe as receptivity. As a matter of fact, it might prove so simple that you achieve it even while driving your automobile or riding in a streetcar or bus. It is just as simple as touching your ear, indicating that you are opening consciousness to the inflow of this truth–just opening the ear; or sitting down for a moment in silence and declaring, "I am receptive to the Christ" or "I am a state of receptivity to the Christ." Any little thing that you do, any little thought that you think, will open your consciousness to that inflow.

It must be repeated three, four or five times a day to keep the flow going, because there is a mesmerism out there in the world. Every time you read a newspaper or listen to a radio, you get a little of that hypnotic suggestion thrown at you of a sinful world, of a fearful world, of a diseased world. And so, with that pouring in all the time, there must be some counter-influence. That counter-influence is your receptivity to the Christ, your conscious receptivity to the Christ. It has to be an activity of consciousness–specifically, definitely, consciously. You may either sit down or stand up or walk, but open that inner ear and realize your receptivity to the Christ.

In proportion as you do that, you find something wonderful happening. You will be able to sit down in the morning and at night, and for five or ten minutes find yourself in a wonderful state of peace, in a wonderful state of receptivity and there begin to feel the inflow of the spirit, to feel the spirit coursing through the whole body. This a real experience, an actual one. Many people in this work have had this, and do have this continuous experience of the soul, spirit, pouring itself through. It does it much better in silence than in speech. Speech sometimes stops it. The more of silence we have, the better and more power there is in the speech when we do speak. Silence is of tremendous power when silence is tied up with receptivity. With that listening ear: "I will listen for thy voice." Remember that? Or, "Speak Lord, for thy servant heareth."[7] Or listen for "the still, small voice."[8] All of those things.

Watch our friend, the old Hebrew prophet, whose servant was so doubtful, so fearful, that he caused his master to pray. And just listen to that master's prayer: "Open his eyes that he may see."[9] That is the prayer. Don't send us more warriors, don't send us more help, don't send us more supply. "Open his eyes!" What happens when the servant's eyes are opened? Then he knows that even the clouds round about are filled with warriors, and we find that the streets round about us are filled with customers, students, patients, an audience–for whatever our line of work may be. Not if we pray for those things, however! The truth is that these things are already there–health, wealth, harmony, opportunity, peace, joy, power, dominion. They are all right here. Your consciousness is full of them. There is only one thing hiding them. The seeing takes inner eyes. You remember that there were those that had ears but they didn't hear, and those that had eyes but they didn't see? That is what I mean. We have eyes, certainly. But do we see those hidden warriors? Do we see this infinite supply of good? No, you cannot see those with these eyes; you see them only with that inner eye, when your attention is centered on receptivity to God.

In that inner vision you can behold everything here. It is all here. You don't have to have a customer added to your list. You don't have to have a single new thing added to your experience to make it full. You have only to open your spiritual eyes to see the fullness and completeness of God's universe—which is already here and which is already now.

Scriptural References and Notes

Chapter 1
1. From an inscription in the Stanford University Chapel, Palo Alto, California.
2. John 5:30.
3. John 14:10.
4. Galatians 2:20.
5. John 5:30.
6. John 14:10.
7. Galatians 2:20.
8. John 19:11.
9. See Note 1.
10. John 5:30.
11. John 14:10.
12. Galatians 2:20.
13. Exodus 20:3.
14. John 19:11.

Chapter 2
1. Matthew 11:3.
2. Matthew 11:4,5.
3. Matthew 6:33.
4. Galatians 2:20.
5. John 14:10.
6. Galatians 2:20.
7. Isaiah 26:3.
8. John 12:32.
9. Matthew 18:20.
10. John 10:27.
11. I Corinthians 3:19.
12. John 5:30.
13. Galatians 2:20.
14. Galatians 2:20.
15. Isaiah 26:3.

Chapter 3
1. Galatians 2:20.
2. Galatians 2:20.
3. John 5:30.
4. John 14:10.
5. Luke 15:31.
6. Matthew 28:20.
7. Matthew 18:20.
8. John 18:12.
9. John 14:6.
10. John 11:25.
11. John 14:9.
12. John 12:45.
13. John 10:30.
14. Psalms 139:8.
15. John 11:25.
16. John 19:10.
17. John 19:11.
18. Luke 15:31.
19. Galatians 2:20.

Chapter 4
1. John 14:6.
2. Matthew 16:23.
3. John 10:30.
4. John 10:30.
5. Luke 15:31.
6. Luke 17:21.

Chapter 5
1. John 14:6.
2. John 6:35.
3. John 14:9.
4. John 10:30.
5. John 7: 16.
6. John 5:31.
7. John 5:30.
8. Luke 15:31.
9. John 10:30.
10. John 19:10.
11. John 19:11.
12. John 18:11.
13. Galatians 2:20.
14. John 5:30.
15. John 16:7.

Chapter 6
1. Exodus 3:5.
2. Matthew 6:33.
3. Luke 12:30.
4. Luke 12:32.
5. Zechariah 4:6.
6. Luke 12:22.
7. Isaiah 26:3.
8. John 10:30.
9. Matthew 6:33.
10. Friends of Joel's.
11. Matthew 6:33.
12. Matthew 6:31.
13. Matthew 6:32.
14. Matthew 12:48.
15. Matthew 14:46.
16. Matthew 22:39.
17. John 10:30.
18. Luke 15:31.
19. Exodus 3:5.
20. Luke 12:22.
21. Zachariah 4:6.
22. Isaiah 43:10&12.
23. Isaiah 44:8.
24. Exodus 20:3.

Chapter 7
1. Luke 15:31.
2. Exodus 3:5.
3. John 10:30.
4. Matthew 28:20.
5. Matthew 13:46.
6. Psalms 24:1.
7. Luke 15:31.
8. Matthew 6:33.

Chapter 8
1. John 8:12.
2. John 19:6.
3. John 5:30.
4. John 7:16.
5. I Corinthians 15:31.
6. John 10:30.
7. Galatians 2:20.
8. I Corinthians 5:1.

Chapter 8 (Continued)
9. Matthew 28:20.
10. John 10:10.
11. John 12:45.
12. John 10:30.
13. Isaiah 45:2.
14. John 16:7.
15. John 16:24.
16. Luke 17:21.
17. John 20:17.
18. John 14:12.

19. Mark 16:20.
20. John 14:6.
21. Galatians 6:7.
22. Luke 17:21.
23. Matthew 23:37.
24. John 14:27.
25. Matthew 28:20.
26. Mark 12:30,31.
27. Philippians 4:7.

Chapter 9
1. Matthew 7:16.
2. 1Samuel 3:9.
3. Psalms 46:10.
4. John 14:9.
5. Isaiah 2:22
6. John 16:33.
7. John 5:30.
8. Philippians 4:13.
9. Exodus 20:3.
10. Isaiah 2:22.

11. Psalms 146:3.
12. John 16:7.
13. 1John 4:8.
14. Luke 23:34.
15. John 8:11.
16. Matthew 17:21.
17. Luke 15:31.
18. Matthew 26:39.
19. Matthew 19:17.

Chapter 10
1. Isaiah 2:22.
2. Luke 12:22.
3. John 16:33.
4. Alfred, Lord Tennyson,
   The Higher Pantheon

5. John 10:30.
6. John 8:32.
7. Isaiah 54:17.
8. John 16:33.

Chapter 11
1. John 14:6.
2. Job 19:26.
3. Exodus 20:3.
4. Romans 8:17.
5. Luke 15:31.
6. John 10:30.
7. Isaiah 26:3.

8. 1 Thessalonians 5:17.
9. 1 Timothy 6:10.
10. Galatians 2:20.
11. Luke 17:21.
12. John 14:6.
13. John 16:7.
14. John 16:33.

Chapter 11 (Continued)

15. By Joel Goldsmith.
16. John 14:10.
17. By Joel Goldsmith.

18. Philippians 4:13.
19. Isaiah 55:8.
20. I Samuel 3:9.

Chapter 12

1. Alfred, Lord Tennyson, *The Higher Pantheism*
2. John 10:30.
3. Luke 15:31.
4. Luke 17:21.

5. Exodus 3:5.
6. John 18:36.
7. Matthew 19:17.
8. John 10:27.

Chapter 13

1. Galatians 6: 7,8.
2. Ezekiel 18:32.
3. John 10:30.
4. 1 Corinthians 10:31.
5. John 16:7.
6. Galatians 6:1-3.
7. Galatians 6:6,10.
8. Exodus 20:3.

9. Mark 12:31.
10. Matthew 26:52.
11. Isaiah 59:1.
12. Galatians 6:10.
13. Philippians 4:7.
14. Matthew 7:14.
15. 1 Samuel 3:9.
16. Isaiah 26:3.

Chapter 14

1. 1 John 3:2.
2. Isaiah 40:11.
3. Proverbs 3:6.
4. Isaiah 26:3.
5. 1 Thessalonians 5:17.
6. Exodus 13:21.
7. Galatians 2:20.
8. Philippians 4:13.
9. Mark 4:39.
10. John 14:6.
11. John 10:30.

12. John 12:45.
13. Matthew 16:13.
14. Matthew 16:16.
15. Matthew 28:20.
16. John 1:14.
17. Matthew 19:17.
18. John 5:30.
19. John 5:31.
20. John 7:16.
21. Exodus 20:3.
22. Matthew 19:19.

Chapter 15

1. John 12:24.
2. John 12:25.
3. John 12:25.
4. John 12:27.

5. John 12:28.
6. Proverbs 3:5,6.
7. John 12:27.
8. John 12:28.

Chapter 15 (Continued)

9. John 12:29.
10. John 12:30.
11. Philippians 4:13.
12. John 5:30.
13. John 12:40. (Isaiah 6:9,10.)
14. John 12:42.
15. John 12:42,43.

16. Matthew 11:9.
17. John 12:44,45.
18. John 12:49.
19. John 12:45.
20. John 14:2.
21. John 15:16.

Chapter 16

1. Matthew 5:45.
2. John 5:14.
3. Job 26:7.
4. John 4:14.
5. John 4:32.
6. John 12:49.

7. John 12:45.
8. John 8:58.
9. Zechariah 4:6.
10. Exodus 14:13.
11. Exodus 14:13.
12. John 4:32.

Chapter 17

1. Matthew 6:25.
2. Luke 15:31.
3. II Kings 6:17.
4. Exodus 3:5.
5. John 10:30.

6. John 12:45.
7. Psalms 139:7,8.
8. John 19:11.
9. Psalms 91:1.
10. Matthew 10:39.

Chapter 18

1. John 17:5.
2. John 5:30.
3. Galatians 2:20.
4. John 8:58.
5. Matthew 28:20.

6. II Corinthians 5:1.
7. I Samuel 3:9.
8. I Kings 19:12.
9. II Kings 6:17.